THE TRADER, THE OWNER, THE SLAVE

James Walvin taught for many years at the University of York. He has published widely on slavery and the slave trade. His book *Black and White* won the Martin Luther King Memorial Prize and his book on the Quakers was named as a 'Notable Book of the Year' by the *New York Times*. Walvin's book *The People's Game* has long been the standard work on the history of football.

JAMES WALVIN

The Trader, The Owner, The Slave

Parallel Lives in the Age of Slavery

VINTAGE BOOKS
London

Published by Vintage 2008

4 6 8 10 9 7 5 3

Copyright © James Walvin, 2007

James Walvin has asserted his right under the Copyright, Designs
and Patents Act 1988 to be identified as the author of this work

First published in Great Britain in 2007 by
Jonathan Cape

Vintage
Random House, 20 Vauxhall Bridge Road,
London SW1V 2SA

www.vintage-books.co.uk

Addresses for companies within The Random House Group Limited
can be found at: www.randomhouse.co.uk/offices.htm

The Random House Group Limited Reg. No. 954009

A CIP catalogue record for this book
is available from the British Library

ISBN 9780712667630

The Random House Group Limited supports The Forest Stewardship
Council (FSC), the leading international forest certification organisation.
All our titles that are printed on Greenpeace approved FSC certified paper
carry the FSC logo. Our paper procurement policy can be found at:
www.rbooks.co.uk/environment

Printed and bound in Great Britain by
CPI Cox & Wyman, Reading RG1 8EX

Cover details: portrait of a African once thought to be Olaudah
Equiano © Royal Albert Memorial Museum; chains © Wilberforce
House; slave auction in Virginia © Peter Newark American Pictures;
American abolitionist emblem; Granville Sharp © Guildhall Art
Gallery; shipping bill for a slave boy © Michael Graham-Stewart All
photos © Bridgeman Art Library

For Caryl Phillips

Contents

PART THREE
The Slave: Olaudah Equiano (1745–1797)

Illustrations

John Newton, portrait by J. Russell, engraved by J. Collier (*Mary Evans Picture Library*).

Africans below deck on a slaver, from the *Illustrated London News*, 1857 (*Mary Evans Picture Library*).

African insurrection aboard a slave ship, 1794 (*author's collection*).

The slave ship *Brookes* (*author's collection*).

Granville Sharp, portrait by George Dance, 1794 (*Mary Evans Picture Library*).

Thomas Clarkson, portrait by A.E. Chalon (*Mary Evans Picture Library*).

William Wilberforce, portrait by J. Rising, 1790 (*Mary Evans Picture Library*).

Slaves planting sugar cane on a Caribbean plantation (*author's collection*).

Slave gangs preparing the ground for planting cane (*author's collection*).

Slaves at a sugar mill, drawing from William Clark, *Ten Views in the Island of Antigua*, 1823 (*author's collection*).

Inside a sugar plantation's boiling house (*author's collection*).

'West India Fashionable': 'On a Visit in Style' and 'Taking

a Ride', by William Holland, 1807 (*private collection,* ©
Michael Graham-Stewart/Bridgeman Art Library).

The Jamaican Maroon leader, Leonard Parkinson, 1796
(*Jerome S. Handler and Michael L. Tuite Jr, The Atlantic
Slave Trade and Slave Life in the Americas - A Visual Record,
a project of the Virginia Foundation for the Humanities and
the University of Virginia Library, http://hitchcock.itc.
virginia.edu/Slavery/Index.php*).

'The Poor Blacks Going to Their Settlement', published
by E. Macklew, 1787 (© *City of Westminster Archive Centre/
Bridgeman Art Library*).

'Lowest Life in London: Tom, Jerry and Logic among the
Unsophisticated Sons and Daughters of Nature', by
George Cruikshank, from *Life in London* by Pierce Egan,
1821 (*Bibliothèque des Arts décoratifs, Paris, Archives Charmet/
Bridgeman Art Library*).

Grave of Scipio Africanus, 1720, in St Mary's churchyard,
Henbury (*author's collection*).

Frontispiece and title page of *The Interesting Narrative of
the Life of Olaudah Equiano, or Gustavus Vassa, the African,*
1789 (*British Library,* © *British Library Board, all rights
reserved/Bridgeman Art Library*).

Acknowledgements

In writing this book I built up debts to many people. My first is to the late Douglas Hall whose pioneering work first introduced me to Thomas Thistlewood. It was only when I began to write about Thistlewood that I fully appreciated the importance of Professor Hall's work. I am doubly indebted to Trevor Burnard, first for his marvellous study of Thistlewood, and secondly for his personal kindness in letting me use his microfilm copies of the Thistlewood diary. The late Tony Clarke was a welcoming host and guide as I tried to retrace Thistlewood's life in western Jamaica. Tony Seward kindly introduced me to the world of John Newton at Olney in Buckinghamshire. Jim Horn again allowed me the run of the Rockefeller Library at Colonial Williamsburg: for that and many other kindnesses I am very grateful. Vincent Carretta's meticulous scholarship made me think more critically about Equiano. My agent Charles Walker liked the idea for this book from the moment I first discussed it with him. So too did Will Sulkin whose growing interest, as I explained what I had in mind, gave me the confidence to embark on the project. But this book's greatest debt is to Jörg Hensgen whose detailed and sympathetic editing helped the emergence of the final version of what follows. To Gad Heuman I owe more generalised thanks for many years of shared interest in the scholarship of slavery, and for his friendship.

James Walvin
November 2006

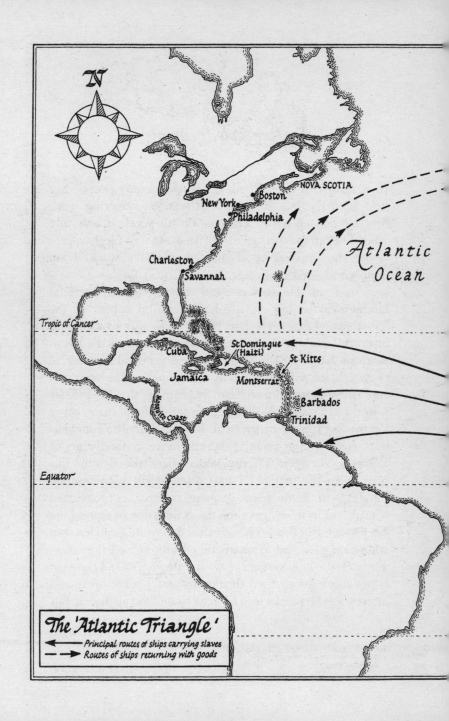

N

Atlantic Ocean

NOVA SCOTIA

Boston
New York
Philadelphia

Charleston
Savannah

Tropic of Cancer

Cuba
St Domingue (Haiti)
St Kitts

Jamaica
Montserrat
Barbados
Trinidad

Mosquito Coast

Equator

The 'Atlantic Triangle'

← Principal routes of ships carrying slaves
- - → Routes of ships returning with goods

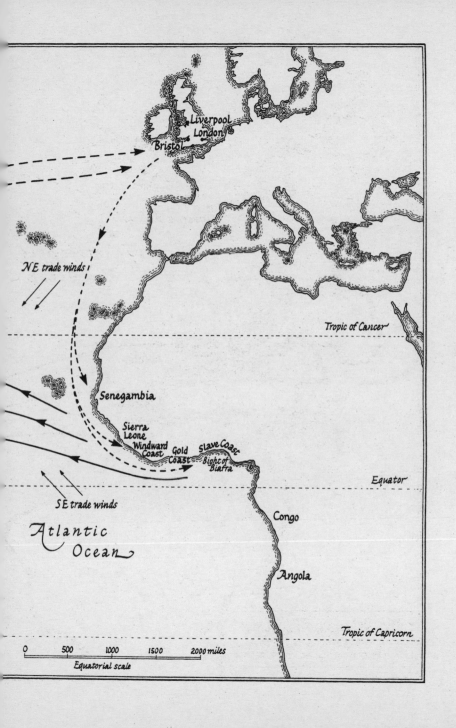

Liverpool

London

Bristol

NE trade winds

Tropic of Cancer

Senegambia

Sierra
Leone
Windward
Coast   Gold   Slave Coast
        Coast   Bight of
                Biafra   Equator

SE trade winds

Atlantic
    Ocean   Congo

                               Angola

                                                Tropic of Capricorn

0   500   1000   1500   2000 miles

        Equatorial scale

Introduction
Three Men Among Millions

The broad outlines of the story of Atlantic slavery are familiar and have been told many times, in many different ways. Over more than three centuries European and American traders loaded some 12 million Africans on to slave ships destined for the Americas. More than 10 million Africans arrived, many of them sick, all of them traumatised by the hellish experience of the previous few months. The Africans were then resold and most of them settled on to the plantations to cultivate the tropical and semi-tropical produce which the Western world consumed in ever increasing volume. The great majority of Africans worked in sugar, tobacco, rice and, later, cotton, though many spilled out into all corners of the economies of the colonial Americas.

Although African slavery was a dominant feature of the history of the Americas, it was initiated and sustained by European political and economic institutions. It was also a system which brought widely based prosperity (in some cases, very great wealth) – though never to the Africans. Stated simply, between *c.*1550 and 1860 slavery was integral to the way the Western world lived, functioned and prospered.

The Trader, the Owner, the Slave

The British did not initiate this Atlantic slave system, but by the mid-eighteenth century they dominated it; by about 1750, slavery had established itself as an unquestioned institution in the British way of life. Hundreds of British ships, thousands of British sailors, tens of thousands of British settlers – not to mention British workers, merchants, financiers – and millions of consumers, all depended on, or benefited from, slavery.

The word 'slavery' sounds neutral – a word that simply describes an institution – but it masks a complex social and human reality. What the Western world came to rely on were Africans and their descendants, enslaved in unprecedented numbers, and consigned to a lifetime's bondage which they bequeathed to their offspring born in the Americas. Of course slavery had existed since time immemorial. But *black* slavery in the Americas was very unusual. It was a unique form of bondage which, from an early date, was highly racialised. By 1750, to be black in the Americas (and often in Europe) was to be enslaved. Never before had the institution of slavery been so shaped and defined by colour, or, more properly, ethnicity. Many consequences of this racialised system have survived down to the present day.

To transport so many Africans, to force them to work, generally in the most difficult and oppressive of environments, Europeans and their American descendants devised systems of excruciating violence and cruelty. From the beginning of American slavery, soon after the arrival of Columbus, to its final demise in Brazil in 1888, Africans were the victims of the system. They resisted it, fought it, ran away or found a myriad other means of coping with their brutalised condition. There were, of course, great varieties of slavery, but in essence it remained a brutal system which was conceived in violence, maintained by draconian punishments, and all for the material betterment of the Western world.

Despite this, it was very easy for most people not to notice it. Unless you worked on a slave ship, or lived in a slave colony, it was possible not to be aware of the grim human realities at the heart of slavery. This was largely because the focus of Atlantic slavery was far away from the metropolis. Slavery was at its worst in West Africa, on the mid-Atlantic slave ships and on the plantations scattered across the colonial Americas. For Europeans, here was a system which was distant and remote: a colonial experience many thousands of miles away. Yet the metropolis was, from the first, intimately involved. British legislation, finance, insurance, institutions of all kinds, British towns and industries – all and more were intimately linked to Atlantic slavery. To take a single example, we know of large numbers of Acts of Parliament passed to facilitate and help the growth of the slave trade. Parliament played an active role in shaping Atlantic slavery long before it outlawed the trade in 1807.

The story of Atlantic slavery is so unrelentingly bleak that it is sometimes hard to grasp the enormity of what took place. Modern readers might be forgiven for wondering how such suffering could be visited, so persistently, on so many people, for so long. Even more perplexing, in retrospect, is the fact that Atlantic slavery was the invention of Christian nations. Today, it seems so manifestly wrong, so obviously inhuman and unethical; but it did not appear that way to contemporaries. It is perhaps one of Atlantic slavery's most perplexing features that very few people objected to it until quite late in its history. There was, it is true, a small descant of complaint, mainly religious, sometimes ethical – but rarely economic. The power of slavery was its ability to deliver profitable trade and production; profit silenced slavery's critics.

Then, quite suddenly, all this began to change. When our story begins, in the middle years of the eighteenth century, few complained about slavery. When it ends, in

1807, the British slave trade had been abolished by Parliament.

I have tried to tell this story in a different way; to get away from the big, metanarrative (the tens of millions of people, spread over centuries) by narrowing the historical focus on to three individuals. The aim is to tell a big story through what seems at first to be the small experiences of three men. As will become clear, these individual experiences encompass astonishing stories. What follows is the story of British Atlantic slavery from its mid-eighteenth-century apogee through to the first fatal blow against it in the early nineteenth century, but it is a story told through three parallel lives, three men who were critical actors in the broader story: a slave trader, a slave owner and a slave.

In many respects these three men were unusual. They were literate, sophisticated men who loved books. They were also authors; all three left substantial papers. But all three speak to other, broader groups. They were contemporaries who might easily have met each other at certain critical points in their lives. But it is the *trajectory* of their lives, linking three continents – Europe, Africa and the enslaved Americas – which gives shape and movement to their collective story. Their lives provide different themes to the same story – parallel lives in the world of Atlantic slavery.

John Newton (1725–1807) was a slave-trade captain, responsible for buying and transporting Africans across the Atlantic. But he was many other things besides; most famously he was author of the hymn 'Amazing Grace'. Thomas Thistlewood (1721–1786) was a slave owner in a remote corner of Jamaica whose voluminous diary provides a unique account of his life among enslaved Africans. And Olaudah Equiano (c.1745–1797) was perhaps the most powerful African voice to emerge from the world of Atlantic slavery in these years.

Introduction

Let us begin with John Newton – 'the Old African blas-phemer' to use his own description – perhaps the most celebrated of the three, by looking at events he did *not* wish to celebrate: his life as a slave-trade captain.

PART ONE

The Slave Trader

John Newton (1725–1807)

1 *A Wayward Youth*

If he had never written another word, John Newton would have been famous for 'Amazing Grace', the hymn he wrote in December 1772. At the time, he thought it an unremarkable piece: just one of the many hymns and sermons he wrote down as a matter of weekly routine, and intended for delivery to his packed, enthusiastic congregations. He had a particular audience in mind: the humble working people who flocked to his church at Olney in Buckinghamshire. Newton wanted his hymns to be attractive to 'plain people' and he cranked them out by the dozen, each hymn written to accompany one of his sermons. Seven years later, in 1779, a collection of Newton's hymns, along with a good number written by his close friend and neighbour, the troubled poet William Cowper, was published as the *Olney Hymns*. The first edition ran to 428 pages and contained 348 hymns. Some established themselves as the most abiding and popular of hymns in the English language, but one in particular is in a league of its own. Translated into dozens of languages, sung and recorded by many of the world's greatest singers, performed at some of the most memorable occasions – state funerals, national ceremonies, times of national grief and remembrance, almost a second national anthem in the USA – it is hard to recall the humble origins of 'Amazing Grace'.

Today, many millions of people know by heart these simple verses. It is all a very long way from what its author intended as he sat in the rectory in Olney that early winter of 1772. Newton made no great claims for his hymn-writing skills, indeed he spoke very modestly of his work, never assuming for example that he had the dazzling literary talents of his friend, Cowper; 'There is a style and manner suited to the composition of hymns, which may be more successfully, or at least more easily, attained by a versifier, than by a poet.'[1] 'Amazing Grace' is a hymn that has attracted some remarkable analysis but its appeal still remains elusive. What precisely has given this simple tune and its taut verses such universal appeal, over so long a period? The verses were hardly original, their memorable phrases and concepts transposed from biblical texts, and they had often appeared in previous settings before they took on the form we recognise today. The music was not Newton's but was added in the early nineteenth century in the USA, the country which adopted the hymn more quickly and more completely than any other.

Newton intended 'Amazing Grace', like all his hymns, to reinforce a main, parallel argument in his sermon, delivered at the same service, telling the story of a Christian's pilgrimage from an awareness of sin, through repentance and on to eternal life. The key was grace. 'Since the sinner can't seek God, God seeks him and sheds grace upon him.'[2] Other hymn writers had used similar imagery, employed similar language before. But this one immediately stuck in the mind of people who first heard it. It soon rippled out, from its original birthplace in the Buckinghamshire countryside, and was carried, through the rapidly proliferating world of cheap print and universally available hymn books, to congregations across the English-speaking world. It was a hymn which inevitably attracted change and alteration – stanzas were added, words changed, new music appended.

The opening lines were in fact a reflection of John Newton's early life.

> Amazing grace! (how sweet the sound)
> That saved a wretch like me!
> I once was lost, but now am found,
> Was blind, but now can see.

John Newton was forty-seven when he wrote this hymn. Twenty years earlier, his daily writings had been of an entirely different nature. In December 1752, Newton wrote the following:

> By the favour of Divine Providence made a timely discovery to day that the slaves were forming a plot for an insurrection. Surprized 2 of them attempting to get off their irons, and upon farther search in their rooms, upon the information of 3 of the boys, found some knives, stones, shot, etc and a cold chisel . . . Put the boys in irons and slightly in the thumbscrews to urge them to a full confession.[3]

The young John Newton had been a slave trader, and although he had changed fundamentally by the time he wrote 'Amazing Grace', it was to be another decade before he felt able to speak publicly about his life and deeds on board the slave ships. Some things were best kept secret, and in 1772 Newton – despite the confessional mode of his preaching, openly admitting past sins and misdemeanours – was not yet ready to reveal the full truth about his past.

Born in 1725 in Wapping, a riverside corner of the capital which thrived on maritime trade and its myriad industries, John Newton was destined for the sea. His father, also John Newton, was a sailor, and every occupation and skill associated with ships and shipping lived or passed through Wapping. It was on the edge of the City of London, itself the commercial and financial heart of maritime trade and business, and close to the taverns and, especially, the coffee houses, which were a hive of information and gossip about the sea and seafarers. Later in life, long after he had quit the sea, Newton enjoyed the company to be found at the Jamaica Coffee House, a favourite hang-out for sailors and captains from the slave ships. The sea was in his blood.

At Wapping, the Thames was at its most crowded: packed with every conceivable kind of vessel, with flotillas of small boats serving them and lining both banks of the river. Local industry and business prospered on the remarkable growth of the Thames-based shipping trades. Wapping was home to a string of thriving ship-chandlers and, like so much of dockside London, was a place which teemed with 'Seafarers and shipwrights, caulkers and coopers, scavelmen, joiners, boatmakers, plumbers, pump-makers and pitchbearers . . .'⁴ It was also home, or temporary resting place, for the thousands of men – Africans, Lascars, slaves from the Americas and those leathery men from across Britain – whose main abode were the crowded crews' quarters of Britain's floating empire.

Newton spent his early years in a London which was in its economic and commercial ascendancy, just before other British regions – the North, the North-East, the Midlands and, of course, Scotland – burst into their own era of growth and transformation. But at the time it was through London and along the Thames that the great bulk of British trade and commerce passed back and forth, on and off the ships whose dense crowd of masts dominated the skyline. Something like 80 per cent of the nation's imports, and 70 per cent of its exports, passed through London – all those exotic items from Asia, Africa and the Americas which, within an old person's lifetime, had been transformed from dazzling luxuries of the rich to the daily essentials of the common folk: tea, china and spices from Asia; ivory, wax and gum from Africa; rice, tobacco, sugar and rum from the slave plantations of the Americas.

Commercial and governmental life thrived on this flux of imports and exports; banking, insurance, customs, excise and taxes, like the myriad industries living by the side of the river, all boomed as never before. Even that great arm of the state which secured (and expanded) Britain's maritime wealth, the Royal Navy, was itself part of the river-borne ebb and flow of men and ships along the Thames. It was impossible to live in Wapping and remain untouched by Britain's seafaring life.

John Newton's father was a captain of merchant ships trading to the Mediterranean. Consequently, the boy saw little of his father, though he ultimately steered the younger John towards a seafaring life. Newton Senior had (unusually) been educated by Jesuits in Spain but he remained unaffected by religion. Newton's mother, Elizabeth, on the other hand, was a God-fearing woman, a regular worshipper at the Nonconformist chapel in Gravel Lane. With his father at sea for long periods, the boy inevitably fell closely under his mother's influence, and from the first she raised him in a deeply spiritual and highly disciplined manner. John read early, and she hoped to send him to university in Scotland where he could train to be a preacher (as a Nonconformist he would have been unable to attend Oxford or Cambridge).

While his mother read Bible stories, his father, back from the sea, would regale him with seafaring yarns (at least those suitable for a child). But his mother's lessons were perhaps the more influential. John Newton learned to recite, and to provide word-perfect answers to children's catechisms, and memorised hymns and poems written for children. Newton's early years were, then, steeped in religiosity, but especially in a new kind of hymn with growing popular appeal. Elizabeth was especially fond of the hymns of Isaac Watts, who insisted on writing hymns that used 'the common sense and language of a Christian'. His mother's choice of contemporary hymns, chosen specifically for children, gave John Newton the basics which were to bear fruit, half a century later, in his own hymns, but most spectacularly in 'Amazing Grace.'

But the influence and company of his mother were short-lived. When he was seven, Elizabeth developed tuberculosis and though she was moved out of London to be cared for by old friends at Chatham, she was dead within months.

Following his mother's untimely death, his father quickly remarried and started another family. John was dispatched for two years to a school in Essex, which he considered the unhappiest time of his life. It was a cruel time for the boy: removed from the one person who had provided him with security and love, and who had supervised his education and religious upbringing, he now found himself taught by a harsh martinet of a schoolmaster. In the arid, hostile atmosphere of that Essex schoolroom, Newton's early love of books and learning simply dried up. In later life, when he wrote about his childhood from the vantage point of evangelical old age, Newton was thoroughly dismissive of his Essex education and disdainful of his new family. To the end of his days, he was acutely aware of the suffering he endured by being parted from his mother. Yet, not many years after his own loss, he would tear apart children and parents – time and again, and on a massive scale.

* * *

Newton's unhappy childhood ended in the summer of 1736 when at the age of eleven he joined his father and a crew of twenty on a voyage to the Mediterranean. Other voyages quickly followed and Newton was regularly at sea throughout his teens. But he found it a troubling time spiritually and, lacking the steadying hand of his mother, he swung wildly from extreme piety to complete religious apathy. He later described himself as 'religious in my own eyes; but, alas! This seeming goodness had no solid foundation, but passed away like a morning cloud, or early dew. I was soon weary, gradually gave it up, and became worse than before: instead of prayer, I learned to curse and blaspheme, and was extremely wicked . . . All this was before I was twelve years old.'[5] Occasionally he tried to prove himself to his Maker by displays of rigid personal discipline, before once again lapsing into religious indifference. But throughout these years at sea he retained his interest in the printed word; he remained an avid reader, especially of the Bible. Reading was important on board eighteenth-century British ships: many sailors travelled with their own books, they borrowed from other crew members, and picked up new volumes in port. Doubtless there were many men who did not or could not read, but there were enough readers on most ships to form a small literate community.

It was one such casual encounter with a new book on board ship which helped transform John Newton's religious outlook at the age of seventeen, when he read *Characteristicks*, a collection of philosophical essays written by the 3rd Earl of Shaftesbury (who had himself been taught by John Locke). Shaftesbury's writing enjoyed a degree of popularity at the time, with his mocking of excessive religiosity and his critique of the contemporary Church. For the young Newton, sensitive to religious appeal yet deeply uncertain of his own true faith, Shaftesbury's writing was a revelation. Newton described how he 'saw the second volume of his

Characteristics in a petty shop at Middleburghe in Holland'. The book, 'suited to the romantic turn of my mind', became his daily companion: 'always in my hand; I read it, till I could very nearly repeat the Rhapsody [the second part] verbatim . . .' Newton was startled to learn, for example, that high moral standards did not necessarily depend on Christianity. The idea that morality might be founded not in religious laws but in human instinct, and that behaving out of fear of God's wrath was selfish, not righteous – all this struck the intense, young Newton as a liberating discovery.[6] It helped to steady a man who had religious inclinations but who was uncertain and confused about the exact nature of his Christian faith. Newton was looking for guidance, and Shaftesbury provided it. Newton wrote that Shaftesbury's work operated 'like a slow poison, and prepared the way for all that followed'.[7] What Shaftesbury's book had achieved was to release Newton from orthodox faith: it also made him feel superior to those who simply accepted the teachings of the Church. Thus, still only seventeen, Newton struck out, intent on being his own man. It was a characteristic which was to mark his faith, and his life in general, thereafter.

Equipped with Shaftesbury's book, John Newton gained strength and confidence. He felt able to set aside religious orthodoxy, a quality that was to prove a key element in the making of the mature cleric in later life. But if Newton had acquired a new security in his faith, his private and working life remained as unsure and indisciplined as ever. As long as his father was close to hand, John Newton seems to have knuckled down to the rigours and demands of shipboard life. But discipline clearly did not come naturally to him. In middle age he looked back regretfully on his youthful failings: '. . . I was capable of anything. I had not the least fear of God before my eyes, nor (so far as I can remember) the least sensibility of conscience. I was possessed of so strong a spirit of delusion, that I believed my own lie . . .'[8]

Newton's father, determined to overcome the boy's lack of application, secured a place for him with a merchant friend in Alicante. But Newton was no more settled there than he had been at sea and suffered the first of many working rebuffs when he was sent home. In later life he openly admitted that he was lazy and indisciplined, and did not take kindly to authority. He was much happier when left to his own devices, and allowed to pursue his intellectual and religious interests.

Though his mother had succeeded in encouraging his attachment to theology, his encounter with Shaftesbury's ideas left him, in those early years, with a serious disadvantage: he found it very hard to work for others, or to do anything other than what he wanted. Such a life was possible for young men of means, but John Newton had nothing except his aversion 'to the thought of industrious application to business'.[9]

John Newton Senior, keen to spend more time with his second family, retired from the sea. But a pressing concern was to see his son settled in work. An old friend, Joseph Manesty, now a Liverpool merchant, had thrived on the Atlantic trades, prospering both as a shipper and from investments in Jamaica. As a favour to his father, Manesty offered the young John Newton a position in Jamaica, the booming colony which lured boatloads of hopeful emigrants (among them, ten years later, the young Thomas Thistlewood). John was due to depart from Liverpool at the end of 1742 to take up an appointment contracted for five years. But as so often in this young man's life, something more attractive presented itself.

In December 1742, Newton was invited to visit the Catletts in Chatham, the family who had cared for his dying mother. Here he fell in love with one of the children, the fourteen-year-old Mary (Polly to the family). It is hard, at this distance, and especially in the light of Newton's odd reluctance to write about her, to know the secret of Mary's appeal, though she had a reputation for social charm and for putting people at their ease. Whatever the cause, John Newton immediately fell under her spell, and was completely smitten by the young woman. Both John Newton and Mary Catlett were young and innocent, yet this meeting set the seal on their future.

> Almost at the first sight of this girl (for she was then under fourteen), I was impressed with an affection for her, which never abated or lost its influence a single moment in my heart from that hour. In degree, it actually equalled all that the writers of Romance have imagined; in duration, it was unalterable.[10]

Newton's infatuation must have seemed obvious and alarming to Mary's parents. He was manifestly intoxicated by her and simply forgot that he should be heading north to Liverpool, to board his ship bound for Jamaica. Under Mary's spell, Newton reverted to type, overlooking his obligations and simply drifting in whatever direction seemed more congenial. After three weeks, and having missed his ship, Newton set off to face his father at his home in Essex. Surprisingly, Newton Senior was sympathetic to his son's plight, despite the embarrassment he had caused him. Manesty promptly found the boy another position, on a merchant ship trading in the Mediterranean. This time, however, the young John Newton was not destined for the relative comfort and privilege of sharing the captain's cabin, but was thrown into the crude company of ordinary sailors. It was a world which provided little room for self-indulgence.

It was on this voyage that Newton had a powerful dream that haunted him for years. After his ship had visited Venice, Newton dreamed about meeting strangers in that city, one offering him a ring, another telling him to throw the ring in the lagoon. When he did, the city was instantly ringed with fire. A third stranger appeared, dived to retrieve the ring and the city's flames were extinguished. When he looked back, later, Newton thought he could easily interpret the meaning of the dream: the ring was biblical truth, offered to him as a child, but which he periodically rejected for easier, more tempting pursuits. The evangelical John Newton thought the dream was a warning he had failed to heed.

On his return to England in November 1743 Newton set off, not to his father in Essex, but to Mary Catlett in Chatham. Many young men would have done much the same, but Newton's decision was to have serious consequences. Chatham was a Royal Naval town, a hive of activity in the building, repairing and equipping of British warships. Finding crew for those ships was a permanent problem for the navy and the press gangs – no more than a crude version of compulsory military service – trawled the docksides of English ports for victims to be dragooned on to the warships. We do not know exactly what happened to Newton, but he later acknowledged that he put himself in harm's way at Chatham, perhaps by hanging around the wrong places, or displaying his sailor's garb, both likely to catch the eye of a press gang. Whatever the cause, Newton was forced on to HMS *Harwich* along with seven other men.

He managed to send a despairing letter to his father, begging him to intercede. Although Captain Newton, now working for the Royal African Company, had no clout with the navy, he succeeded in securing some preferential treatment for his son. John desperately wanted a transfer to a merchant ship, but all his father could manage was elevation from the rank of ordinary sailor to one of the ten midshipmen. The young Newton now found himself in a hazardous world with the danger of combat in the looming war with France. He soon got into spiritual arguments with fellow sailors. There were those, like him, who had a deep-seated if often simple faith. Others, however, gnawed away at his beliefs with their open cynicism, dismissing his faith as mere superstition. Newton later admitted, that 'my mind was unsettled, and my behaviour very indifferent. I met with companions who completed the ruin of my principles; and though I affected to talk of virtue, and was not as utterly abandoned as afterwards, yet my delight and habitual practice was wickedness . . .'[11]

Newton blamed such doubters for weakening his resolve and undermining his beliefs. This was a recurring theme in his life: he tended to blame his failures and shortcomings on others. Temptations which came his way were blamed on the tempters, and not seen as a consequence of his weakness in succumbing to temptation. But whoever took the blame for his lapses, Newton found his faith sorely tried below decks on HMS *Harwich.*

In December 1745, the ship received orders to escort a convoy bound for Gambia, thence to pick up an East India Company fleet heading for India. John Newton, who had been expecting a stint of no more than twelve months on the *Harwich,* realised that the voyage would last five years. He was given twenty-four-hour shore leave, but rode to Chatham to see Mary where he stayed for several days. Newton had already tested the patience of his commanding officer, Captain Carteret, and his failure to return on time confirmed his reputation as an indisciplined young man who might be more trouble that he was worth.

As the awful prospect dawned on him that he might not see Mary for years, he wrote her a love letter, confessing his ambitions to win her, but recognising that others too might find her attractive in his absence: 'I will not mortify myself to think I shall return to find you in another's possession, before I have an opportunity of showing what I could do to deserve you . . .'[12]

It was the start of a remarkable series of love letters from John Newton to Mary, a flow of written affection which lasted throughout their life together.

2 In Africa

John Newton was hopelessly besotted with Mary Catlett. Yet he was trapped on board a warship and Mary had been unable to reassure him about her future plans. Her mother had asked him not to see her until they were more mature – and to stop pestering her with letters. But Newton was nothing if not persistent; such resistance did not deflect him. He made his own position worse when he returned to his ship many days late, to the understandable anger of his captain, 'and lost me his favour, which I never recovered'. Newton's ship was part of a huge convoy, slowly assembling on England's south coast, before dividing into fleets bound for North America, Lisbon, India and Africa. Severely damaged by a storm while anchored in Torbay, the fleet was delayed and brought to safety at Plymouth. It gave young John Newton the chance to seek the help of his father, who had hurried to the West Country on his own business to oversee some of the damaged ships heading for Africa. Once again, his headstrong son made a decision which he must have known was wrong: leaving his ship without permission to find his father. It was an obvious act of desertion – and in wartime at that. He was quickly apprehended by soldiers, brought back to the *Harwich* in chains, and flogged before the assembled crew. Such brutal floggings were commonplace, a basic means of maintaining the necessary discipline in the harsh environment of an eighteenth-century warship. In addition, Newton was removed from the ranks of midshipmen and demoted to that of an ordinary sailor. There would have been little sympathy in the rough world below decks for Newton's preoccupations with theology, or for his yearnings for Mary Catlett.

In mid-April, as the *Harwich* began its voyage to Africa, Newton watched the most westerly point of Cornwall disappear. He felt suicidal, 'But the secret hand of God restrained me.' Newton's gloom deepened the further they sailed. His captain, understandably, had turned against him and life below decks was squalid and often brutal. One of his shipmates was whipped 'for striving to commit sodomy with ye carpenters boy'. The same man was punished by the whole crew two days later 'for striving to commit sodomy with a black man. He run three times round ye lower deck. Peter de Cruse, a black Portigee, had the same punishment for committing sodomy with a sheep.'[1] At the end of April 1745 the convoy docked in Madeira to take on supplies before the last leg down to West Africa. Some British merchant vessels in the harbour were keen to exchange sailors, having transferred some of their more undisciplined men to the warships in the hope that the Royal Navy might be able to beat some obedience into them. Captain Carteret, keen to offload Newton, agreed to let him go the other way. The transfer took a mere thirty minutes, a sure sign that his officers were glad to see the back of him.

The captain on the merchant ship knew Newton's father but Newton soon got himself into more trouble. He wrote an account of his dissolute life many years later, when he was happily married and a much respected cleric. In his memoirs, written in the form of letters to friends, he masked the details of his sins and transgressions by employing biblical quotes and leaving the reader to imagine what he had got up so. He confessed that

> I now might be as abandoned as I pleased, without any controul: and from this time, I was exceedingly vile indeed, little if any thing short of that animated description of an almost irrecoverable state, which we have in 2 Peter ii.14. I not only sinned with a high hand myself, but made it my study to tempt and seduce others open every occasion: nay, I eagerly sought occasion sometimes to my own hazard and hurt.[2]

He said more than enough, to tell us how much he enjoyed female company ('having eyes full of adultery'), and made the most of whatever opportunities came along. In the dockside world of transient seafarers, John Newton, to use the words of an early biographer, 'could sin without disguise'.[3] He described his life in this period thus: 'my whole life, when awake, was a course of most horrid impiety and profaneness. I know not that I have ever since met so daring a blasphemer.' Though never fond of drinking, 'I lived long in excess of almost every other extravagance . . .'[4]

Newton seemed unable to learn from experience. Once again, he alienated his superiors, not merely by his behaviour and his corrupting influence on his shipmates, but by devising rude and witty songs directed against the captain. John Newton was apparently devoid of any common sense, or any instinct for self-preservation. And as if to prove the point, he had volunteered to be transferred to that most dangerous and risky of maritime ventures – a slave ship.

Life on the slave ships was notoriously brutal. The work, involving lingering for protracted periods on the West African coast, loading the ship with distressed Africans destined for the American slave colonies, was unpleasant at the best of times. But it was also dangerous: large numbers of sailors died of disease on the coast; African slaves posed a permanent rebellious threat; and even if all those dangers had been overcome, and the ship turned west into the Atlantic, slave ships quickly became a fetid, stinking stable – a floating nightmare of human filth and degradation.

John Newton had changed ships in order to get away from a hostile captain and to avoid serving on a battleship in wartime. But he had simply exchanged one danger for another. As Newton's ship traded on the African coast, the captain fell sick and died. His successor, the first mate, was also ill-disposed to him and Newton resolved to move on once again. He worried that once the ship had delivered its human cargo in the West Indies, he would simply be handed back to the Royal Navy.

His ship was the 200-ton Bristol slaver, the *Levant*, captained first by James Phelps, then by William Miller. After six months on the African coast, as the holds filled with Africans, the *Levant* was ready to depart for Jamaica from Banana Island, off the coast of Sierra Leone. Newton did not want to sail, however, and when he was offered a post working for an English merchant on Banana Island, he accepted, persuaded perhaps by the man's plans to branch into other slave-trading ventures. It may have seemed an ideal opportunity for Newton to make his way in the world and finally persuade Mary Catlett's family that he was worthy of her hand.

It proved to be a disastrous move. Far from thriving, Newton was soon reduced to utter wretchedness: sick, poor and badly treated, no better, he said later, than a slave. Here, on the African coast where tens of thousands of Africans were consigned to the hell of the slave ships, a young Englishman endured the nadir of his miserable fortunes. He described himself as 'destitute of food and

clothing, depressed to a degree beyond common wretchedness . . .'⁵ He looked back on the experience as a period of
enslavement and of grotesque maltreatment.

His new English employer planned to establish a slaving
base on Plantain Island, a bleak inhospitable spot, but close
to the supply routes for Africans from the mainland. A few
miles away from the River Nuna, it was a good spot for
ferrying slaves from Sierra Leone on to the waiting
Atlantic vessels. Newton, his employer and local workers
set about creating a new settlement, a warehouse for
storing and selling Africans to the Atlantic slave ships.
Newton seems to have enjoyed his first weeks there. But
it was not to last.

Like so many Europeans on the African coast, Newton
fell sick. There followed two years of misery, 'an absolute
blank in my life'. To be sick in Africa was bad enough, but
Newton soon found that he had other problems to contend
with. Looking back, he thought that the Lord had placed
him in this miserable spot in order to bring him down: 'I
was big with mischief, and, like one infected with a pesti-
lence, was capable of spreading a taint wherever I went.
But the Lord wisely placed me where I could do little
harm.'⁶

His employer, like so many Europeans on the coast,
lived with a local African woman who quickly took a great
dislike to Newton. His latest nemesis was a powerful
woman in her own right, who belonged to a prominent
local family with long-established links to English traders.
Frequently, Africans and Europeans came together to
create personal and trading dynasties on the coast, mainly
with an eye to filling the inbound ships with Africans
destined for the Americas. With a mastery of the local
language and English (or other European languages), and
with offspring born of African mothers and European
fathers, such commercial families were connected both
with African trade systems along the coast and into the

interior, and with foreign companies and shippers. It was these local trading systems that provided European and American ships with their cargoes of slaves, and which in return haggled for imported goods to be fed into the local and regional African economies.[7]

When Newton fell sick (almost certainly with malaria) he was left behind in the care of his employer's African wife, known as P.I. Her initial care for him quickly turned into indifference and then into hostility. Newton was quite helpless, and reduced to utter misery. He slept on a mat, with a log as a pillow, and was often denied even the water he needed. P.I. refused to feed him properly, instead sending him scraps from her own plate. At times he was so hungry he ate raw roots he pulled from the ground. At his low point his condition was so wretched that even the chained slaves, awaiting transfer to slave ships, shared their food with him: 'I have sometimes been relieved by strangers; yea even by the slaves in the chains, who have secretly brought me victuals (for they durst not be seen to do it) from their own slender pittance.'[8] In addition, P.I. ridiculed and insulted him, laughing at him in his moments of distress, mocking his incapacity and frailty. 'She would call me worthless and indolent, and compel me to walk, which when I could hardly do, she would set her attendants to mimic my motions, to clap their hands, laugh, throw limes at me . . .'[9]

When his employer returned, Newton's complaints fell on deaf ears: the man simply would not hear criticism of his wife. Worse, when Newton recovered and travelled on his employer's vessel, trading along the coast, he was accused of dishonesty, chained on deck and given meagre rations. By this time his clothing had been reduced to rags: 'my whole suit was a shirt, a pair of trowsers, a cotton handkerchief instead of a cap, and a cotton cloth about two yards long, to supply the want of upper garments . . .' He was kept in this pitiful condition, both on ship and on

In Africa

Plantain Island. Throughout his ordeal, Newton tried to keep his sanity by reading a book by Euclid, which he had bought at Portsmouth and which he had managed to preserve through all his troubles.

There is something very puzzling about this whole affair. Why should two people, English husband and African wife, treat him so badly? Or was all this merely a literary device, designed by the older Newton in his memoirs to portray an Englishman reduced even below the level of nearby captive Africans? No student of Newton's life has doubted this account; all accept it as an accurate version of the low point of his fortunes. If it is true, it was an experience which seems not to have affected Newton's own behaviour a decade later, when he returned to the region as a slave trader and was responsible for loading and shipping Africans in conditions remarkably similar to the ones he had endured, and which he had so hated and despised.

It is striking that John Newton looked back on his own debasement, not as a means of assessing his own treatment of Africans, but as a means of calibrating his spiritual rise. In later life, Newton was a respected and famous cleric, his powerful oratory attracting huge congregations, and his publications and hymns reaching legions of people. When he recounted his life in Africa and afterwards, he told the story of one man's fall and subsequent rise: an inspiring account of what could be achieved with the Lord's blessing. Newton knew that his plight had been of his own making, the result of a sequence of foolish and rebellious acts. But he also believed that he had escaped from his miseries not simply through good luck or determination, but thanks to the Lord's benevolence. As he explained in 'Amazing Grace':

> I once was lost, but now am found,
> Was blind, but now can see.

Newton's wretched state continued for more than a year. He wrote to Mary and to his father, hoping he might be able to secure his release. His father thought that his son had become yet another victim of the slave coast and asked traders working the coast to find out what they could of his fate. Eventually Newton was allowed to transfer to work for another slave trader, nearby at Kittam River. His job was to travel upriver to inspect enslaved Africans, buy them in exchange for European goods, and bring them back to the base to await transfer to the Atlantic ships.

Newton's new work took him into African communities where he enjoyed local company and began to admire local customs. He came to recognise the virtues of the way Africans governed and ordered their family and community life. In old age, he spoke fondly of African life: 'I have lived in peace and safety amongst them when I have been the only white man amongst them for a great distance.'[10] He even considered staying in Africa. He had initially promised himself that he would return to England only if he had made a success in the world, and would be in a position to secure Mary's hand in marriage. But that all seemed as remote and unlikely as ever. There was a local phrase that 'a White man is grown black', not by complexion, but simply by adopting local routines and customs. Newton went the same way: 'I entered into closer engagements with the inhabitants, and should have lived and died a wretch amongst them, if the Lord had not watched over me for good.'[11]

Newton used a coded language to describe his life in Africa, especially in hinting at his associations with local women. Although liaisons with African women were the norm among men working on the coast, it was not an issue he wanted to parade too blatantly before his readers in later life. But even his guarded comments are clear enough. Europeans had long been transfixed by what they took to be the relaxed nature of sexual relations in Africa, though in large part such fascination stemmed from confusion about family and community systems. They also took full advantage of what they regarded as African sexual licence, though as often as not these sexual liaisons were a result of white domination and power, rather than African sexual freedom.

It seems that after his early terrible ordeals, John Newton had made his peace with Africa. After flirting with the idea of staying, thoughts of Mary Catlett resolved the issue: he was now desperate to leave, and wrote beseeching letters to traders to help him. One of his letters had, despite the odds, managed to reach his father in England. His father asked his old friend Joseph Manesty for help, who ordered one of his outbound ships, the *Greyhound*, to search for Newton. Just when it seemed that Africa would never let him go, Newton was rescued, or to use his own words, 'the Lord providentially interposed ... [to] ... save me from ruin, in spite of myself'. Captain Gother of the *Greyhound*, deputed to find Newton and bring him home, arrived to trade along the coast of Sierra Leone. By an extraordinary set of circumstances, Newton was discovered.

In February 1747 he joined the *Greyhound* as a passenger, though the vessel had only just begun its protracted trawl along the African coastline in search of a range of African commodities, notably gold, ivory and timber. Newton found the slow trawl along the coast a tedious affair and quickly fell back on his old shipboard tricks. When he claimed to be able to outdo his fellow sailors in the excess of his blasphemies, the captain had to caution him against his extreme profanities.[12] When he joined various expeditions on shore he was invariably a troublemaker, getting himself drunk and losing the way with other sailors. The captain quickly tired of him: 'he would often tell me that, to his great grief he had a Jonah on board; that a curse attended me wherever I went ...'[13]

Finally, in January 1748, the *Greyhound* picked up the currents and winds to head home. That involved heading first towards Brazil, thence north towards Newfoundland before the last easterly leg back to Britain. It was a voyage of about seven thousand miles. The ship had long been away from home, and the journey and the time on the African coast had obviously taken its toll: it was in no fit state for the tempest that engulfed the ship when they left the Newfoundland fisheries on 1 March for the final leg to Britain.

The *Greyhound* sailed into a massive Atlantic storm which threatened to send them all to the bottom. Newton was jolted from his sleep by the sudden onset of the storm and by water filling his cabin. He rushed on deck to help, one man was swept overboard but they 'had no leisure to lament him'. The vessel was badly damaged, the pumps were overwhelmed, and part of the ship's structure swept away. Newton and the crew struggled through the night to keep the ship afloat, bailing out seawater when the pumps were overwhelmed. They plugged the leaks with bedding and clothing and by early morning the worst had passed. Unconsciously Newton found himself saying, 'The Lord have mercy on us.' He realised that it 'was the first desire I had breathed for mercy for the space of many years'. Lashed to the ship by ropes, Newton continued at the pumps throughout the morning, but now he was also struggling with his own conscience, looking back over his previous sins and wickedness to 'the licentious course of my conversations, particularly my unparalleled effrontery in making the Gospel history . . . the constant subject of profane ridicule . . .'[14]

Newton was now steering the ship, and the storm returned to threaten them, but finally, in the evening of the second day, they seemed clear of the worst danger. By six in the evening, 'the ship was freed from water, there arose a gleam of hope. I thought I saw the hand of God displayed in our favour; I began to pray.' He also began to reflect on his sinful life, and recognised the errors of his ways. In what spare time he had as the vessel ran towards Britain, Newton turned to his Bible.

The ship was terribly damaged, the food and livestock washed overboard or ruined. As they approached Ireland they were again attacked by a storm and driven among the western isles of Scotland. They eventually docked in Lough Swilly in Ireland on 8 April. Down to their very last rations, no sooner had they entered port than another violent storm blew out at sea. Had they been in open water they would surely have been doomed. John Newton later wrote: 'About this time I began to know that there is a God, who hears and answers prayers.'[15]

It had been a close run thing. The *Greyhound* and its crew had come close to destruction. Hardened sailors had wept at their imminent death, and Newton thought their survival could only be explained by divine intervention. Reprieved, the crew repaired the ship, making it ready for the last short leg back to its Liverpool base. Newton took the opportunity of attending church − twice daily − in Londonderry. There, '[I] with the greatest solemnity, engaged myself to be the Lord's forever and only his'.[16] Henceforth John Newton was converted: he thankfully renounced his former ways, repented the sins of his past life and he resolved to be the Lord's servant. To the end of his days, Newton commemorated his rescue and redemption. When he was seventy-five, for example, he again gave thanks: 'My Gracious Lord, Thou hast preserved me to see another anniversary of that great, awful and merciful day, when I was upon the point of sinking with all my sins and blasphemies upon my head into that pit which has no bottom, and must have sunk, had not Thine eye pitied me . . . O I have now cause to praise Thee for that terrible storm . . .'[17]

Until its arrival in Ireland, there had been no contact

with the *Greyhound* for months, and all concerned, including Newton's father, had given it up for lost. He was now delighted to receive a letter from his wayward son, but father and son would never meet again. The older man was about to depart to take up the post of governor of York Fort in Hudson's Bay where soon after his arrival he would drown while swimming. The son was never given the chance to show his father how much he had changed, and to prove that he was capable of making a success in life.

The *Greyhound* finally docked in Liverpool at the end of May 1748. Four years had passed since Newton had been forced into service on the HMS *Harwich*, and three years since he had last seen Mary Catlett. Although he was home, safe and sound, and despite having survived a litany of sufferings, John Newton had nothing to show for the past four years. He longed to marry Mary, but what could he offer her? 'I have been confounded and disappointed in all my schemes hitherto and am as far back as ever . . .' he wrote. He was still unable 'to make her suitable proposals'.[18]

In the early summer of 1748 Newton travelled to London, but when he finally met Mary he was utterly lost for words: 'I scarcely durst look at you. I was tongue tied.' It was an unpromising meeting, and the only agreement he emerged with was permission to write to her. He headed back to Liverpool, unable even to afford the coach fare, trudging all two hundred miles on foot. But then Joseph Manesty once again came to his rescue. Manesty offered Newton command of his slave ship, the *Brownlow*, destined for Africa and South Carolina. It was a remarkable offer given Newton's relative youth and inexperience. What he had in his favour, however, was a remarkable experience of living and working in Africa. A critical part of any slave captain's life was not merely commanding a slave ship, but conducting successful and protracted trade with

Africans, and John Newton was well versed in life and trade on the African coast.

Nonetheless, Newton sensibly thought himself too inexperienced a sailor, and opted instead to sail as first mate. In late July 1748, the *Brownlow* left Liverpool bound for West Africa and thence to the slave markets of South Carolina. John Newton had embarked on his new career as slave trader.

3 Slave Trader

John Newton had already spent a great deal of time on the African coast working in the slaving business. But in the summer of 1748 he embarked on his first foray into the full cycle of an Atlantic slave-trade voyage, a journey that might last up to eighteen months. The route looked simple: from Liverpool to West Africa, thence to South Carolina for delivery of the human cargoes, and finally home many months later. The execution was inevitably more complex and uncertain. In the 1740s Liverpool had pushed aside Bristol to establish itself as Britain's major slaving port. In that decade 239 ships from Bristol shipped 60,378 Africans across the Atlantic, but in the same period 322 ships from Liverpool transported 78,890 Africans.[1] One of them was the *Brownlow* with John Newton as first mate.

That the twenty-three-year-old Newton should occupy so high a rank (and having been offered the captaincy), with so limited maritime experience, was itself a sign of the boom in the Liverpool trade. It is true he had been at sea throughout his teens, had spent a long time on the African coast and had weathered the worst storms the Atlantic could throw at a vessel. But he had never before exercised command over men or a ship, still less experienced the unique complexities and dangers of loading, transporting and maintaining control over a ship filled with sick and rebellious Africans. Slave trading on the African coast was a unique form of oceanic trade requiring an uncommon mix of qualities and disciplines. There was, quite simply, nothing like it.

However, Newton came to the *Brownlow* equipped with experience of bartering and trade with merchants and middlemen on the African coast. He had haggled for slaves, had mastered negotiations and exchanges of imported goods with Africans, and he had been involved in the complex and protracted process of accumulating Africans ready for the Atlantic slave ships.

At the time, the Atlantic slave trade was enjoying a remarkable boom which was to last, despite blips (normally caused by wartime disruptions), until the end of the century. Europe's maritime nations all scrambled to gain a stake in the slave trade. Britain became the dominant trader, partly because of the rise of British economic and military power, but also because of the massive expansion of their own slave-based economies.

The British West Indies turned to sugar – and slavery – just as the tobacco plantations of Virginia and Maryland came to rely on slaves. Later, the rice economy of the Carolinas added a new American market for African labour. The success of plantation production in British America saw slavery spill out into most corners of the local economies. Slaves worked in the field gangs, in artisan trades, in distribution and transport, in domestic work and in a range of jobs in American towns and ports. Other colonial powers followed the same trajectory: Spanish, Portuguese, Dutch and French colonies used African labour to tap the commercial potential of their colonial settlements. And the British maritime fleet, expansive and backed by the power of the Royal Navy, was happy to supply the African labour force, often trans-shipped from their initial landfall on a British island.[2] The numbers involved were staggering. Between 1662 and 1807 British ships carried 3.25 million Africans across the Atlantic.

Of all the Africans transported, perhaps 70 per cent were destined for the sugar economies of Brazil and the Caribbean. By the mid-eighteenth century the Western world consumed sugar on an enormous scale. And the more sugar the colonies produced, the more Africans they required as slaves. In part this was because of the simple expansion of the sugar industry, but it also stemmed from the inability of the slave population in most of the sugar colonies to increase naturally. The slave populations there grew because of importations of new Africans. It was a circular pattern. New plantations were settled, especially in Jamaica and, most dramatic of all, in the French colony of Saint Domingue (Haiti after 1804), and those planta-tions needed ever more Africans. John Newton was, then, one of many Europeans anxious to provide Africans for the plantations of the Americas.

This demand for Africans created sharp competition among traders on the African coast, and knowing how to trade effectively was an enormous advantage (it was perhaps this quality that Manesty saw in the young John Newton). But the most difficult of all tasks was main-taining order and control on board the ship itself: of knowing how to keep Africans, penned below, in peaceable and reasonably healthy condition before finally preparing them for sale to planters in the Americas. At its simplest, it was an exercise in brute control, an intimidating regime designed to threaten and overawe the Africans, and to preserve as many as possible from the dangers and threats endemic on all slave ships. John Newton was to prove himself as brutal and severe a master as any, never hesi-tant to inflict pain and suffering on his human cargoes if he felt it necessary to maintain order. His first slave voyage on the *Brownlow* was to prove a fiery baptism for the young slave trader.

But when he later looked back on those events, Newton was more interested in describing his spiritual and moral struggles. Apart from the profanity, which he had successfully abandoned, many of life's temptations continued to sweep over him as the ship sailed from Liverpool. Newton was enticed by 'those brutish lusts by which I was once so long and deeply enslaved'.³ But the brutal business of slaving Newton preferred not to mention, and when he did, he tended to hide his own role behind a veil of religiosity. However, we have an abundance of material which tells us in precise detail what Newton did. In addition to his letters, sermons and memoirs, we have the logbooks of the slave ships he served on. There, in Newton's own hand, lies a full account of his days as a slaver.

Newton's aim of sailing on the *Brownlow* was to gain experience for future ventures in the slave trade, all in the hope that he could make enough money to win the hand of Mary Catlett. It proved a difficult voyage. He sailed back to the scene of his recent humiliation, Plantain Island; he revisited P.I., his tormentor not so long ago; and he found himself again lured by what he described as a 'rain of temptations'. He fell ill and he clearly succumbed to enticements, almost certainly sexual involvements.⁴ Sailors at sea for months on end made the most of the opportunities available on land, and Newton seems to have been no different from the men around him. By the time his ship had reached the Gold Coast, where most of its African victims were taken on board, Newton confessed, 'I seemed to have forgotten all the Lord's mercies.'

After eight months sailing up and down the coast in search of slaves, the *Brownlow* set sail for Charleston, via

Antigua. There were 218 Africans shackled below decks. It was a troublesome voyage but Newton mentioned it only in passing. We know from the logbook that there was an attempted slave uprising, which resulted in the death of one crew member and four Africans. Insurrection was the greatest worry on the slave ships: about 10 per cent of all slave voyages experienced some form of slave revolt, mainly on the African coast. Some ships were overwhelmed and destroyed by rebellious Africans.

The slaves greatly outnumbered the crew, who, in their turn, felt able to control the Africans only by draconian and inescapable violence. Shipboard routines always took place under the watchful eye of the ship's swivel guns. Every crew member, on every slave ship, knew that survival depended on vigilance and violence: hence the chains, manacles and the ever-present guns. When the crew dropped their guard, the results were disastrous. Slave revolts saw black and white butchering each other with callous savagery. The sailors feared the slaves, and the slaves hated the sailors. This produced a volatile and inflammable brew which simmered on every single slave ship.

The *Brownlow* was also troubled by the other great threat on the slave ships: sickness and death in the slave holds. The ship suffered serious losses – sixty-two Africans died, effectively one-quarter of those taken on board.[5] This was an exceptionally high level of mortality for the 1740s. The whole purpose of this trade in African humanity was to deliver as many Africans as possible, in a healthy condition, to the planters, and to get the best available price at the American slave auctions. But it was not always possible.

Africans fell sick from a range of ailments, some brought on to the ship from Africa, some acquired in the long delays on the African coast. But most were a result of the filth which quickly engulfed the slave decks.

Communal eating, communal lavatories, polluted food, but above all polluted water, sent dysentery racing through the manacled slaves. Africans lay in their own waste, infecting others around them. Not surprisingly, the 'bloody flux' (amoebic dysentery) was the scourge of the slave decks. However, gradually the slave traders learned how to cope with the problems of shipping so many people such huge distances by ship. Average losses of 20 per cent in the early seventeenth century had been reduced to 10 per cent by the late eighteenth century. The death rate on the *Brownlow* was, then, unusually high for the period.

The crew was always delighted to see land. It meant they had survived one of the most dangerous of all oceanic crossings, and that they would soon be rid of their volatile cargoes. The Africans, however, had no idea where they were, or what would happen to them. The crew set about preparing them for landing and sale; washing them, feeding them, shining their skin with oil to add lustre to faded appearances. Imperfections were cleverly disguised, and grey hair dyed, although purchasers were usually alert to the cosmetic tricks of the slave traders. The Africans were sometimes given extra rations of tobacco and rum. One commentator noted that slaves on one Liverpool ship 'had been made up for market, by having their skins dressed over three or four times with a compound of gunpowder, lime juice, and oil'. The men were shaved, and sometimes those with dysentery were bunged up with oakum to give the appearance of good health. Sometimes healthy Africans were taken ashore as a sample to whet the appetite of waiting merchants and planters. One man took a large group ashore 'to give them an airing, but more with the intent of letting the planters see what fine slaves we had'.[6] The Africans were utterly confused: happy at being back on land but terrified at the prospects facing them.

The new arrivals were sold in different ways. Sometimes the sale took place on the freshly scrubbed deck of the slave ship, or close to the quayside. Most frightening of all was the 'scramble', sales where buyers rushed into the crowd of Africans, seizing the ones they wanted in a confused tumult, with Africans grabbed and corralled into groups by their future owners. Yet, whether brutal or smooth, the sale was just the latest of a string of frightening ordeals which had dominated the Africans' lives for months past.

On 14 August 1749, the *South Carolina Gazette* reported the arrival of the *Brownlow*. A week later, the following advertisement appeared in the same newspaper:

A choice parcel of healthy slaves, just arrived from the Windward Coast of Africa in the snow *Brownlow*, Captain Jackson, to be sold on reasonable terms, at their store in Broad Street, by Kennan and Campbell, who have a parcel of choice Madeira wine to sell.

Kennan and Campbell were general merchants, not specialists in slave sales, and like other Charleston merchants sold Africans alongside their other commercial offerings, in this case wine from Madeira. The Africans were all sold in six weeks, thereafter being moved onwards, by foot or boat along the complex waterways of the region, almost certainly destined to work on rice plantations. John Newton seemed uninterested in their fate. Later, he only recalled his own search for spiritual peace (and good company), though not at the expense of enjoying himself. In Charleston he loved to walk into the woods, when the day's work was finished, where 'I began to taste the sweets of communion with God, in the exercise of prayer and praise and yet I frequently spent the evenings in vain and worthless company'.[7] This was to be a dominant theme in Newton's recollection of his life as a slaver: he wrote about his spiritual state and social life, but made no mention of the Africans. They passed through his hands unnoticed and unmourned. In early October, the *Brownlow* cleared for Liverpool, arriving there almost two months later on 1 December 1749. They had been away eighteen months, and Newton lost no time in heading south to propose marriage to Mary Catlett.

Theirs had been a long, protracted courtship, Newton having been told to prove himself by Mary's parents. Despite the rebuffs, Newton continued to pine for Mary through all his travels and troubles. In her absence he had not lacked for female company on his voyages, but his thoughts always returned to Mary Catlett: the prospect of winning her hand had been his only spur in his bleakest moments. Now, at the end of 1749, with a successful slave voyage under his belt, he felt that he had done more than enough to persuade the Catlett family of his good intentions and his worthiness.

When he met Mary, intent on proposing, he was lost for words. 'I sat stupid and speechless for some minutes.' When he finally found the courage to speak, Mary refused him, twice, but he persisted with a third effort and was successful. Finally, on 12 February 1750, after seven years of courtship the two were married at St Margaret's Church, Chatham, and the newlyweds moved in with Mary's parents. Newton had secured Mary's hand by promising her material comfort, which he could only guarantee by returning to sea – and to the slave trade. Joseph Manesty had offered him the command of his own vessel, and thus, a mere three months after the wedding, Newton headed back to Liverpool – this time as captain.

As he rode north, Newton peppered Mary with letters. From St Albans he told her, 'I cannot express what I feel. Do me the justice to believe my affection goes beyond any words I can use.' From Liverpool he begged to know her domestic routines: when exactly she rose, dined, went to bed, all so that he could synchronise his own day with hers.[8] It was the beginning of a lifetime's correspondence between man and wife: hundreds of letters spread over thirty-five years, many of them later published by Newton after Mary's death in 1790. Whenever they were apart he wrote to her, at length and profusely. Newton's letters were, understandably, filled with declarations of his love for her, and it seems strange that he chose to reveal such personal details to a wide-reading public. By the 1790s, when he published the letters, he was a public figure, a cleric of national renown and a powerful voice among contemporary evangelicals. Why publish such private letters, most of them concerned with affectionate and intimate matters?

Less strange perhaps was what he chose *not* to reveal. Though willing to recite his most personal thoughts to his wife, he was much more hesitant to reveal details about his working life as a slave trader. Newton's letters to his wife were extravagant displays of virtue, affection and religious sentiment, but they steered clear of his seafaring life, filled as it was with bleaker, more disagreeable information. This contrast was revealed most sharply on Newton's next voyage, his first as a young married man, anxious to return to his absent wife, miserable about being separated from her, but intent on making money for their joint future.

On 11 August 1750, the *Duke of Argyle*, a snow of 140 tons under Captain John Newton, departed Liverpool bound for the Windward coast. There was a crew of thirty men, and room below decks for hundreds of Africans. It was an unattractive ship which Newton described as 'a very old and crazy vessel . . . hardly fit to lye in a dock or make a Gravesend voyage'. That such a ramshackle vessel should cast off for a voyage to Africa and the Americas, for a period of many months, speaks to the boom conditions of the Atlantic trade. It was a good time for the slavers, and especially for the ascendant city of Liverpool, its merchants rarely able to get enough vessels or crew to satisfy the voracious demand of the American plantations for ever more Africans. Newton's cargoes of Africans formed only one small part of almost 80,000 people shipped into the Americas in the 1740s on Liverpool ships. As staggering as these figures were, they were to be dwarfed by the numbers in the years just before abolition in 1807. In the last seven years before the trade was outlawed, Liverpool slave ships delivered a quarter of a million Africans to the American slave markets.[9]

In 1750 then, the twenty-five-year-old John Newton and his decrepit ship were among a veritable flotilla of men and ships lured to the African coast in search of human cargoes and the profits they generated. Newton recorded the daily comings and goings on the African coast, with ships from all nations crossing each other's paths: Dutch, French, American and plenty from Britain – all helping each other, swapping crew and supplies, exchanging information. Newly arrived ships carried mail and new instructions from their owners, for ships already trading on the coast. The slave coast was a marketplace for the Western world's maritime traders, all of them intent on filling their holds with Africans bound for the Americas.

Newton was instantly faced with a host of problems. The ship was old, battered and infested with rats, and the crew spent all their waking hours preparing the vessel for the arrival of Africans. Worse still, however, was the crew. Newton had more than the usual share of drunk, insolent and disruptive men, all of them keen to exploit the inexperienced young master. But he was ready for their challenge, responding with draconian severity to each and every infraction, and ready to hand over any incorrigible man to the first Royal Navy warship. He knew from bitter personal experience that the Royal Navy had its own means of bringing even the hardest of men to heel. His boatswain was especially harsh on other crewmen, all of whom complained to Newton. Newton, anxious to sort out the man before the Africans came on board, put him in irons for three days, releasing him 'upon his submission and promise of amendment'.[10] A week later Newton gave two of the crew 'a good caning' and put one in irons 'for his behaviour in the boat and likewise being troublesome last night, refusing to keep his watch and threatening the boatswain'.[11] When the same man, William Lees, tried to escape to an island off the coast, Newton was only able to retrieve him by giving local Africans a gallon of brandy to find him. A week later Newton handed Lees over to the HMS *Surprize*. In return, Newton took Will Lapworth, but soon discovered he had acquired a thief; Lapworth broke into the stateroom stores to get at the brandy. Two days in irons produced a confession, followed by a dozen lashes.[12] It was little comfort when Newton heard from other slave captains that they too were plagued by indiscipline among the crew. He pondered why it was that the three ships he had known had such 'piratical crews'.[13]

Life for slave traders on the coast was dangerous for a variety of reasons. There were the natural dangers of the inshore waters – of the rocks, shoals, currents and sudden storms – but the most persistent and unpredictable threat came from the Africans. Newton's crew, like all others, were on permanent guard against attack, especially when they worked on shore and, as the number of slaves increased, when they worked below decks. The shipboard routines involved regular exercise of guns and firearms, ensuring that all was in place for any threat or danger. When he learned that a French slave ship, trading not far from their own location, had been totally overwhelmed and destroyed by Africans, Newton suspected that some of the slaves he bought had been retrieved from the French vessel by the locals and sold on to other slavers.

There were other African dangers which were beyond the power of man to anticipate or prevent. West Africa was infamous for the destructive speed of its diseases. Crew members and Africans alike were regularly struck from the ships' logs. Men who were active and alert one day could be given a hasty burial a day later. Some lingered longer, suffering tropical agonies which contemporary medicine (and even the presence of a ship's doctor) could do little to remedy or alleviate.

When William Lawson died on 18 December after seven days of fever, Newton recorded that he 'was obliged to bury him immediately, being extremely offensive'. Three weeks later he was joined by the ship's carpenter, Andrew Corrigal, after ten days of 'nervous fever'. By then, Newton complained that he had '5 whites not able to help themselves'. A week later his mate, John Bridson, died after 'the most violent fever I have ever seen...' Bridson was a great loss because he was an experienced trader with Africans[14] and Newton worried that such a rate of attrition would endanger the whole enterprise. But so too would the deaths among the Africans, corralled below decks.

Slaves were acquired in ones and twos. Local traders pulled alongside in their canoes offering Africans in exchange for imported goods. Sometimes, Newton's ship would put out a signal that he was ready to trade, inviting offers of new Africans from traders. He also regularly sent out the *Argyle's* small boats to trade for slaves further along the coast, or up neighbouring rivers. Sometimes, crew were gone for days on end before returning with small coffles of Africans. It was a slow, protracted process, sometimes helped by news from neighbouring ships, though sometimes hindered when competitors put out false information in the hope of securing slaves for themselves.

The *Duke of Argyle* spent seven months ranging along a huge stretch on the African coast, sailing south from Sierra Leone along the Windward coast. Like most slave ships, the *Argyle* began to lose Africans soon after they came on board, many succumbing to the 'bloody flux'. Long before he turned his ship towards the Americas, Newton's log began to record its inexorable impact. On 9 January 1751 he wrote: '. . . buried a fine woman slave, No. 11, having been ailing some time . . . she was taken with a lethargick disorder . . .' A few weeks later, 'In the morning buried a boy slave (No. 66) who was taken ill with a bloody flux . . .' Ten days later it was the turn of 'a man slave (No. 33), having been a fortnight ill of a flux, which has baffled all our medicines'. This first wave of slave deaths from the 'bloody flux' faded away, but returned again in April.[15]

Despite the deaths, Newton and his crew slowly filled the ship with its complement of Africans, new arrivals filling the gaps left by the dead. They were purchased in return for the drink, foodstuffs, metal goods, that range of items stored in the ship's holds, and brought out from Liverpool for barter and exchange. Sometimes they even exchanged slaves with other European ships. Throughout, Newton exercised that crude, impersonal yet intimate inspection of Africans to see if they matched his valuation and got his approval. Some were rejected and sent back (sick, small, too old, women with 'sunken breasts') but all of them, those who passed Newton's scrutiny and those who failed, had to endure the most intimate and humiliating of physical inspections.

The eight months between 23 October 1750 and 22 May

1751, Newton traded on the slave coast of West Africa. Such a protracted stay was not unusual: the trade was a slow, piecemeal business, competitive and uncertain. Yet despite all these problems, Newton and his backers, and an army of similar traders, merchants and investors, stuck to the task. The same ships and their surviving crews returned time and again; the same merchants dispatched voyages to the same region, time and again. And all because they felt that the profits, or the prospects of profit, far outweighed the risks, and certainly outweighed the human cost involved. The real cost of course was borne by Africans; by those who did not survive, and whose numbers were scratched from the ships' ledgers, and by those who did, and who were soon to find themselves cast ashore into a lifetime's bondage in the American plantations.

By the end of November, the *Duke of Argyle* had gathered twenty-six slaves. On the 28th, the longboat arrived, carrying '11 slaves, viz. 3 men, 1 woman, 2 men boys, 1 boy (4 foot), 1 boy and 3 girls (undersize)'.[16] This was a characteristic entry: no names, few personal details save for some physical remarks. All along the coast, other slavers did much the same thing, entering the simplest of details about newly acquired Africans into their ships' logs and ledgers. It was a cold, economic exercise, the perfect reflection of the process of enslavement and purchase. In mid-December two local traders came on board, stayed overnight and sold Newton '2 small girls . . . 1 of 3 feet, the other, 3 feet 4 inches . . .' (Newton was generally keen to record their exact heights.) Two weeks later he acquired another six Africans: '6 slaves, 1 woman, 2 boys, and 3 girls, all small, No. 38 to 43.' And so on. People who, not long before, had names and kin, loved ones and friends, were reduced to mere numbers in a white man's logbook.

As his ship nosed along the African coastline, John Newton pined for his young wife back in England. When he retired to the master's cabin he wrote regular letters to her, handed over for delivery to other ships about to leave for England. Soon after his arrival in Sierra Leone he told her: '. . . I generally devote some time, twice a week at least, for writing to you . . .'[17] And Mary replied, her letters arriving courtesy of newly inbound merchant or slave vessels.

Sometimes business got in the way of his love letters ('I have been cruizing about in the boat in quest of trade . . .'), and when he wrote, he said it was 'the most pleasant way of filling up a leisure hour'. His working days were 'distracted with the noise of slaves and traders, suffocated with heat, and almost chop-fallen with perpetual talking'. His work was a stark contrast to 'the sweet agreeable evenings I have passed in your company'.[18] Newton bombarded Mary with the details of his thoughts, of his feelings for her, sprinkling his letters with classical references, parading his learning in a display of sensibility. He clearly loved Mary, missed her and longed to be back home with her.

As he prepared to leave for the Caribbean he told her about the difficulties of his life:

Two hundred people confined in a small vessel, in bad weather, occasion noise, dirt, and trouble enough. Besides common business and care incident to other ships, we have a large number of slaves, that must be attended, fed, cleaned, and guarded against . . .[19]

With 161 Africans on board, Newton finally turned westward and struck out for landfall in Antigua. A week later Africa had slipped behind them, its dangers 'by the goodness of God, happily over . . . I now think myself every hour drawing nearer to you . . . It is now ten in the evening. I am going to walk the deck, and think of you . . .'

The *Duke of Argyle* lost twenty-five Africans on the Atlantic crossing. At regular intervals, as they sailed westward, the crew pitched an African corpse overboard. Number 34 was the first to go, on 23 May. A week later, 'Buryed a boy slave (No. 86) of a flux.' Perhaps most telling of all was Newton's entry for 13 June: 'This morning buryed a women slave (No. 47). Know not what to say she died of for she has not been properly alive since she first came on board.' A week later a man (No. 140) and a boy (No. 170) were buried.[20] And so it continued, clean across the Atlantic, dead Africans cast overboard, almost like markers as the vessel cut a deathly route across the ocean. On 3 July, the *Duke of Argyle* docked in St John's, Antigua. Each African death had been recorded, a subtraction from the slave lists, a number scratched out, a loss on the balance sheet of the whole enterprise. It was also a failure: the purpose was to sell Africans in the slave auctions.

On the next leg of the voyage, as the *Duke of Argyle* was a few days out of Antigua, heading back to Liverpool, he wrote to Mary on 14 August: 'You will not wonder that I write in a serious strain, when I tell you that I am sitting by a person in his last agonies, and who, only five days since, was healthy and florid. This is my surgeon . . . But I fear he must go . . .'[21] Two days later, 'At 6 a.m. Departed this life Mr Robert Arthur, our surgeon, of a fever which seized him a few days before we left St Johns . . .'[22]

Newton missed Arthur not merely because he was a reliable doctor, but also because he had listened patiently for hours as the ship's master had spoken at length about his young wife back in England. Now, Newton had no one left to confide in: 'I have none with me now but mere sailors . . .' No African death was ever accorded such detail, or invested with such a sense of loss. Here was one of the many strange aspects of Atlantic slavery: a man of learning and some sophistication, oblivious to his actions: a God-fearing man energetically going about a godless job. Newton, the star-struck lover, spent his waking hours at the centre of a daily cycle of brute inhumanity. Yet he, and all who worked with him, seemed not to have noticed.

4 Finding Grace in Slavery

When Newton brought his ship into St John's he was delighted to find letters from Mary waiting for him, and he, in turn, posted his usual stream of letters to her via ships leaving for England. He wrote in the spare moments between offloading his African cargo and readying the ship for its long haul back to Liverpool. To today's reader, Newton's letters seem rather self-indulgent missives, displays of lavish affection larded with extremes of sentimentality and godliness. Every two or three days, he spent an hour writing to her, spicing accounts of his daily life with grandiose declarations of love: 'gaining you, I secure the principal of my life'. He wrote of dreaming about her, 'a pleasing illusion' which was shattered at daybreak by the cacophony of a slave ship. If others could read their letters, they 'would smile at me for writing so often, and at *you* for accepting my frequent and long letters so favourably as I know you will'.[1] On leaving the African coast, he had told Mary that 'I now think myself every hour drawing nearer to you'. (The same journey took the Africans shackled below his feet further from their loved ones.) Alone, he would often mutter her name, 'My dearest M***, and find music in the sound.'[2]

49

Through all these letters, which arrived in huge bundles, God was always close at hand, an ever-present strength and guide in Newton's emotional and business life – blessing his marriage, saving him from the manifold dangers of slave trading. It is, of course, possible that writing letters may have provided an escape from the misery all around him: a way of retreating from rebellious Africans, a troublesome crew, and from the death and disease threatening everyone on board. Some critics have enjoyed Newton's letters and described them as 'fine feelings in very fine English'.[3] But they are also letters which seem to be abstracted from place and circumstance. They are, at once, revealing and perplexing: outpourings of a deep passion and longing, written in, yet curiously oblivious of, the most gruesome of circumstances: love letters from a slave ship.

The *Duke of Argyle* cleared its cargo of Africans and embarked on its return voyage to Liverpool on 13 August 1751. It was a battering, dangerous voyage, with the ship running from one Atlantic storm to another. The winds, which Newton liked to think were driving him ever closer to Mary, at times threatened to destroy the vessel. That he survived the lashings of the deep was, again, the Lord's work: 'Need we go farther for the proof of a Providence always near . . . ?'[4]

By early October they sighted the southern tip of Ireland, and on 7 October they reached Liverpool. They had been away almost fifteen months. John Newton's reward (on top of his wages) was a handsome £257 dividend; for those officers who survived this hellish business, slave trading could be a profitable concern.

In later years, when he had spoken out as an abolitionist, Newton felt obliged to explain his life as a slaver. Needless to say, there was a religious justification to his work:

I felt the disagreeableness of the business very strongly. The
office of gaoler, and the restraints under which I was forced
to keep my prisoners, were not suitable to my feelings, but I
considered it as the line of life which God, his providence,
had allotted me and as a cross which I ought to bear with
patience and thankfulness till he should be pleased to deliver
me from it.

Newton's explanation makes no mention of his wages and
handsome bonuses.

While he argued in public that he tried to be a humane
slave trader – 'I will treat them with humanity while under
my power and not render their confinement unnecessarily
grievous'[5] – his business papers provide a very different
view on Newton in the 1750s. After the discovery of a
plot among the slaves chained below decks on the African
coast, Newton wrote in his ship's logbook on 11 December
1752, 'Put the boys in irons and slightly in the thumb-
screw to urge them to a full confession . . .'[6] Thirty-two
years later, in his tract *Thoughts upon the African Slave
Trade*, a major contribution to the abolitionists' argument,
Newton told his large abolitionist readership: 'I have seen
them [slaves] agonizing for hours, I believe for days
together, under the torture of the thumbscrews; a dreadful
engine, which if the screw be turned by an unrelenting
hand, can give intolerable anguish.'

What he did not say was that he had not only seen it,
he had ordered it – and on more than one occasion. In
February 1753, still on the African coast, he had a tip-off:
'The boy slaves impeached the men of an intention to rise
upon us.' Having identified the plotters, Newton 'punished
them with the thumb screws and afterwards put them in
neck yokes'.[7] Newton used thumbscrews on Africans not
merely to extract information about potential plots, but
also as a form of punishment. Yet years later, he wrote:
'I am persuaded that every tender mother, who feasts her

51

eyes and her mind when she contemplates the infant in her arms, will commiserate the poor Africans.'

John Newton's first voyage on the *Duke of Argyle* had been his apprenticeship as a slaver. Despite all the problems, the death and disease among Africans and crew, it had been a profitable venture. It clearly satisfied the ship's owner, Joseph Manesty, and had served Newton's own purpose in bringing wealth to his new marital home. Flush with money, Newton headed straight home to Mary. But after the past year on his ship, life in Kent, for all the pleasures of being with his wife, soon proved a little too dull, though it gave him plenty of time to study and read. This domestic interlude only lasted to the summer of 1752 when Manesty offered him the command of a brand-new Liverpool slave ship, the *African*.

Newton took command of the *African*, 'one of the strongest vessels that can [be?] built for money' in April 1752. They sailed on 30 June for the Windward Islands via the Gold Coast, and by mid-August were prowling for slaves off the coast of Sierra Leone. It was, by now, a familiar routine. Local traders and rulers promptly appeared to offer their latest human wares, haggling over the price, and securing the goods loaded on board at Liverpool. Newton knew what he wanted, rejecting the old and the lame, holding out for what he thought a reasonable price when African traders asked too much. There were plenty of slaves available, but prices were high, in part because of the competition from other European slave ships. On 24 August a canoe brought four 'prime slaves', but when Newton was paying for them the African trader 'took an exception to the smallness of the powder cags' and Newton withdrew from the deal. 'I was determined not to shew so ill a precedent.' A month later, Newton recorded in his journal, 'I have refused 7 slaves yesterday and today, being either lame, old or blind.' Much the same happened on 14 November: 'refused them all, 2 being too old, and 2 too young'. Prices were very high. At the end of the year he bought 'a fine boy slave from a little Monserado canoo, but very dear'.[8] Newton tried to steer clear of the knots of British competitors looking for slaves, heading instead to other, clearer locations. When he saw '2 other vessels passing down', he feared 'that they might otherwise hurt my business' and set out to pre-empt them.[9]

The familiar problems of slave trading quickly surfaced. Two crew members, James Wilkinson and Richard Griffith, escaped in a stolen boat, and the coast was awash with rumours of insurrections on other ships. Illness attacked the crew. Peter Mackdonald died in mid-November after a week 'in a continual delirium', but though others were periodically sick, the *African* did not sustain the number of deaths suffered under Newton's last command. The most serious threat came, initially, not from the slaves, but from his own crew. Newton was convinced that they had been thrown into an insurrectionary mood by the widespread illness among them, and planned to seize the ship. He needed to be on guard 'against the slaves and the round robin gentlemen [the plotters] . . .' These were, he said, 'ticklish times' and he dared hardly leave the ship to accept invitations on shore or on other vessels.

Newly arrived vessels brought fresh sailing instructions. A letter from Manesty told Newton not to sail to Antigua as planned but instead to head for St Kitts. Although ships trading thousands of miles from their home base were away for years, there was a slow trickle of news and orders. The system sometimes failed, with vessels missing each other and instructions going uncollected. But with so many ships plying the Atlantic routes there was a much more efficient system of postal communication than we might imagine. Slave captains were able to respond to fresh orders, and in their turn keep their owners informed of current trading conditions on the African coast.

As the number of Africans below decks grew, the problems of discipline and control, and the importance of vigilance increased accordingly. When crewmen were trading on shore, the ship was often badly undermanned. Africans, on the lookout for chances to escape or overpower their oppressors, quickly noticed the gaps in a ship's defences. Newton uncovered a planned insurrection on 2 December 1752, with slaves hiding knives, stones, shot and a chisel. He does not say what he did when he 'examined' the ringleaders, but it was unlikely to have been a gentle interrogation. He used thumbscrews on the boys to extract the full details.[10] His difficulties were made worse by a recalcitrant crew and he was glad to be able to offload the troublemakers to other ships and thence to Royal Naval warships. He feared that his crew troubles would jeopardise control over the slaves: 'Such a mark of division amongst us was a great encouragement to the slaves to be troublesome, and for ought I know, had it ever come to extremity, they might have joyned hands . . .'[11]

Throughout, Newton was busy buying Africans, worrying about their escalating cost, and concerned that he was being outbid by competitors. He was unsure about whether to stay where he was, or head further south along the coast. Each decision was shaped by rumour and news: gossip and tips from other vessels, information picked up from traders on shore. Trading on the African coast involved a great deal of guesswork and luck, all mixed with the intuition and hunches which only experience could bring. But although he was still only twenty-seven, he was by now an old hand on the coast.

Occasionally Newton went ashore to parley with local traders or rulers, sometimes staying overnight before picking out the slaves he wanted, and settling on the value of the exchange of goods he had brought. Trading was always unpredictable, sometimes even haphazard. Newton bought one African after a chance encounter along a pathway as he walked towards a distant African village. More common, slaves were offered by African traders sending out smoke signals to indicate that slaves were available, and they were ready to trade: 'I went on shoar seeing a smoke, was shewn 2 men slaves, but not liking them both, could get neither.'[12]

In all this there was of course strong competition among the Europeans. It was not unknown for foreign competitors to attack the small boats ferrying Africans from the shore, and simply confiscate them as their own cargo, which must have added another dimension to the terrifying uncertainties of the victims' lives.

Traders knew that they would almost certainly lose slaves. No sooner had new Africans been added to the ranks than illness depleted their numbers. Sometimes, Africans took matters into their own despairing hands: 'When we were putting the slaves down in the evening, one that was sick jumped overboard. Got him in again but he dyed immediately between his weakness and the salt water he had swallowed, tho I imagine he would have lived but a little while being quite worn out.'[13] Slave suicides were common, even though the traders did everything to prevent them. The ships had nets rigged round the decks at obvious spots, and the crew were on permanent guard against slaves flinging themselves into the ocean. But they could not totally eliminate suicides.

In the teeth of the many dangers and risks, Newton imposed a strict discipline on his ship and its men, but despite his severity, sometimes things got badly out of hand. On 31 January 1753 Newton recorded that

In the afternoon while we were off the deck, William Cooney seduced a woman slave down into the room and lay with her brutelike in view of the whole quarter deck, for which I put him in irons. I hope this has been the first affair of the kind on board and I am determined to keep them quiet if possible.

If anything happens to the woman I shall impute it to him,
for she was big with child. Her number is 83 . . .[14]

In the midst of this misery and violence, Newton's
passion for Mary remained undimmed and he scratched
away at his regular missives to her, bombarding her not
merely with effusions of love, but parading his learning
and theological interests through most of his letters. The
extremes of his daily life ran side by side. On Christmas
Eve he bought an expensive boy slave. The day after, he
sat down to write to Mary, 'to wish you a happy Christmas;
a merry one, is a frequent phrase, but that falls far shorter
of my desire . . . It grieves me to think, that this is usually
a season of festivity and dissipation . . .'[15] Occasionally his
letters to Mary revealed more than Newton perhaps
intended. By March 1753 the ship had still not acquired
enough Africans, and Newton wrote to his wife:

I have been now nearly seven months upon the coast, and
am yet unable to judge when I shall probably leave it, and
must expect to make a losing voyage at last . . . As to what
concerns myself: how far two unsuccessful voyages may affect
my interest, or diminish my expected profits, I am tolerably
easy . . . As to money, you know my thoughts of it. In itself,
and as an end, it is of no value; but of use, as a means of
procuring the conveniences of life . . .[16]

Newton took spiritual comfort from his daily
communion with the Almighty, and he may have found
some sort of justification for his life in the regular letters
to his beloved wife. But the essence of his working life
was simple and undeniable: he was a harsh slave trader,
willing to dole out the fiercest of draconian punishments
(to both black and white) to make a profit for himself and
his employers. He kept careful financial management of
every aspect of the ship, right down to how much they

could afford to spend on food for the enslaved Africans. By late March, his budget was so tight that he cut back on their food: 'Give the slaves bread now for their breakfast for cannot afford them 2 hot meals per day.'[17]

A month later, on 26 April 1753, 'they weighed with a fresh brease at SW bound by God's permission for St Christophers'.[18] Newton was relieved that the dangers posed by his African slaves seemed to have passed. Indeed, he was now struck by 'the remarkable disposition of the men slaves', whose mood had changed:

> I was at first continually alarmed with their almost desperate attempts to make insurrections upon us . . . However from about the end of February they have behaved more like children in one family, than slaves in chains and irons and are really upon all accounts more observant, obliging and considerate than our white people . . .

Still, they had to keep up their guard: the crew 'were not wanting in such methods of guarding against them as custom and prudence suggest . . .'[19] After a crossing of less than six weeks, on 2 June the *African* anchored off Basseterre, St Kitts. Newton was keen to sell all his Africans as quickly as possible there, and was most unwilling to embark on another lengthy voyage to sell slaves further north: 'as for Jamaica or America, I should be extremely loth to venture so far, for we have had the men slaves so long on board that their patience is just worn out, and I am certain they would drop fast had we another passage to make'.[20] He was in luck; there was a keen market for his Africans in St Kitts. The first batch was sold on 6 June, and by 20 June all 167 had changed hands.[21]

Contrary to his earlier fears, it had proved a profitable voyage. 'Most of the cargo is sold,' he told Mary in a letter of 8 June, 'and at a good price.' But he was about to warn Manesty 'that I cannot undertake to do any thing upon the Windward Coast next season, the trade is so overdone. If they will send me, I am ready to go; but I will not be blamed, in case of ill-success.' Newton was prepared to go anywhere his employers instructed, but reassured his wife 'it is all for your sake . . .'²² As if to prove the point, on 3 July he sent Mary bills of exchange for £40 and for £207, 'the amount of my Guinea commissions and privilege'.²³ Whatever he might say or write about it, then or later, Newton was in the slaving business for money.

Everyone involved in the world of Atlantic slavery, from the captains of the ships through to slave owners in the Americas and the British-based shippers – all of them, measured in their thousands, were lured to the world of Atlantic slavery by the hope of profit. Today, this seems obvious. But what is surprising perhaps is that few of them seemed to have any moral or religious qualms about what they were doing. Few saw anything wrong or unacceptable in their own behaviour, or in the behaviour of others intimately involved in Atlantic slavery. It was, quite simply, an unquestioned, widely accepted, morally neutral form of trade which yielded profits for some and pleasure for millions. That it also created misery on an epic scale for untold numbers of Africans barely registered among people who ran and worked in the Atlantic slave system. Moreover, many of those same people prided themselves on their sophistication and civility. Few were more conscious of his refined feelings, and of his finely tuned sense of being the Lord's servant, than the captain of the *African*. When he returned to Liverpool on 29 August 1753, fourteen months after he had departed, Newton thought it had been a voyage 'with entire satisfaction to myself, my friends and my employers'.²⁴ He stepped ashore without a scruple.

While in St Kitts, Newton had spent a great deal of time in the company of a fellow slave captain, Alexander Clunie, who lived in Newton's birthplace at Wapping. Clunie was a keen student of the Bible, and the two men enjoyed long, intense discussions about theology. For almost a month, they spent evenings on board each other's ships conversing on the subject. Newton wrote to a friend, from St Kitts, 'We spend the whole time we can command from our business together at the sacrifice of almost all our common acquaintances . . .'[25] Newton had long prayed that he would be given the chance to speak and live as a Christian, and Captain Clunie gave him the confidence to do just that. Clunie was especially helpful in encouraging Newton to pray without the use of formal written prayers. More importantly, he explained the concept of 'grace' to Newton. Newton looked back on his weeks in St Kitts in Clunie's company as a major turning point in his religious life. 'Your conversation was much blessed to me at St Kitts, and the little knowledge I have of men and things, took its first rise from thence.'[26]

Newton felt that Clunie 'gave me a general view of the errors and controversies of the times' and he came to see that he had been running away from God, and indeed had rebelled against Him throughout his life. Clunie persuaded him to accept that the Lord had chosen him – had pursued *him*, John Newton, wherever he had travelled: in Britain, in Africa, on the high seas.[27] Newton had always worried that his various lapses in life – his periods of immorality, his licentiousness and sinfulness – would deny him the salvation he sought, but he now accepted that he had been saved not by his own doing but by grace. He came to accept (reluctantly at first) that his own life was proof of God's grace. He was not a member of any church, yet God had pursued him, 'had rescued him, preserved him, and drawn him'. Newton wrote, 'I now began to understand the security of the covenant of grace and to expect to be preserved, not by my own power and holiness, but by the mighty power and promise of God, through faith in an unchallengeable Saviour.'[28]

What seems like a convoluted theological discussion, between two slave traders, in the slave colony of St Kitts in 1753, was to leave its traces down to the present day. It embedded firmly in Newton's mind the concept of grace, placing it right at the centre of his faith. Thereafter, the word itself was lodged in Newton's everyday language, becoming part of the vernacular he relied on when he discussed religious issues, but more especially when he described the story of his own faith. Above all, of course, it was to find its most memorable and abiding use in the hymn he wrote in 1772. Few today realise that the concept began to take shape in Newton's mind as he rested after his latest trans-Atlantic slave voyage, the stink of the slave holds fresh in his nostrils, and when he found himself instructed in theological matters by another slave-trade captain at Sandy Point, St Kitts.

5 From Slaving to Preaching

John Newton arrived back in Liverpool at the end of August 1753. Throughout his last voyage he had longed to be with his wife, but he been at home a mere three months when he was again called back by Manesty, to captain another voyage on the *African*. The last venture had been very lucrative, and Newton showed no obvious reluctance to end his slave-trading career. This time he was instructed to trade along the Windward coast, from the Sherbro River south to Cape Palmas. It was to be a much shorter trip which may explain why, unusually, the *African* suffered no casualties. When the ship quit the African coast, it had only eighty-seven slaves on board; on its previous voyage it had carried 207. Newton had predicted that trade would be tight and unyielding, and that slaves would be difficult and costly to come by. He was proved correct.

Newton again faced problems with the crew. Men were caught pilfering, those involved put in irons and then lashed. Later, he had to whip the carpenter (twenty-four 'stripes') for behaving 'very mutinously in my absence, daring the officers and refusing his duty . . .'[1] When they reached Sierra Leone, they heard the by now familiar tale of rebellions among the Africans on board other slave ships. The *Adventure* from London, for instance, had been run aground by the slaves, though most of the crew escaped. As Newton had presaged, the price of slaves had risen greatly. What he now paid for four slaves would, only a short while before, have bought ten.² Newton was pessimistic from the outset about making a profit on the trip. He wrote to Mary in late January 1754: 'I expected, before I left England, that the present voyage would not prove successful, in point of profit; and I was not mistaken.'³ He anxiously looked around for other means of salvaging the mission. He was attracted to the *Racehorse*, a forty-ton snow, rebuilt three years before in London and now lying idle at Sherbro. His plan was to load her with his own surplus goods, unused because of the trading problems on the coast, and have her trade independently on the coast before she returned direct to Liverpool. It seemed the only way of cutting his losses on what was emerging as a barren voyage. By the new year of 1754 Newton had bought the *Racehorse* for £130.

This illustrates the complexity of the African trade. The popular image of the slave trade as a triangular affair does an injustice to what was in fact a network of over-lapping trading routes and systems linking Europe, Africa and the Americas. Newton's third voyage as master also reveals the remarkable flexibility which owners sometimes gave to their captains. Newton had sailed with strict instructions to leave the African coast by April, yet he was also authorised to pay for an unexpected commercial opportunity which he encountered on the coast. By now, Joseph Manesty, back in Liverpool, had very good reason to trust Newton's judgement. After all, he had delivered a good return on both his previous commands. It was a remarkable turnaround given Newton's record of indiscipline, rebelliousness and generally disagreeable conduct.

John Newton kept his wife informed of the latest voyage

in another stream of letters penned in idle moments. They were much like his earlier outpourings, about love, theology, and all laced with Newton's philosophical musings. He urged her not to worry about the apparent financial failure of his current venture: 'this failure in dirty money-matters, is the only abatement we have hitherto met with . . .' That he should again adopt a lofty indifference to moneymaking was strange, because it was clear from the beginning that it was his only reason for being on board a slave ship. Throughout his letters he again took shelter behind his faith, and behind the happiness of his marriage ('We have blessings which riches cannot purchase, nor compensate for the want of'). He told Mary that money did not matter. 'Perhaps we may not be rich, – no matter. We are rich, in love.' Yet even on such a poor trip, Newton expected to make a decent return. All was not as bad as he sometimes claimed: 'Besides, what I may get by an indifferent voyage, would, by many, be thought a great sum.'[4] But there were times when Newton was less than open in his discussion about the profits of slave trading.

So, in the new year of 1754 buying Africans was a costly enterprise. One man cost Newton '120 bars, through the positiveness of competitors'[5]* and to secure this particular African, one of Newton's crew had to walk two days to inspect him. Newton doubted whether such costs could to recovered in the Americas. As time passed it became clear that this stretch of coast had been badly over-traded and Newton decided to sail south to Cape Palmas. There, he found other problems waiting for him: 'they have got such a head in their first villany thereabouts, that it is judged precarious for a single ship to venture near them'. Newton only agreed to sail there in the safe company of

---

* 'Bars' were the pieces of metal which acted as a means of exchange and against which all other commodities were measured and valued.

another vessel, 'to take our chance of trade, and assist and protect each other . . .'⁶

Slave traders were always in an odd position. They were competitors for trade and for Africans, and were constantly jockeying to outdo each other. But there were times when they needed to liaise and coordinate against the common threats posed by Africans. Year after year European slave traders in their thousands descended on the coast, in search of human cargoes which could only be secured by direct dealings with other traders on the coast. These middlemen and rulers sanctioned, organised and profited from the local slave trade. Viewed from the European slave ships, it was, from first to last, a highly risky and dangerous venture. The crew had, it is true, the security of their ships, and their powerful armoury of weapons, though these were sometimes of limited use. And as the ships began to fill with slaves, the dangers increased. There were potential rebels below decks, and unpredictable Africans on shore. To parley, negotiate and trade, Europeans had to leave the relative security of their ships, travelling in smaller boats, to rendezvous with African traders: on beaches, in villages, settlements and even in distant locations, further along the coast or days away up river systems. They were often absent from the mother ship for days – sometimes weeks – on end. Newton was forever worrying about the time his men spent ashore, hoping they had come to no harm and would return as and when agreed. In late March he recorded that '. . . Mr Dickenson in the *Greyhound*'s yaul was cut off last week by Robin Will at Kittam, himself and his 2 white people all murdered and the boat halled on shoar . . .'⁷ There were any number of places and moments when Europeans could be overwhelmed as they traded: on land, when they had coffles of Africans on small craft, and – of course – when rebellious slaves rose on the slave ship itself. They dropped their guard at their peril, and this need for vigilance continued right across the Atlantic. Slavers were not able to relax until they had sold their Africans in the Americas. Planters were to find that they inherited very similar problems.

By early April 1754 Newton had wearied of trading so fruitlessly. In any case, Manesty had given him strict instructions to leave Africa that month. Having ensured that his recent purchase, the *Racehorse*, was suitably manned and supplied for the rest of its time on the coast, Newton turned the *African* westward on 7 April, 'bound by God's permission to St Christophers'.[8] Six weeks later, on 21 May they anchored off Basseterre, St Kitts.

They had carried only eighty-seven Africans, but had suffered not a single fatality. Nor had a single member of the crew of twenty-seven died. On his first voyage on the *Duke of Argyle*, Newton had lost seven crewmen and twenty-eight Africans. A clean sheet was an unusual occurrence and Newton was understandably pleased. It was such an unusual voyage that later, back in Liverpool, 'I had the pleasure of returning thanks, in all the churches, for an African voyage performed without any disaster, or the loss of a single man ... This was much noticed, and spoken of, in the town; and I believe it is the first instance of the kind.'[9]

No one in Liverpool expected a slave voyage to pass unscathed by human loss. But what they were celebrating primarily was the absence of *white* fatalities: the loss of Africans generally went unnoticed in British home ports except, that is, in the ledgers of the local trading company.

Predictably enough Newton felt that his good fortune had other explanations: 'Neither in the wilds of Guinea, nor in the pathless ocean, am I wholly without his gracious presence.'[10] St Kitts had a special place in Newton's affections and over the coming years he frequently returned to the issue he had discussed with Alexander Clunie on his last visit – the question of 'grace'. His letters to Mary frequently mentioned the role of grace in his own life: 'By his grace he brought me from a state of apostacy, to the knowledge of his Gospel . . . He brought me, as I may say, out of the land of Egypt, out of the house of bondage; from slavery and famine on the coast of Africa, into my present easy situation.'[11]

Similar ideas, similar phrases, were to echo throughout the prayers and music of black American spirituality over the next two centuries. Hymns and spirituals were suffused with biblical imagery of slavery, redemption and escape from slavery; and they naturally struck a powerful chord with black congregations. They too had escaped bondage, had been freed from the land of Egypt, and they too praised the Lord, in music and prayer, for their emancipation. Especially in North America, images of Moses blended easily with images of Jesus to provide a powerful theme of deliverance among slaves and their descendants. By a quirk he could never have predicted, Newton, slaves and the offspring of slaves were united in celebrating the liberating power of Christian faith, and giving thanks to the Saviour.[12]

John Newton wrote these lines at sea, in July 1754. Having just successfully delivered eighty-seven Africans to the slave market of St Kitts and now halfway home across the Atlantic, he used the biblical imagery of slavery to describe his own salvation, to discuss *his own spiritual* state, not the *actual* bondage of the Africans. It was to be another thirty years before the reality he knew so intimately – the brute violence, and stinking squalor of the slave ships – came back to haunt him, and to propel him to speak out against the trade which had brought him such comfort and material success.

By August 1754 Newton was back in Liverpool. He was glad to leave the *African*: 'I have quitted her because she is such a heavy sailer.' But another ship was already waiting for him. Launched on exactly the same day as the *African*,

'I may have her if I please, and probably I shall not refuse
her, though I know not what to do with her at present.'
Newton thought it best to wait six months before heading
back to Africa but worried that Manesty thought he
wanted to delay departure simply to spend more time at
home with his wife. It would have been hard to blame him.
Since marrying Mary in February 1750, he had been at
sea for almost three years, and had spent only sixteen
months in England, and for some of that time he had been
away from Mary on business.

Newton may have thought that the time was not ripe for
a return to the slave coast, but he was not opposed to sailing
there on principle, or for family reasons. In fact, he was on
the point of departing on his new vessel, the *Bee*, when his
plans, and future, were suddenly thrown into confusion. Two
days before the intended departure date, John Newton
suffered what seems to have been a stroke. In the words of
an early biographer, 'as he was one afternoon drinking tea
with Mrs N. he was seized with a fit, which deprived him
of sense and motion'.[13] The seizure lasted for an hour, and
left him with head pain and dizziness. It was immediately
obvious that Newton could not be entrusted with the
command of an ocean-going ship, and he resigned as master
just one day before the *Bee* was due to depart.[14]*

John Newton's flourishing career as a slave trader had
come to an end but the experiences of the past few years
would remain with him. What he had been responsible for,
and what he had done with his own hands, was nothing
unusual for a white sailor on the slave coast of West Africa.
But it formed a catalogue of brutality which, though
generally acceptable in the 1750s, had begun to look
morally and spiritually threadbare a generation later.

*   *   *

* It was a providential illness. His replacement, Captain Potter, died along with
many of the crew, in a slave rebellion on the African coast.

Although Newton quickly recovered from his stroke, the shock of his illness tipped Mary Newton into a serious depression. For the best part of a year Mary was sunk in a deep gloom which no amount of medical and family care could ease. Though apparently triggered by her husband's seizure, the length and severity of her depression suggests deeper problems. She lost strength, became emaciated and at one point could barely walk across a room unaided. Newton could not manage her care alone and Mary was nursed by family, allowing her husband to return to Liverpool to take up a new post.

It was a time of great stress for John Newton but, as ever, he found something positive in Mary's suffering. Along with his own stroke, Mary's illness forced Newton to withdraw from the sea. Joseph Manesty again came to his rescue by finding a new position for him. In August 1755 Newton became the 'surveyor of tides' at Liverpool, though the job was not what its title suggests: he was in fact employed in the Customs House: 'I have a good office, with fire and candle, fifty or sixty people under my direction, and a handsome six-oared boat and coxswain, to row me about in form.' He asked Mary not to worry about his safety when he was out on the water: 'Remember that I am in the path of duty, and under the protection of Him whom the winds and seas obey.'[15] Newton's role was to board inbound ships, inspect the cargoes and ensure that customs duties were paid on imported goods. An ex-sea captain was clearly suited for such a role: Newton was wise to the tricks of seafarers, all the more important in an age when smuggling had became an industry in itself. It was an important position, which reflected the rapid expansion of Liverpool, as the city grew into a major international port on the back of the African and American trades. But Newton worked only one week in two, allowing him the leisure time to read and study, and to follow his interest in theology.

Newton spent as much free time as he could in local churches, sampling whatever congregations and sects were available, devouring theological literature and arguing the finer points of theology with whoever was interested. His time with Alexander Clunie in St Kitts had proved a revelation, and he was anxious to pursue some of the ideas the captain had planted in his mind. Newton also wanted to make contact with some of the devout people Clunie had recommended. He began to talk of himself as 'evangelical'; this was at a time when evangelicalism was beginning to make a significant impact in Britain and North America.

Clunie's contacts enabled Newton to meet a number of prominent contemporary preachers. He spent time with George Whitefield, founder (along with the Wesley brothers) of the Methodist movement, in both Liverpool and London. Newton was intrigued by the Methodists and was familiar with their writings, but what really impressed him was Whitefield's ability to attract huge crowds and his effect on his congregations: 'that composure, that elevation, and that assurance of faith which shone in his frame and discourses were in some measure diffused over the whole assembly'. Newton also liked Whitefield's attachment to hymns and hymn-singing. 'He made many little intervals for singing hymns – I believe nearly twenty in all.'[16] Years later, when Newton had his own congregation, hymns were to play an important role.

John Newton was living through an extraordinary period of religious revival. The crowds, the fervour, the conversions, all and more shook the established Anglican Church to its very foundations. The traditional Church of England, its dominance not seriously challenged since the religious and political upheavals of the seventeenth century, initially found it hard to respond to the evangelicals. Anglicans were troubled by many features of evangelicalism, by the literalist interpretation of the Bible, by the preaching for conversion, the insistence on a strict sabbatarianism, and by the emphasis on human sinfulness and personal salvation. A later generation, personified by William Wilberforce, took evangelicalism to the heart of the Anglican Church, but in the period when Newton was searching for his own spiritual home, evangelicalism was viewed with hostile suspicion by many Anglicans.

What sustained the mid-eighteenth-century evangelical upsurge was its emphasis on conversion, the idea that men and women were expected to follow the gospel's demand that they fundamentally change their life.[17] Few people were more susceptible to such an appeal than John Newton, a man acutely conscious of his past weaknesses and sins, anxious for salvation, and who had undergone an extraordinary transformation from licentious and blaspheming seafarer to self-taught cleric.

Newton devoted himself to religion on a broad scale. He visited assemblies, churches and prayer meetings organised by Anglicans, Baptists, Independents, Presbyterians, Congregationalists, Methodists and Moravians. And everywhere he went and worshipped, he made his presence felt. Word began to spread about his own remarkable life. Of course, there was nothing remarkable about being a slave trader in Liverpool – the more prosperous sat in their own designated pews in the town's most prestigious churches – but Newton's story was different. Even by the hair-raising standards of seafaring life, Newton's life had been extraordinary. Among Liverpool's many slave traders and sailors, how many had been enslaved in Africa, and how many had been transformed from slave trader to preacher? Mid-eighteenth-century England was awash with self-made preachers, but how many of them had captained a slave ship, or had so narrowly escaped the physical dangers of life in Africa and of Atlantic storms? Newton had passed through dangers which most people could barely comprehend.

Moreover he had emerged a new man, redeemed by the Saviour's grace. People began to look to Newton himself for religious guidance and inspiration. He had a presence, his powerful oratory was riveting, and he had a story to tell. But he also had a story to hide.

From childhood John Newton had been an avid reader: of classical texts, theological disquisitions and even studies in mathematics. In many ways he showed all the virtues (and vices) of the self-taught man: filling his head with information, excited by new ideas, keen to discuss newly discovered theories with interested parties, and always anxious to impress others with the range of his learning. At the same time, there remained an element of indiscipline even to his learning. It was as if he vacuumed up information for mental storage, sorting and application. But he also seemed unsure which intellectual route to follow. This hesitation clearly emerged in his theology. He was not certain which direction he was taking, though significant encounters with other theologians and scholars steered him, eventually, towards the career which dominated the rest of his life.

Much of the inspiration for the evangelical movement stemmed from deep dissatisfaction with the established Church of England. Its failings were many and obvious. There were too many placemen, too many sinecures and absentee clerics, too many parsons who knew little and cared less about their parish and parishioners. The Church elite, its bishops, with their quota of places in the Lords, often abused their patronage on a flagrant scale. With their links to England's other political and propertied elites, they gave an impression of institutional corruption and venality. The Church of England seemed to reflect eighteenth-century England's overall ills, yet showed no willingness or ability to address or solve them. To many, England was, in the words of Adam Hochschild, 'a nation that had lost its moral bearings'.[18]

In all this, however, the world of Atlantic slavery was oddly missing. Those who felt the need for spiritual and social reform looked closer to home for flaws and for solutions. Later in the century, Britons would come to see slavery as one of the nation's great ethical and religious failings, but in the 1750s, as evangelicalism began to spread, it paid little notice to the slave ships or the plantations. As we have seen, the swirl of theological debate at the heart of early evangelicalism caught up two men who spent their waking hours attending to cargoes of enslaved Africans. As Newton wrote in a letter to Alexander Clunie in 1761, 'Your conversation was much blessed to me at St Kitts, and the little knowledge I have of men and things, took its first rise from thence.'[19] It appears that Africans and slavery did not even begin to encroach on the world of their much-vaunted sensibilities.

John Newton went about his customs work in Liverpool with all the efficiency of a successful naval captain, but his heart lay elsewhere. Encouraged by friends and clerics, and prompted by the response he provoked when he rose to speak at religious gatherings, Newton determined to become a minister. His main problem, however, was that he did not have a degree. In the years when potential clerics would have been studying at Oxford or Cambridge, Newton was leading his dissipated life at sea. It is true that he had more than made up for his lack of formal education by reading, studying and taking part in serious theological debate. He also spent as much time as possible simply listening to preachers and clerics, in Liverpool or London. He was a serious critic of many, a devotee of some, but he learned something from all of them: about theology, about preaching, and about the neglected world of choral singing. Above all, perhaps, he appreciated the vital need for preachers to appeal to that audience of British people who were desperate for spiritual leadership and inspiration.

It was obvious to all who knew him that Newton was the kind of man the Church badly needed. When John Wesley met him in 1760, he wrote in his diary:

> His case is very peculiar. Our church requires that clergymen be men of learning, and to this end have university education. But how many have university education and yet no learning at all? Yet these men are ordained! Meantime one of eminent learning as well as unblamable behaviour, cannot be ordained, 'because he was not at a university'! What a mere farce this is!

When it came, the solution to Newton's problem was slightly fortuitous.

Newton had written a series of eight biographical letters to his friend John Fawcett, a Baptist preacher at Hebden Bridge. Amazed at what he read, Fawcett circulated the letters among friends, including Thomas Haweiss, curate to a London hospital. Haweiss was so impressed by the letters that he immediately contacted Newton, urging him to write more fully about his remarkable experiences. Newton replied with a string of fourteen letters written in three days. Haweiss passed Newton's letters on to Lord Dartmouth, a powerful politician, and perhaps England's most high-ranking evangelical. Dartmouth, equally astonished by the story Newton told, sponsored the publication of the letters. Edited by Haweiss and published anonymously in 1764, they were in effect Newton's autobiography: *An Authentic Narrative of Some remarkable Particulars of the Life of ******** .

More critically, Lord Dartmouth also owned large tracts of Buckinghamshire, and had the patronage of a number of local parishes, one of them at Olney. Dartmouth called Newton to London for an interview for the vacant position at Olney, before handing over the formal ordination proceedings to the Bishop of Lincoln. Newton had been periodically rebuffed in earlier applications for Anglican positions, but this time, backed by a powerful aristocratic patron, he was successful. His seven-year search for a post in the Church of England was over.

6 *The Slave Trader as Cleric*

In April 1764, at the age of thirty-nine, John Newton was ordained curate of Olney, and was appointed priest in June of that same year. It had been a remarkable transformation. The former slave-trade captain, his brutal past safely behind him, was now comfortably placed in a small Buckinghamshire town. Only ten years earlier, he had transported hundreds of Africans across the Atlantic. Forgotten for the time being, they would return to trouble Newton in later years.

John and Mary Newton moved south from Liverpool to Olney, a small town of two thousand souls, and home to a domestic lace-making industry. After Liverpool, the gateway to Britain's Atlantic empire, it must have been like stepping back in time. Although he was now a local parish priest, within four months, Newton found himself catapulted to national fame with the publication, in August that year, of his *Authentic Narrative*. Despite the text being formally anonymous, it was widely known that Newton was the author. At a stroke, he acquired celebrity as a national voice of evangelicalism. Though he was as surprised as anyone else by his new-found fame, it was, he felt sure, the Lord's doing.

Newton was acutely conscious of his debt to Lord Dartmouth, who had both subsidised the autobiography and granted him the Olney position. Dartmouth was also, he noted, 'wonderfully kind in giving me so many opportunities of his company and engaging me so often in his house'. Newton hoped to repay his debt by bringing a distinctive, more attractive form of preaching to Olney. 'One thing I hope, at Olney we shall not find such barren tedious Sabbaths as have been our usual appointment at Liverpool.'[1] Newton was delighted to find his Olney congregation filled with 'a considerable number of lively, thriving believers ...'[2] Though tempted by a position in Hampstead (better paid and closer to Mary's family) soon after moving to Olney, Newton turned it down. His family fortunes, however, took a turn for the worse when Joseph Manesty went bankrupt in 1766, taking with him Newton's assets: 'I suppose what I had in his hands is quite lost. It was not much, but it was my *all.*' Even though he had left the Africa trade, Newton had maintained some investment in the business with Manesty. Newton had embarked on his slave-trading career to establish himself economically; now, twelve years after leaving the sea, he had nothing to show for the dangers and risks of a career in the slave trade. Newton's stipend at Olney was meagre but he did not seem to resent losing his savings: 'I repine not at this ... the Lord will not want means to give me what he sees necessary ...'[3] Secure and happy in a position he had coveted for years, money seemed not to matter.

What did matter was his work as a parish priest and preacher. He had mastered the art of public speaking, preparing carefully and scouring the Scriptures for appropriate ideas and quotes to use as an entrée to a sermon. The Olney congregations clearly took to their new minister, and increasing numbers came to hear him preach. Newton found himself speaking to people of little learning, but who nonetheless had a zest for faith.

Sometimes they had pronounced views of what was theologically acceptable. It was a challenge he rose to with gusto.

Impressed by the great preachers he had watched so closely in recent years, Newton was keen to attract more people to his church, and he set out to woo his congregations. One problem was that sermons had a bad reputation: 'A large majority of our congregations are, I fear, sermon-proof − they come to the house of God, and return like a door upon the hinge.' Newton wished to appeal to local people by telling 'the world from my own experience that there is mercy . . . for the most hardened'.[4] His sermons were liberally sprinkled with tales from his life at sea: maritime imagery, naval phraseology, storms, navigation − all were used to make a point.[5] He thought he was at his best when an idea suddenly caught his attention when he was in full flow, in the middle of a sermon, and he allowed his thoughts and words to move with the inspiration.

As Newton refined and honed his preaching skills, more and more people came to his church. For special occasions, people walked many miles to hear him. Slowly but surely, John Newton emerged as a great preacher, and it was his style − confessional, down to earth and plain − that became his main appeal. He spoke to ranks of ordinary people in terms and in a tone they recognised and appreciated. The most unusual of all of Newton's qualities as a preacher, which distinguished him from most other Anglican clerics, was that he consciously aimed at the lower orders, and not at the respectable, propertied and well-to-do. Few humble people felt uncomfortable or out of place in his church. Newton also established a reputation as a dutiful, caring parish priest, always ready to visit the poor and the sick, often in distressing conditions, and never repelled by some of the more unpleasant scenes awaiting him. Even the homes of the most wretched could never have been as repellent as the daily life Newton had experienced on board his slave ships. As a result, his congregations grew bigger and the church had to be extended to cope with the numbers of worshippers. It appears that at Olney both Newton and Mary were happy.

Newton's services were unusual for their choral music. He had always loved hymns and hymn-singing, but he was spurred to write his own by the arrival in Olney of the poet William Cowper. Cowper is now recognised as a major figure in English letters, but when he arrived in Olney in 1767 at the age of thirty-six he cut a pathetic figure, his health and sanity both delicately balanced. A well-educated man from a privileged background, Cowper was plagued by mental unrest, and after a series of dangerous episodes had been consigned to an asylum in St Albans. Throughout his time there he had wrestled with theology and the Bible. One of his major mental torments was his obsession that God would not forgive him for his sins, and he would not accept that he could be saved until and unless he alighted on a biblical quote that would prove the point. He searched the Bible in vain, and consequently believed he was doomed. Adopted by a family in Huntingdon, the Unwins, Cowper at last seemed to find personal peace in their caring company. The accidental death of the Revd Unwin left him alone with the young widow, and for propriety's sake, they moved to Olney.

Cowper moved in with the Newtons and he was later joined, in a rented house, by Mrs Unwin. This unremark-able coming together of two men, the eminent preacher and the delicate, anguished writer, led to a close friend-ship. As the crowds for Newton's services increased, they spilled out into bigger rooms – Lord Dartmouth's 'Great House' for example – and it was for these crowds of eager Christians that Newton and Cowper began to write hymns, giving musical voice to the eighteenth-century evangelical revival. The Anglican Church itself remained unsympathetic to hymn-singing, but Cowper and Newton took their freshly written hymns *outside* the church building, and had large crowds singing in Lord Dartmouth's house.

Newton tried to write a hymn each week for use along-side his weekly sermon, and sometime in late December 1772, he wrote 'Amazing Grace'. He could never have imagined that he had drafted a few simple verses which would grow in power and popularity over the next two centuries.

'Amazing Grace' was first presented to his congregation in Olney in January 1773. But it was also the last time Cowper attended church. Newton and Cowper had spent part of every day together since 1767 but in 1773 Cowper slid into a new bout of bleak instability. He remained gripped by a belief that he was damned, and no amount of dissuasion by doctors or friends could change his troubled mind. After 1773, Cowper was too sick to join Newton in his regular weekly hymn-writing: 'Ask not hymns from man suffering despair as I do.'[6]

The publication of the *Olney Hymns* – a collection of 428 pages – in 1779 also marked the end of John Newton's time at Olney. His national reputation had grown so much that he was now a sought-after preacher. Friends and supporters thought he would be better employed in London where he could reach a much wider audience, and perhaps exercise greater influence, than working in a small town in Buckinghamshire.

Newton had been at Olney for more than fifteen years and in that time he had received regular offers of posts elsewhere, but he resolutely stuck to Olney. Yet in 1779 a new offer proved irresistible. He was offered the parish of St Mary Woolnoth, close to the Bank of England. He preached his last sermon at Olney in January 1780.

The translation to London plunged Newton into the busy life of the capital. He lived close to the centre of commercial and financial life, hard by the river which fed the nation's thriving maritime trades – of which he had, twenty years before, been so active a member. He brought to St Mary's the gusto and evangelical fervour which had so revitalised worship at Olney, though his new congregation found it hard to adjust to the new man and his style – and to the large crowds packing the church. Huge numbers continued to want to see and hear Newton. Many arrived early to get a seat, and were not too worried about taking over the pews of regular parishioners – to their great annoyance.

The noise and clamour of city life was utterly unlike the peace and quiet of Olney, but the new post had its rewards. Newton had access to an amazingly varied company of worshippers and admirers: clerics, visitors, MPs, among many others, came to his breakfast prayer meetings, or sought out his personal counsel. Looking back, his most important influence was probably exercised over the man who was to dominate – personify even – the campaign against the slave trade: William Wilberforce. Wilberforce was also to be the catalyst which prompted Newton to confront his former life as a slave trader.

Following his seizure in 1754, John Newton had abandoned the slave trade. For the next thirty years his energies and intellectual vigour were directed elsewhere. During that time he paid little attention to the slave trade in his enormous *oeuvre* of sermons, letters, pamphlets and hymns. Yet it was no secret that Newton had been a slaver. Indeed, his transformation from slave trader to eminent evangelical preacher added to his fame and appeal: it was hard to point to a more staggering change of personal fortunes. But his early life and his experiences on the slave ships gained a new and more political significance in the 1780s when the first British political organisations were launched to bring the slave trade to an end. As the early abolitionists struggled to make their case, what better ally could they have than a man of God, famous for his preaching and his good works, friend to the influential and the well placed – but who had, as a young man, been a slave trader? John Newton was about to undergo yet another remarkable change when he became an influential voice for abolition. The slave poacher was about to become abolitionist gamekeeper.

7 *Reluctant Abolitionist*

In the twenty years since John Newton had left the sea, the Atlantic slave trade had expanded enormously, taking tens of thousands of Africans to the plantations, and generating untold wealth and economic advantage for Britain. Newton's home port of Liverpool took the lion's share of the business in those years. During the 1780s the city dispatched 646 slave ships to Africa, compared to 166 from London and 111 from Bristol. Year after year, thousands of Africans were dragooned into British ships bound for the Americas: 136,000 from Sierra Leone in the 1760s; a similar figure from the Bight of Biafra in the same decade. In the years 1766–75, British ships delivered 411,300 Africans to the Americas.[1] Liverpool and Britain boomed on the back of the slave trade: a lucrative, buoyant industry, which maintained its appeal to traders, merchants and manufacturers, and which attracted very little complaint. Moreover, whatever complaints people made about the slave trade, they were generally drowned by the cacophony of commercial activity. The slave trade was good business.

But something began to change in the 1780s. For the first time, major objections to slavery began to make an impact. This was the decade when the tectonic plates of British political and social life began to shift; only a little, but with enormous consequences. Issues that had gone unchallenged for many years began to attract growing criticism. An early sense of disquiet about slavery had surfaced in London in the 1760s and 1770s, notably because of the slave cases in English courts. Guided by that indefatigable friend of blacks in England, Granville Sharp, a number of legal cases addressed the thorny issues of black rights, especially the right to freedom in England, and challenged the slave lobby's claims to move their human possessions freely in and out of the country as they saw fit. The turning point was the Somerset case of 1772, which, though not the full victory for black freedom that many believed, nonetheless established a critical legal right: that slave owners could not remove black people from England against their wishes. In these cases, and in broader social agitation, the gross maltreatment of some black servants and slaves came to the attention of the British public. Throughout, Granville Sharp was a vital figure, helping blacks in need, bombarding the good and the great with the news of the latest outrage he had discovered, and seeking throughout to extend the defences of English law to black as well as white.[2]

These were not obscure, marginal matters relegated to the law courts, but received widespread coverage and popular discussion in the press, with an active involvement from London's black community. It was difficult to live in London in those years and not notice the emergent issue of slavery. John Newton's church in Lombard Street, and his home, in Coleman Street Buildings, were only a short distance from the centre of London's commercial and legal life. It is inconceivable, given his background, position and social activities, that Newton remained unaware of the debates about black freedom, and of the mounting concern about the slave trade. We should also remember his long-standing friendship and religious debates with William Wilberforce.

The eight-year-old Wilberforce had first met Newton in London, in the company of his aunt, Hannah Wilberforce, a friend of Newton's, and they later paid regular visits to Olney. The boy instantly liked Newton, who always went out of his way to pay attention to children, in church and in his home. Wilberforce soon revealed his exceptional intellectual talents (he went to Cambridge at the age of fourteen) and Newton watched his progress with interest and admiration, though they rarely met as Wilberforce grew up. By the time he was twenty-one, Wilberforce had been elected MP for Yorkshire. Thereafter his political star was in the ascendancy; a brilliant conversationalist, a close friend of the rich and powerful (he was a wealthy man in his own right) and a regular subject of gossip in the newspapers and magazines. No one doubted that Wilberforce was destined for high office or similar.

He had a prodigious intellectual curiosity (and energy to match) which, in the mid-1780s prompted serious doubt about his religious beliefs. He began a journal to record his spiritual life and what unfolded was a deepening religious crisis. Wilberforce had everything a man could want, but he came to realise that he needed something more. 'I believe', he wrote in 1785, 'all the great truths of the Christian religion, but I am not acting as though I did. Should I die in this state I must go into a place of misery.'[3] It was a religious crisis similar to the one experienced by Newton many years before. Troubled by profound religious questions, and unable to resolve them alone, Wilberforce felt the need to renew his friendship with John Newton. He knocked on Newton's door, but he had to do so furtively, for fear of being associated too openly with a preacher many distrusted because of his oratory and 'enthusiasms'. Wilberforce promptly found himself locked in serious theological debate with the older man. Newton manage to dispel his young visitor's doubts, and, equally important, urged him not to follow his instinct to abandon Parliament, but instead to remain in politics. It was a defining moment. Wilberforce wrote in his diary: 'When I came away my mind was in a calm, tranquil state, more humbled, looking more devoutly up to God.'

In 1785–6, Wilberforce moved into lodgings close to Newton's church so that he could easily seek his advice. As his religious crisis eased, Wilberforce gradually became aware that he should offer himself to the Lord, for whatever service was required of him. And as he talked to Newton, and as he discussed matters with his close friend, William Pitt, the Prime Minister, it became apparent that the cause he should adopt was the slave trade.

As the issue of the slave trade edged closer to the centre of the political stage, John Newton must have realised that his past would catch up with him. He had included some basic details of his slave-trading career in his autobiographical sketch, *Authentic Narrative*, published in 1764, less than a decade after he quit his last slave ship in Liverpool. Six years later, he took a critical stand towards British colonialism.

> We are taught from our infancy to admire those who, in the language of the world, are styled great captains and conquerors, because they burned with a desire to carry slaughter and terror into every part of the globe, and to aggrandize their names, by the depopulation of countries, and the destruction of their species . . .[4]

Newton did not, however, direct such a hard hitting critique at the one form of colonial expansion he knew best: the Atlantic slave trade. Again, we face a genuine puzzle: on the one hand Newton took great pains to tell the public about his moral shortcomings and his former sins, in sermons and writings; on the other hand he remained oddly silent about the slave trade.

Throughout his career at sea there had been no hint that he thought slave trading sinful, but that position was to change fundamentally in the 1780s under the impact of early abolition sentiment. Quakers, notably American Quakers led by Anthony Benezet in Philadelphia, were especially agitated against the trade. Along with other prominent American Friends, Benezet was a regular visitor to London, travelling and speaking on British Quaker circuits and pressing home the issue of slavery wherever he spoke. Benezet was also an active correspondent with Granville Sharp. The result was a transatlantic anti-slavery movement emerging in the 1760s and 1770s. Small-scale and restricted as it might seem, and limited almost uniquely to Quakers and a small band of sympathisers, it provided the organisational foundations and networks on which the nationwide and popular abolition movement was built.

The main debate about slavery was driven forward by the upheavals caused by the American Revolution between 1776 and 1783, and by the ideology of freedom at the heart of that revolution. The ideals of the Founding Fathers (many of whom were slave owners themselves) did not, however, extend to their slaves, a fact capitalised on by the British colonial power in rallying Africans to their side in the war. There was an inevitable flight of slaves to the British, but the British lost the war, and the defeated power was left with large numbers of freed slaves on their hands. The American war and its consequences, one of which was to leave large numbers of black poor on the streets of London, brought home as never before the nature and consequences of Atlantic slavery. After 1783 slavery was no longer a geographically distant, remote consideration, but had become a pressing domestic political issue in London itself. There followed a growing

British debate about slavery, but John Newton still maintained his silence on the issue.

Many of Newton's friends and acquaintances, however, now turned publicly against slavery. John Wesley, a long-time admirer of Newton's, had been influenced by the Quaker-inspired debate about slavery, and in 1774 published his own contribution, *Thoughts Upon Slavery*. It was a highly derivative tract, but was to prove hugely influential in swinging the growing number of Methodists behind the campaign against the trade. To this was added the voice of former slaves. There was Phyllis Wheatley whose poems were published in 1773, financed by the Countess of Huntington, an acquaintance of Newton. One of those poems was dedicated to Lord Dartmouth, the man who had given John Newton his first position at Olney. Even Newton's close friend from Olney days, William Cowper, had turned his pen to the early anti-slavery cause. Newton was familiar with Cowper's abolitionist poetry: he wrote a preface for the published version in 1782.

The spur, eventually, seems to have come from the man he had known since he was a child: William Wilberforce. The two men met regularly after their initial discussions in late 1785. Each time Wilberforce felt strengthened by Newton's wise counsel, yet he remained troubled by the problem of knowing how (or if) to combine his faith with a political life. He finally found his political cause, when he read an essay written by Thomas Clarkson.

Thomas Clarkson, the son of a Wisbech schoolmaster, had studied at Cambridge and planned for a clerical career. In 1785 he won a Cambridge prize for an essay on the slave trade composed in Latin. Clarkson had undertaken extensive research for the paper, interviewing former slave traders, and others who had seen slavery at first hand. What began as an intellectual exercise turned into a personal revelation. Faced by a mounting catalogue of horror stories, he turned against the slave trade. As he rode to London in June 1785 after winning the prize, Clarkson became ever more convinced that he must commit himself to abolition: '. . . a thought came into my head, that if the contents of the Essay were true, it was time some person should see these calamities to their end.'[5]

Others had made similar resolutions, but Clarkson's intervention was to be of an entirely different order. He proved to be the catalyst for the transformation of abolition sentiment into a major political campaign. At first, it did not look promising. Thomas Clarkson was young, politically inexperienced – and his essay was in Latin. Helped by his brother, he translated it into English, and then had it published by the Quaker publisher, James Phillips, whose presses were already busy spitting forth anti-slavery material on a huge scale. Clarkson, surprised to learn that he was not alone, had in fact joined the well-orchestrated, if relatively small, Quaker abolitionist effort. In June 1786, a year after his revelation on the ride to London, Clarkson's essay was published as *An Essay on the Slavery and Commerce of the Human Species, particularly the Africans, translated from a Latin Dissertation, which was honoured with the First Prize in the University of Cambridge for the year 1785, with Additions.*

Later that same month Clarkson joined a small group of opponents of the slave trade which gathered in Teston, Kent, convened by the Reverend James Ramsay, to consider how best to move forward. Teston was effectively the birthplace of evangelical abolitionism.[6] The group included Clarkson, some Quakers, Granville Sharp, Bishop Porteus of London and other prominent evangelicals. But Ramsay was the critical figure. He had been a naval surgeon in the 1750s, and had seen the seaborne sufferings of Africans at their most extreme. He resolved thereafter to preach among the slaves, and for twenty-five years he ministered in St Kitts, though, inevitably, his work was obstructed by local planters. Ramsay also published a denunciation of slavery, *An Essay on the Treatment and Conversion of African Slaves in the British Colonies,* in 1784. Like Newton, Ramsay knew slavery in its daily, most brutal form, both on the high seas and on the plantations. It was a world, he wrote, where 'Every man may beat, abuse, ill treat, maim and starve the [slaves] at the suggestion of his lust, his avarice, his malice, his caprice'.[7]

The Teston group decided to bring the issue of the slave trade to the attention of Parliament and all agreed that Wilberforce should undertake the task. Others too, quite independently, urged Wilberforce to promote abolition in Parliament, most notably the Prime Minister, William Pitt: 'Wilberforce, why don't you give notice of a motion on the subject of the Slave Trade?' This gradual coalescing in the 1780s, of Quakers and evangelical Anglicans, keen to promote abolition finally took political shape on 12 May 1787 when twelve men (most of them Quakers but including Granville Sharp and Thomas Clarkson) met together to form what became the Abolition Committee, 'for procuring such Information and Evidence, and for distributing Clarkson's Essay and such other Publications, as may tend to the Abolition of the Slave Trade, and for directing the application of such monies as are already, or may hereafter be collected, for the above Purposes'.[8]

There were disagreements within the committee about their tactics and aims. All agreed that their long-term ambition was to end slavery, but the first step in that direction was to abolish the slave trade. Most of the early abolitionists felt, though it was hard to prove, that cutting the supply of fresh Africans to the plantations would oblige planters to treat their slaves better. And then, once the slave trade had been abolished, they could turn their attention to slavery itself. But even the immediate goal of abolishing the trade was a daunting undertaking. This small band of men, all alert to the brutal reality of the slave

ships, all of them conscious of the troubling ethical and
religious issues involved, and all aware of the economic
consequences of abolition, needed first of all to rally
support for their arguments. The Abolition Committee
needed no persuading that the slave trade was wrong, irreligious and possibly uneconomic, but how could they
persuade the country at large?

The first requirement was suitable literature and there
was no shortage of talent to write tracts and essays against
the slave trade. But what they really needed was powerful
personal testimony: voices from inside the slave system.
Two in particular sprang to mind: John Newton, the ex-
slave captain, and Gustavus Vassa (Equiano), the ex-slave.

Newton still hesitated. His friend William Cowper,
despite his private turmoil, had no such hesitation, adding
his talents to the rising abolitionist tide. His latest book
of verse, *The Task* (1786), now regarded as his greatest
work, had finally established his name as a serious poet,
and the abolitionists approached him, via John Newton, in
the hope that he would contribute to the new campaign.
The result was the ballad 'The Negro's Complaint', which
was widely reprinted in the press and in pamphlet form,
and quickly established itself as a popular abolitionist
song.

> Forced from home and all its pleasure,
> Afric's coast I left forlorn,
> O'er the raging billows borne.
> Men from England bought and sold me,
> Paid my price in paltry gold;
> But, though slave they have enrolled me,
> Minds are never to be sold.

Cowper wrote other anti-slave trade songs and poems,
though he doubted their effectiveness. As he wrote to
Newton, 'General censure of the iniquity of the practice

will avail nothing, the world has been overwhelmed with such remarks already.'⁹

Cowper was wrong. His work was just one of many varied contributions to a remarkable and expanding popular outpouring of abolition sentiment. Indeed, the pioneering committee was taken aback by the widespread mood they had tapped into. In 1787 they found themselves inundated by requests from supporters across the country, especially from churches and chapels, from men and women, and from groups which had never before flexed their political muscles. This was strikingly the case in the Midlands and the North, where the rise of new forms of dissent, and the first signs of embryonic industrial change, created a new social context for British political life: abolition found its voice in urbanising and industrialising Britain. It was also female as well as male, and, from within London's black community, the voice of black as well as white.

This coalition of abolitionists had taken on a powerful, entrenched opponent. The slave lobby had traditionally been well represented in London. The West India Committee had long been the well-oiled metropolitan machine for broader Caribbean interests, a federation of planters, traders and merchants which had for so long been able to bend the ear of London's politicians and statesmen to promote their cause. Now, quite suddenly in 1787, they found themselves aggressively confronted by an equally well-managed organisation. Using Quaker networks – printers, publishers, local outlets and critical contacts in London and the provinces – the Abolition Committee very quickly created a nationwide pressure group. It proved to be an extraordinary system which was able to tap into a rising public sentiment against the slave trade, mainly via cheap publications and lectures.

Much of the impetus for abolition was local, especially from chapels and churches, but one critical ingredient was the work of Thomas Clarkson. No longer the solitary young scholar, writing in Latin for a Cambridge prize, Clarkson emerged as an indefatigable abolitionist speaker, criss-crossing Britain on exhausting lecture tours, covering thousands of miles, speaking at hundreds of venues to packed audiences, the room's capacity often the only limit on the numbers in attendance. Wherever he went, Clarkson gathered evidence against the slave trade, most notably – and most dangerously – in the slave ports of Bristol and Liverpool. Clarkson's voice and the data he gathered, sometimes at great personal risk, were important in transforming the abolition debate, in encouraging national popular opposition to the slave trade, and in collecting the grim details of life on the slave ships.

As Clarkson trekked around the country, Wilberforce, emboldened initially by John Newton's words and advice, and encouraged by the Prime Minister, promoted abolition in Parliament. To persuade the Members that the people really *did* feel strongly about the slave trade, the abolitionists called for a petitioning campaign.

Drafting petitions was an old, well-established system of rallying opinion on a range of political issues. But no previous petitioning movement could compare with the unexpected success enjoyed by abolition in 1787–8. The petitions raced ahead of the wildest expectations of the abolitionists, attracting huge numbers of names. Abolitionist petitions descended on Parliament from all corners of the land. By May 1788, one hundred appeals had arrived. Manchester's petition alone had attracted a remarkable 10,639 signatures and even in Bristol – the old heart of the slave trade – it was well supported. Parliamentarians could not deny the authenticity and strength of feeling behind the movement. Indeed, there were few people, inside or outside Parliament, who doubted that opposition to the slave trade had taken on a genuinely popular, widely based support.

There was an unquestioned national revulsion against the slave trade, partly because of the stark information which the abolitionist movement had scattered across the country in tens of thousands of pamphlets. The British people also felt a growing sense of religious outrage when they were told the grim details of the trade. Churches, congregations and churchmen were increasingly at the forefront of abolitionist sentiment, and when worshippers learned about the brutal realities of life on the slave ships, they hurried to express their collective disgust. Nonetheless, persuasive voices were still needed to win over a dogged Parliament.

In the midst of all this abolitionist activity, John Newton finally decided to add his voice to the cause. For a brief moment only, the former slave captain was transformed into an abolitionist. It is likely that it was Wilberforce who persuaded him to take a public stand, and in 1788 Newton published his pamphlet, 'Thoughts upon the African Slave Trade'. It was a stunning event, not least because among the nation's abolitionists, only Newton had been a slave-trade captain. In his own convoluted prose, 'The experience and observation of nine years would qualify me for being a competent witness upon this subject . . .'[10]

One of England's major contemporary clerics, a preacher of great renown, a man whose word had reached thousands, laid bare, as never before, his life as a slave trader. Readers learned not only about Newton's disapproval of the slave trade, but discovered that as a young man, he had been a slave trader – and a slave ship's captain to boot. But what was curious about Newton's attack on the slave trade was that it was not couched in theological terms; Newton's was an almost secular denunciation, which concentrated on the ethical and practical arguments against the trade. It was also a public confession: 'I am bound in conscience to take shame to myself by a public confession, which, however sincere, comes too late to prevent or repair the misery and mischief to which I have, formally been an accessory.' Newton wrote in the hope that his personal story 'will always be a subject of humiliating reflection to me, that I was once an active instrument in a business at which my heart now shudders'. Newton openly confessed that he only quit the slave-trading business because of ill health, '... but I think I should have quitted it sooner, had I considered it, as I now do, to be unlawful and wrong. *But I never had a scruple upon this head at the time; nor was such a thought once suggested to me by any friend.*'[11]

In the 1750s, Newton the slave captain, and most of his friends, had raised no objection to the slave trade. Now, in 1788, critics were lining up in their tens of thousands, to sign petitions, to listen to speakers, and to lend their own voice to the abolitionist cause. The tide had turned. When the British people learned in detail about the slave trade, they overwhelmingly spoke out against it. And they were able to do so largely because of a highly effective campaign run by the abolitionists and by the transformation taking place in the nation's religious culture.

John Newton's published testimony against the slave trade provided powerful weaponry for the abolitionists' armoury. Newton belonged to no political faction, yet he was a national figure who was lionised for his preaching and godliness. His attack on the slave trade was an unimpeachable document from an unimpeachable figure. Not surprisingly, it was warmly welcomed by Wesley and Cowper, by Pitt and Wilberforce. It was inevitable that John Newton would be called on again to speak about his career when Parliament chose to investigate the slave trade.

Newton's 'Thoughts upon the Slave Trade' was (by his standards) a short and snappy essay which was both a denunciation and a public confession. The trade, he wrote, was an 'unhappy and disgraceful branch of commerce'

which formed a 'stain of our National character'. He also
hoped that 'it will be a subject of humiliating reflection
to me, that I was, once, an active instrument, in the business at which my heart now shudders'. Newton admitted
that illness had driven him from the trade, and also
revealed that in addition to causing terrible suffering
among the slaves, the trade killed huge numbers of sailors.
Among the survivors, it helped 'efface the moral sense, to
rob the heart of every gentle and humane disposition, and
to harden it, like steel, against all impressions of sensibility'.[12]

The abolition petitions in spring 1788 were intended
to coincide with a major abolitionist initiative in
Parliament. Wilberforce had prevailed on Pitt to initiate
a parliamentary scrutiny of the slave trade, to be
conducted by a committee of the Privy Council. But many
wanted the House of Commons, not a Privy Council
committee, to take up the issue. As Edmund Burke said,
'If that House neglected the petitions from its constituents,
that House must be abolished, and the privy council substi-
tuted in its stead.'[13] Here began the protracted process,
delayed by bureaucratic and political obstructions,
prolonged first to 1789 and then again until April 1791.
By then the political climate had changed dramatically,
largely because of the revolution in France. As the revolution slid into violence, and as French armies as well as
revolutionary ideals threatened to overturn European
stability, demands in Britain for political change at home
seemed increasingly inappropriate. Revolutionary France
cast an increasingly dark shadow across demands for abolition and helped reinforce opposition. The inquiry into the
slave trade was only the start of a long campaign, lasting
almost twenty years, designed to win Parliament over to
abolition. The first move was to allow abolitionists to
present to the committee eyewitnesses to the full horrors
of the slave ships. These sailors, surgeons, traders, who

had seen the business at close quarters, were men who had manhandled Africans down into the holds and had tended the sick and the dying in the barely sustainable squalor of a mid-Atlantic crossing, who had bought and sold Africans, on the coast and in the Americas. Among the men who addressed the committee was John Newton.

The famous John Newton revealed himself, to a committee of the Privy Council no less, as a harsh slave trader. But for all the shame his confession brought him, it provided perfect ammunition for the abolitionists. Newton was sixty-three when he appeared before the committee. The much younger Prime Minister had been present to greet the revered cleric and to lead him to his seat, and when Newton entered the room (in St James's Palace) the entire Privy Council rose to welcome him. There could have been no greater sign of Newton's status and authority. Newton was typically modest. 'Oh, Lord, it is all Thy doing, to Thee be also the praise. To me belongs the shame and confusion of face, for I am a poor vile creature to this hour.'[14] The witnesses paraded before the committee were carefully organised by Thomas Clarkson to provide an extraordinary range of slaving experience. The aim was to impress the Privy Council, but the evidence was also reprinted in various formats, and used as propaganda throughout the abolition campaign.

Newton's answers were all the more telling for being factual and to the point. When Africans arrived at the coast as slaves, 'They are often under great apprehension at the sight of the sea. They imagine they are being bought to be eat.' Comparing slavery in different locations, Newton thought it 'worse on board ships, and worst of all on our islands'. Newton said he 'believes several captains of slave ships were honest, humane men; but he has good reason to think, they were not all so'. Not surprisingly, he thought *that the Europeans and Africans were in a spirit of mutual distrust*. Describing what happened after shipboard slave revolts, he said, 'it is usual for captains, after insurrections and plots happen, to flog the slaves. Some captains on board whose ships he had been, added the thumb-screw, and one in particular told him repeatedly that he *had put slaves to death after an insurrection by various modes of tortures.'* What Newton did not say, however, was that he himself had put troublesome slaves in the thumbscrews.

Newton told the committee that at the American auctions slaves 'were separated as sheep and lambs by the butcher'. His evidence confirmed what he had recorded thirty years before in his ship's logs: how he bought Africans in twos and threes, that he thought most of them had been captured initially in war, some had travelled hundreds of miles to reach the coast. Newton described the Africans he bought – young, small and mainly male – and all of them terrified. He also made some astonishing comments which cast doubts over the image of Africans long purveyed by the slave lobby: 'I always judged that, with equal advantages, they would be equal to our selves.' Newton also described Africans as 'in a degree civilized, often friendly, and may be trusted where they have not previously been deceived by the Europeans'. This was a far cry from those images of untrustworthy African savagery cultivated by the West India lobby. It is also difficult to reconcile with Newton's own practice as a trader in the 1750s.

By addressing the public and Parliament, John Newton, the former slave trader, established himself as an abolitionist figure. He spoke in secular and rational terms, but his testimony also had a religious impact. His was the story of a sinner saved: an example, for all to see, of redemption. If one single sinner could be saved, if Newton could be transformed from the depths of his slave-trading depravities to the apogee of his clerical fame, perhaps the same could happen to others? And perhaps it might even be possible for the nation to redeem itself – to give up the slave trade and be cleansed of its wicked ways? There is no doubting the significance of John Newton's public confessions in 1788 in advancing the cause of abolition.

There remained the question of the economics of the slave trade. In defence of the slave system, spokesmen for the slave traders and planters tended simply to assert the economic value of slavery. Newton, who had made his own handsome profits in the trade, had a simple response: 'if I had access and influence, I should think myself bound to say to Government, to parliament and to the Nation, "It is not lawful to put it into the Treasury, because it is the price of blood."' [Matthew, 27:6][15]

The British abolition campaign became the first effective, popular movement in modern British history. No other reforming campaign (not the Corresponding Societies in the 1790s, nor even the Chartists in the 1830s and 1840s) could boast such a high proportion of the people – among all sorts and conditions, both men and women – as supporters.[16] In addition, abolition provided a blueprint for how subsequent radical movements might organise themselves: its planning, its methods of campaigning, its links between people and Parliament, its clever use of petitions, lectures and pamphleteering, all pioneered a new means of extra-parliamentary politics. John Newton, for all his fame, was only one in a long (and growing) list of players in these events.

The evidence given by Newton and others was published in April 1789, and a month later, on 12 May, Wilberforce presented his bill for abolition to the Commons. It was defeated, as were many subsequent efforts; but what transformed everything was the shadow of the revolution in France after 1789, and especially the impact of the carnage and upheaval in St Domingue (Haiti) after 1791. The initial debate in France's most important slave colony about political rights and representation quickly led to sectional and racial conflict and violence.

There followed a massive slave revolt under the command of Toussaint L'Ouverture which swept aside all vestiges of colonial and planter power. Terrified refugees, black and white, fled from St Domingue to neighbouring islands (especially Jamaica) and as far north as New Orleans and Charleston. They took with them tales of violence and destruction on an apocalyptic scale. In Britain, the reaction of the slave lobby was predictable: this was what happened when you tampered with the slave system. Abolitionists faced the accusation that they would bring about a similar fate in the British West Indies.

William Pitt, once so sympathetic to abolition, saw the unfolding disaster in St Domingue as a major opportunity to advance British strategic and economic interests in the region. But his government's efforts to seize St Domingue, and to add that colony's remarkably fruitful economy to the British Caribbean possessions, was a catastrophe which led to the loss of 40,000 British military (most of them to disease). St Domingue offered a cautionary tale: it seemed to confirm the slave lobby's argument that tinkering with the slave system could lead only to disaster. The abolition movement thus suffered a serious setback in the 1790s, and it was to take a change of government – and a brief peace with France – before abolition was finally passed in 1807. And it was to be another thirty years before slavery itself was ended throughout the British Empire.

Shortly after his appearance before the Committee of the Privy Council, John Newton was overwhelmed by personal issues. His wife Mary, never a robust woman, had been plagued by illness throughout their marriage, but in 1789 her health seriously declined. Suffering from breast cancer, she was in great pain (described – and then published – in detail by her husband), but both John and Mary took comfort from their long and successful marriage. In Newton's own words: 'How few in the married state live together upwards of forty years! Still fewer who preserve their mutual affection unabated for so long a term.'[17]

Mary Newton died on 15 December 1790. When he published his *Letters to a Wife*, in 1793, Newton included mainly his time at sea and on the coast of Africa, but rounded off the collection with a detailed account of her death, a sample of hymns from her funeral service, as well as some hymns he had written on the anniversaries of her death.[18]

Even his most admiring biographers found something excessive about his public adoration of his wife. There is no doubt that he loved her deeply — 'a sort of lover's passion through life' was the description of an early biographer, Josiah Bull — but there were times when the boundary between the private and the public simply dissolved in Newton's writing. However, there was one area of his life that remained effectively a closed book: his work as a slave trader. In 1788 he had made his great public statement about his slaving past — but then he withdrew again from the debate. It was not an issue he wished to resurrect. Still, he longed for abolition to succeed, telling Wilberforce in 1804, '. . . the prospect of its accomplishment will, I trust, give me satisfaction so long as my declining faculties are preserved'.

Newton had lost none of his zest for preaching, despite his advancing years. As he approached his eightieth year, he shrugged off all suggestions that he should retire: 'What! Shall the old African blasphemer stop while he can speak?' He gave his last sermon in October 1806, but thereafter went into serious physical decline. Suffering from immobility, poor hearing and speech, he was confined to his home. Among his last words, told to a visitor: 'My memory is nearly gone, but I remember two things — that I am a great sinner, and that Christ is a great Saviour.'[19]

John Newton died on 21 December 1807, only months

after the slave trade had been abolished by Parliament. Two days after his death, his obituary in *The Times* remarked on 'his unblemished life'. Newton would never have made so grand a claim for himself. Indeed, he went to his grave all too conscious of his sins and of his youthful depravities – but happy in the knowledge that he had been saved by the Lord's amazing grace.

PART TWO

The Slave Owner

Thomas Thistlewood (1721–1786)

8 A Jamaican Apprenticeship

Towards the end of May 1750, when John Newton took command of the *Duke of Argyle* in Liverpool, readying the vessel for its voyage to Africa and the Americas, another Englishman was settling into his new life in a more remote corner of the Atlantic slave system. The twenty-nine-year-old Thomas Thistlewood had been in Jamaica only a month, residing in the most westerly part of the island, and as he worked on his first job, assistant to a surveyor, he had a memorable encounter:

> Between 8 and 9 miles from Dean's Valley, met Colonel Cudjoe, one of his wives, One of his sons – and Lieutenant and other Attendants. He shook me by the hand and begg'd a Dram of us, which we gave him. He had on a feather'd hatt, Sword at his Side, sun upon his Shoulder etc Bare foot and Bare legg'd. Somewhat a Majestic look – he brought my memory the picture of Robinson Crusoe.

Cudjoe's bizarre appearance should not deceive us. He was a man who had led a fierce guerrilla war against the British and had, only eleven years before, brought the colonial power, reluctantly, to the peace table.

The British found it difficult to gain control over Jamaica. Cromwell's army had seized the island from the Spaniards in 1655 and the first generation of British settlers fanned out along the coastal plains and valleys to work the land. Though they formed the backbone of Jamaica's first planter class, much of the island remained beyond their grasp, and well beyond the formal control of British colonial government. Swathes of the interior were wild and mountainous, inaccessible even to the hardiest of settlers. It was, on the other hand, ideal territory for rebels and runaways.

Slave runaways – initially from the Spaniards, later the British – struck out for the rugged freedom afforded by Jamaica's interior. Small clusters eventually merged into distinct, autonomous communities – Maroons – who, from the earliest day, plagued and threatened colonial and slave societies across the Americas. These were tough, independent people, shaped by forging a life in a harsh environment and fiercely resistant to any political and military effort to bring them to heel. They also offered a natural haven for new runaways. The Jamaican Maroons, especially those in the west of the island, fought the British to an exhausted standstill and to a peace treaty in 1739. In return for a recognition of their own, the Maroons agreed to return future runaway slaves, and to side with the colonial power against local insurrection or foreign invasion. It was a remarkable peace treaty, between former servile people and their erstwhile masters. Colonial government gave the Maroons a grudging respect but many whites in Jamaica remained uneasily conscious of the proximity of the Maroons, not to mention the presence of their own hostile slaves. They knew they lived in dangerous company. One such was the young Thomas Thistlewood.

In 1750 Thistlewood arrived on an island which had become the prize possession in the British Caribbean. Its plantations disgorged prosperity on an unprecedented scale, and the colony offered opportunities for migrants and settlers willing to risk the dangers of oceanic travel and settlement in a hostile climate, followed by a life surrounded by an army of unpredictable Africans and their descendants. It was always a risky venture. Two days after arriving on the island, Thomas Thistlewood was told that of the 136 passengers brought to Jamaica on one ship a mere sixteen months earlier, 122 were now dead.[1] The west of the island was among the most recently settled regions, whereas on the island as a whole, whites were greatly outnumbered by slaves. In 1730, 443 local whites lived alongside 7,137 slaves – a ratio of sixteen to one.[2] Whites were most vulnerable on their own properties, many of them distant from other whites and from whatever help they and the ragged military authorities might be able to muster.

In the summer of 1750, having considered various posts, Thistlewood accepted the position as overseer of the Vineyard Pen in the parish of St Elizabeth, where he lived with forty-two slaves, the majority of whom were African, not Creole (local-born).[3] Thomas Thistlewood had in effect settled in an African community, and as long as Africans dominated, the local culture would necessarily be African and not Creole.

So, a mere month after landing on the island, Thistlewood found himself in charge of a large community of slaves: dozens of men and women he knew nothing about but over whom he now had complete mastery. But such domination was flawed and fissured, as the slaves persistently refused to accept their submission. Moreover, Thistlewood was effectively alone. During his first year in Jamaica, he did not see another white person for weeks on end; when he did, it was an occasion worth noting in his diary. It was almost as if he lived, a lone white man, in Africa. How could so young and inexperienced an

Englishman be expected to maintain control and to exercise effective management over such a large group of alien (and alienated) labouring people, themselves plucked from another continent?

Only twelve months earlier Thistlewood had been unemployed, and penniless, living in his native Lincolnshire, desperate to find some way of making his way in the world. Like many before and after, he had gambled by travelling to Jamaica; there was no guarantee that it would pay off.

Indeed, there was a lot about his earlier years to suggest that he was quite unsuited for the new, harsh world he confronted in 1750. He had good letters of introduction to various people in the region, he was reasonably well educated, and was clearly numerate – an important ability in the bookkeeping and tabulation of people and goods on Jamaican properties. But the key task was handling the slaves, and Thistlewood came to his first major job with no management skills or experience whatsoever. Like all whites, however, he resorted to the full panoply of physical intimidation and violent control. No slave manager, as we shall see, could hope to make enslaved labour work by force alone, but without it, all was lost. African slavery on the plantations was conceived, nurtured and kept in place by a violence that corrupted the masters as surely as it damaged the slaves. Thistlewood's account of his life in Jamaica is the most remarkable testimony we have to this central fact of slavery: that violence was the lubricant of the whole system. There was nothing in Thistlewood's earlier life to suggest he might become a master of casual, cavalier and, sometimes, gross and calculated violence. Life in a slave colony quickly corrupted him, seducing him into a culture of persistent and frequently sadistic brutality. Thistlewood was a very different person before he arrived in Jamaica. Of course, much the same could be said of the Africans.

* * *

Born in Tupholme, Lincolnshire, on 16 March 1721, Thomas Thistlewood inherited £200 at the age of six on his father's death. It was not much by way of an inheritance, but he received a decent education with relatives and at schools in Yorkshire. He was familiar with the classics, developed a competence at mathematics, and clearly acquired a love of books. Indeed, the first item we have in his hand is a list of books he owned. By the time he was in his late teens he owned ninety books and in the years before he settled in Jamaica he bought between fifteen and forty tomes each year. Throughout his life in the island, boxes of books arrived from London, and books remained among his prized possessions. By the late 1770s he had a library of more than a thousand volumes, though it was devastated, like almost everything else, in the terrifying hurricane of 1780. Thistlewood's literacy and learning were important qualities which he applied over the years to the management and improvement of his land, especially to his gardens.

At the age of eighteen Thistlewood was apprenticed to a farmer in his home county of Lincolnshire, but he was restless and unhappy at his meagre prospects. He wandered between different agricultural jobs, spent two years travelling to India with the East India Company, and failed to secure the hand of the woman he wanted to marry: her parents objected to his undeniably poor prospects. By his late twenties, Thistlewood was no more successful or settled than he had been when his schooling had ended ten years before. At this point Jamaica beckoned.

Thistlewood was in the habit of spending time in coffee houses and it was at the Jamaica Coffee House that he had resolved to try his hand in the Caribbean. He took his leave of family and friends early on 1 February 1750 and sailed down the Thames to join the *Flamborough* at Gravesend. He stepped aboard the ship with less than £15 in his pocket.

Thistlewood joined a mixed collection of passengers: a

small band of young men and women destined for the plantations, older men returning to their properties, all pitched together in the uneasy intimacy of a ship 116 feet long and 28 feet across. By mid-April they had made first landfall in Antigua. Thistlewood did not like what he saw. The capital St John's was 'an indifferent sort of place', rough and ready, and costly. The local market was more eye-catching, with its array of tropical fruits and vegetables being hawked by slave higglers. For the first time Thistlewood found himself in the noisy bustle of slave life. He also recorded the first prospects of what was to be a lifetime's sexual encounters with slave women: 'Some black girls laid hold of us and would gladly have had us gone in with them.'[4] On 23 April 1750, Thistlewood's ship approached Morant Bay on the easterly point of Jamaica, and the following day they docked in Kingston. Though he could not know it at the time, Thistlewood was never again to leave the island.

Kingston had emerged as the island's major city after the earthquake of 1692 had destroyed Port Royal, sending much of the old buccaneering port into the ocean. At the time Bridgetown in Barbados was the most important British city in the entire Americas. But in the course of the early eighteenth century Kingston thrived and expanded on the boom in Jamaican sugar. The city developed rapidly after the earthquake, planned on a grid system but boasting few buildings of any great merit, though it enjoyed a fabulous location, looking out across the natural bay of Kingston harbour, and encircled to the north by the beautiful range of the Blue Mountains.[5] When Thistlewood arrived, Kingston was very much a merchants' town, and those merchants were key players in the island's thriving economy, their dealings closely linked to Europe's financial markets, to the appetites of European consumers for tropical staples, and – of course – to the slave markets on the African coast.

Thistlewood took lodgings in Kingston for a few days, exploring the town and its attractions, visiting long-time residents and recording their advice on climate and society, which was notoriously dangerous, especially for new arrivals (both black and white). He visited Spring Path, 'to the westward of the Town, to see Negro Diversions – odd Music, Motions, etc. The Negroes of each Nation by themselves.'[6] He had been transplanted into a different world.

In the previous decade, almost 70,000 Africans had been landed in Jamaica, and although almost a quarter had been shipped on to other slave colonies, the island was now home to some 145,000 Africans and their descendants.[7] They outnumbered whites by more than ten to one,[8] and on the isolated plantations, which created the lion's share of the island's wealth, the imbalance was even greater. There were, however, striking divisions among the slaves, mainly, as Thistlewood observed at Spring Path, along the lines of ethnic or tribal identity. Yet such divisions were as nothing compared to the stark divide which dominated Jamaica: the barrier between the enslaved black majority and the free white minority.

After eleven days in Kingston, Thistlewood continued on to his final destination, Savanna la Mar on the most westerly part of Jamaica, where he stepped ashore on 4 May. When he showed a letter of recommendation to a local sugar planter, William Dorrill, he was promptly offered a post; another planter, Thomas Storer, made another offer a day later. Two offers of work within two days of arriving was testimony not so much to Thistlewood's qualities, or the strength of his supporting letter, but to the paucity of good candidates for life on the plantations.

Plantations needed not merely the battalions of imported Africans to master the harsh landscape and cultivate the sugar, they also required a small cadre of (preferably) educated men as clerks, overseers and book-keepers. There were, however, rarely enough such men available, and even when they were to be found, many did not stay long, unhappy at the isolated and often un-rewarding, miserable lives they led, comforted only by excessive drink and by the sexual pickings to be had among the slave women. Throughout the slave islands, and especially on the sugar plantations, there was, then, an oddly rootless group of white men, ill-paid, always looking for a better opening elsewhere, drifting from one property to another, generally uncommitted, and in-famous for their drunken debauchery.

The world of the eighteenth-century sugar plantation was a very peculiar and dangerous world: a social struc-ture fashioned from harsh inequalities and founded on volatile personal and collective relationships. The majority of its inhabitants, the Africans, were violated at every turn and, as a result, dangerous to the unwary and the uniniti-ated. Placed above them was a small huddle of white workers, badly paid scribblers and managers, responsible for imposing their employers' wishes on the land and its reluctant labour force. At the very top of this human pyramid there was a small white, plantocratic elite, keen to make as much money as quickly as possible, many of them fired by the goal of returning 'home' to Britain. A few became fabulously wealthy, and were able to return to Britain in grand style, becoming a byword for the vulgarity and excess disgorged by Caribbean wealth. Most planters, however, enjoyed much humbler rewards, living in modest, sometimes squalid, homes that often shocked outside visi-tors. But they always lived in hope that the next crop, the next season, the next round of sugar prices in Europe, would at last transform their lives, and enable them to leave behind the harsh and risky routines of sugar culti-vation.

We do not know what Thomas Thistlewood aspired to

when he rode around the hinterland of Savanna la Mar in the early summer of 1750, but he was a choosy man and Jamaica was a land of opportunity. Thistlewood had an eye on being a surveyor, a job for which he had some of the basic skills: he had studied mathematics, and brought a surveying manual with him from London. Western Jamaica was still underdeveloped, with much of its land requiring surveying and documenting. But his plans collapsed when the surveyor he worked with went mad and killed himself at the end of June. So Thistlewood accepted the very different post, of overseer and pen keeper for Florentius Vassell at his Vineyard Pen in St Elizabeth, at an annual salary of £50 a year, plus a regular allowance of rum, sugar and beef. Vineyard Pen was a remote area of 1,170 acres (most of it in swamp), the good land used for cattle and worked by slaves who raised the animals and logged timber.

In his very first days on the island, he had learned what was required to keep slaves in their place. He had seen a runaway slave savagely whipped, the wounds then marinated in salt, pepper and lime juice. The body of another runaway slave had been burned, but not before the head had been cut off and displayed on a pole. Thus he was instantly instructed in the basics of Jamaican life. At Vineyard Pen, his new employer ordered three hundred lashes for one of the slaves in Thistlewood's care 'for his many crimes and negligences'.[9] Later, Thistlewood witnessed the trial of a slave who had drawn a knife on a white man. Found guilty, the wretched man was immediately hanged from the nearest tree, the offending hand cut off and the body left to rot.[10] The inexperienced Englishman would inevitably follow the example of his superiors. There could have been no doubt in Thistlewood's mind that capricious whippings, legalised executions and dismembering all formed the everyday ingredients of a culture of violence and fear which kept the plantation system in place.

Legal violence and dismembering were not unique to the slave islands. The dismemberment of executed criminals was part of England's 'bloody code'. Various body parts, but especially the head, were regularly displayed at strategic locations in assize towns around England, a reminder and warning of the terrible fate which the legal system held in store for the most serious of crimes. Anatomising executed criminals was a feature of English life well into the nineteenth century. (Public executions were not ended until 1868.) It was a well-orchestrated choreography of death and dismemberment played out before large crowds of the morbidly curious, gangs of poor people, of ladies and gents – and of curious scientists anxious to learn more about formal anatomy. In the very year Thistlewood first watched the dismemberment of a slave in western Jamaica, William Hogarth published his own graphic vision of legal dissection, in *The Four Stages of Cruelty* (1750–1). The anatomists were a favourite subject of England's major caricaturists throughout the late eighteenth and early nineteenth centuries, perhaps best captured in some of Rowlandson's grotesque work.[11]

What happened in the slave colonies, however, was utterly different. Formal executions of slaves was part of the local process of law, but the mangling and dismemberment of their bodies, and especially torture, was also a part of labour management and was doled out, capriciously, by men on the spot. Planters, managers and white employees felt free, and unrestrained, to maltreat, hurt and brutalise slaves. The sole restraints were self-preservation, not to provoke the slave to retaliate, and an awareness that excessive violence might be counterproductive. Yet the basic instructions which Thistlewood received in his first weeks in Jamaica, from two of the region's most prominent slave owners, was that the slave system could only function via the most draconian of regimes.

We have no way of knowing whether Thomas

Thistlewood was a naturally sadistic man or whether the raw brutalities of life on the Jamaican frontier appealed to him. But he took to it instantly, and was, in time, to add his own grotesque refinements to the long litany of existing torments. On 1 August 1750, only three months after stepping ashore in the island, he lashed Titus fifty times for hiding a runaway.[12]

This inexperienced Englishman of twenty-nine found himself the only white man on a remote property in St Elizabeth, between Lacovia and Black River, surrounded by forty-two sullen and reluctant slaves. He was just one of thousands of such white men, scattered in isolated locations across the slave islands. They were apparently all-powerful and able to do what they wished to their slaves, yet at the same time also utterly dependent on those same Africans. Thistlewood could not survive without them. Slaves fished and hunted for him, they fetched and carried for him, they taught him how to understand the dangers and potential of the Jamaican environment, and they provided the intimacies of sexual pleasure. Here was an Englishman, who knew effectively nothing about the place which was now his home, dependent on Africans, themselves forcibly transported from another land, and both sides were held together by a system of almost unbelievable abuse and cruelty.

Thomas Thistlewood's home at Vineyard Pen was a modest three-roomed thatched structure, repaired by the slaves using the local system, mixing 'water, soft cow dung, and wood ashes, with a small quantity of fire mould . . .'[13] The whole property sat on the plain of south-east St Elizabeth, shielded by interior mountains from cooling breezes, with an abundance of rocky outcrops reflecting the sun. When he arrived, the region had been suffering a prolonged drought and in addition to their other grievances the slaves were now also hungry. Thistlewood soon learned that they were both the source of his livelihood and the greatest threat to it. His main task was to marshal his reluctant labour force into an orderly system of working the land. He was responsible for everything on the pen: housing, clothing and feeding slaves, supervising their medical treatment, their midwifery, and their burial, organising their work regimes in the house, gardens and fields. He was charged with control over the slaves' movements, both on and off the property, and seeing that the whole system functioned profitably for his employer.

Thistlewood lived and worked at Vineyard for just one year. But it was a vital apprenticeship in the ways of slave management, and in how to make the most of the local habitat. Europeans and Africans were both alien to the region, though some aspects of the tropical environment were familiar to the latter. It posed dangers to both black and white: its extremes of heat and drought, its tropical floods and, worst of all, its periodic hurricanes that could overwhelm all of them. But it also afforded a natural abundance, which was the very reason for the establishment of the tropical colonies in the first place. The land yielded sugar and other important export staples, and enabled black and white to feed themselves. But the fruits and vegetables they planted and ate were, like sugar, alien commodities transplanted from other regions of the globe. Jamaica was a veritable experimental tropical garden where landowners imported and cultivated a huge range of plants, trees, roots and foodstuffs to provide the basics and the luxuries for black and white alike. Together, Africans and Europeans created distinctive Jamaican agriculture, horticulture and food ways.

The garden close to his house, with its range of fruits and vegetables, provided food for his own table and it was there that Thistlewood began his lifetime's passion for horticulture and gardening. In time he was to become one of the island's most accomplished and well-known horticulturists, eagerly awaiting the arrival of new seeds from abroad, and horticultural texts from London, exchanging plants, roots, cuttings and saplings with men of similar interests in other parts of the island. And it was at the Vineyard that he first saw what could be done with that amazingly fruitful tropical climate.[14]

At Vineyard, Thistlewood also learned the accountancy of slave management. He tabulated each and every slave, documenting their lives and conditions, their occupations and their health or sickness. Here, in the ledgers, was the slave as property: humanity reduced to the level and status of an object.

Thistlewood's diary is perhaps most infamous for its meticulous account of his sex life, from his early days with country girls and married women in his native Lincolnshire, to his rapacious, cavalier treatment of slave women throughout his life in Jamaica. Annotated in simple schoolboy Latin, Thistlewood logged each and every sexual congress: where and when, with whom, how often, and in its various permutations. Late one night he had sex 'cum Flora a Congo, *Super Teram*, above the wall head, right hand of the river, toward the Negro ground. She been for water cress. Gave her 4 bits.' A month later it was the turn of another slave woman: 'About 2 a.m. *cum* Negro girl, super floor, at north bed foot in the east parlour.' The inevitable consequences soon followed: 'in the night painful erections, and a sharp pricking, great torment, forced to get up and walk about'. The painful medical treatment did not stop him having sex with other slave women.[15]

This account of a man's sexual activity is unusual in its attention to statistical detail and sexual minutiae, and is a revealing insight into the predatory nature of white sexuality in the world of African slavery. It is impossible to know whether Thistlewood was unusual in the range, variety and voraciousness of his sexual appetite – or whether he was unusual only in recording it in such detail.

Throughout the slave colonies white men took sexual advantage of slave women as the mood took them, but there is nothing on the scale, and in such precise detail, as Thistlewood's sexual descriptions. In his first year in Jamaica, he had sex with thirteen different women, and in his thirty-seven years in Jamaica, his diary records sexual intercourse with 138 women.[16]

It began, in August 1750 at the Vineyard Pen, with Marina, a field slave who lived with him as a lover. Thistlewood built a cottage for her and lavished gifts for a housewarming: 'at night gave Marina some sugar, 4 bottles of rum, some beef and pepper-pot, with 18 pints of corn made into fungi, to treat the Negroes, and especially her shipmates withal at her housewarming'. Here was a slave social gathering, with plenty of drink – 'Marina herself got very drunk as well as many others . . .' – to the usual chorus of music and dancing. Caesar drummed and sang, others 'danced Congo' and Charles did his usual party tricks of fire-eating and striking his arm with the edge of a bill without harming himself. The party ended with Thistlewood lavishing more presents on the drunken Marina: thread, shirts, caps, handkerchiefs, old trousers, a basket, kitchen equipment, furniture, and more food and drink. The revelry ended when he had sex with her. Then, of course, he entered the details in his diary: '*Pro. Temp. a nocte. Sup lect. Cum Marina.*' The day after, he rose early, gave Marina a bottle of rum and some other items and took his leave of her. She was the first and the last of his sexual conquests at the Vineyard. Thistlewood had acquired the taste for instant sexual gratification with slave women, but all set against a steady relationship with one particular woman, in this case Marina. It was a pattern which was to recur time and again over the next thirty-five years.

In his early months at Vineyard Pen Thistlewood took great interest in the slaves' sex lives, and recorded the gossip in his diary. His housekeeper borrowed his razor to shave her pubic hair and he learned how to make an aphrodisiac powder that was alleged to make men irresistible. A slave told him that in Africa it was believed that women were not allowed to tickle their ears with a feather for fear of arousing them sexually; others said that drinking cane juice made women appear just to have had intercourse. Some slave youths used hog's lard 'to make their Member larger'.[17] Such details confirm a widely accepted belief throughout the slave islands: that slaves (and black people in general) were naturally lascivious, and that Africans were more sexually responsive and alert than whites. This view did, of course, provide an excuse and a cover for whatever sexual approaches white men made to slave women.

Whites scrutinised Africans with extraordinary curiosity, noticing (and in Thistlewood's case, recording) each and every aspect of their daily lives, from the food they cooked to the gods they worshipped, from the intimacies of their private lives to the way they danced. It was the curiosity of the ignorant. And here was a central paradox of Atlantic slavery. The white men who operated the system of slavery, using its agents on the slave coast, on the slave ships and on the plantations, knew virtually nothing about these Africans. But in the Americas they needed to know them better if only to get the most out of them, to understand how best to control and organise them. Whites also needed to know more for their own security and well-being. Nowhere in his monumental diary does Thistlewood admit to his fundamental reliance on the slaves, yet, in effect, it tells the story of his education at the hands of his enslaved labour force, both male and female.

This social intimacy between black and white was revealed on Thistlewood's last night at Vineyard Pen, 6 July 1751. It was a snapshot of mid-eighteenth-century slavery in Jamaica. 'They were very merry all night, Mr

Markham's Caesar sang and drummed, Guy and Charles, Phibbah and Wanicker danced Congo etc. Some top performances was had.' Thistlewood clearly enjoyed himself: 'I sat up a good part of the night seeing their tricks.'[18] Marina was the centre of attention and that weekend she received yet more material goods – clothing, furnishings and plenty of foodstuffs – from her English lover. In return, she provided sex, that other physical exchange which bound together slave master and slave woman in all slave societies of the Atlantic world.

On that night of 6 July 1750, Marina shared her enjoyment with her close friends, especially that small group of slaves who were closer to her than others: the ones Thistlewood described as 'shipmates'. These were Africans who had endured the Atlantic crossing together, an experience that had forged the most important of bonds: they were comrades and survivors from the nightmare of the slave ships. The word 'shipmates' recurs time and again in the world of Atlantic slavery and white outsiders recognised its weight and significance. It held together people who, whatever their differences of kinship, language, sex or age, had suffered, communally, in ways which outsiders could barely begin to understand.

A day later, having given more gifts to Marina, Thistlewood left Vineyard Pen. He got up by moonlight, heading west along along the coast road and stayed for a while with William Dorrill, enjoying the by now unusual company of local white people. He needed a new post, but Thistlewood wanted more than a simple job. He was keen to improve himself, and sought advice from established local men, asking about the best prospects of employment and trade, and looking for every opportunity to promote himself. Sugar planters and merchants, like Indian nabobs, had become a byword for the opportunities available in the slave colonies. Thistlewood wanted his share of the cornucopia that was the slave-based sugar boom, but like all before him, he had to begin at the bottom. Despite the boom in the economy of western Jamaica, there were many white casualties: men who fell beyond the pale of frontier life in rural slave society, destroyed by drunkenness, violence and moral collapse. But there was little danger of Thistlewood joining the ranks of such broken men.

Jamaica was a society which bred superiority among those who succeeded. For a start, plantation slavery hinged on the polar opposites of white superiority and black inferiority. In this highly racialised world, the rooted inferiority of the black majority was an article of faith, an economic and racial assumption from which everything else followed. Moreover, the men who made their way to the top of the plantation hierarchy had wrested good fortune and wealth from the most punishing and forbidding of circumstances. They lived in a brutal climate, endured a hostile environment, were surrounded by ranks of dangerous Africans, and their markets and supplies were five thousand miles away. It was hardly surprising that the Jamaican elite felt proud of their attainments, developing the arrogance of self-made men: prickly about their status, thin-skinned about criticism, and quick to take offence. Sparks often flew when such men clashed, and Thistlewood was quick to join this social bickering.

He had quit Vineyard Pen after falling out with the owner and by mid-September 1751 he had accepted a position as overseer on a sugar plantation owned by Dorrill. His salary had increased to £60 a year but he soon discovered the disadvantages: this was a working sugar plantation, not simply a pen.

Sugar plantations were a unique mix of agriculture and industry. They were in effect early, simple industrial operations, serviced by ranks of slaves, who were dragooned into various gangs depending on strength and skill. Most were employed in the labour-intensive field work, but a core of skilled slaves worked in the factory.

Sugar factories and their smoking chimneys dotted the Jamaican landscape; long before such buildings became a characteristic sight of industrial Britain, they were a feature of the West Indian landscape. Sprouting in the middle of luxuriant tropical settings, they eagerly devoured sugar cane, crushing it, boiling it, refining it and finally transmuting cane into raw sugar. Most sugar factories used animal, wind or water power, though by the late eighteenth century early steam engines had made their appearance in the islands.[19]

The crude raw sugar that emerged from the factories was then packed into hogsheads for loading on to waiting boats, thence on to the Atlantic ships bound for Europe. The sugar was refined further for onward sale and consumption in a cluster of refineries built close to the quayside. On both sides of the Atlantic therefore we can see early industrial operations working to process the astounding volumes of sugar harvested by armies of slaves in the Caribbean.

When the Caribbean sugar harvest began each new year, field work had to be synchronised with the mechanical processes of the sugar mill and factory. Cane that took long to be crushed and processed would rapidly deteriorate; timing and coordination between field work and factory was vital. Hence sugar production needed skilled and experienced slaves who were able to process the sugar until all the fields had been cleared of their cane. This unusual mix of agriculture and industry demanded more careful and better planning than had been required from Thistlewood on Vineyard Pen. With no previous experience of managing a fully functioning sugar plantation, and with little more than a year in the island, Thistlewood needed all the help he could get.

He arrived at his new position, on Egypt Plantation, on 16 September 1751, only a few days after a devastating hurricane. (The biblical imagery of Egypt, and the enslavement of Israel, went unnoticed.) Ferocious winds and high waters had damaged everything in sight.[20] Roofs were lifted, windows blown open, buildings utterly destroyed. Trees were blasted and uprooted and, those that remained upright were totally stripped of leaves. The nearby shoreline was strewn with debris from both land and sea, with dead fish and tons of seaweed scattered everywhere. There was not a bird to be heard. News filtered in over the next few days of the devastation across the region, and of stories of narrow personal escapes. Egypt Plantation had been badly managed by the previous overseer and now it had been battered by a hurricane. Yet it presented the challenge Thistlewood was looking for. For all but one of the next sixteen years Egypt would be his home and workplace.

Thistlewood began by listing all the slaves on the property. There were thirty-one men, twenty-eight women, fifteen boys and girls and fourteen non-working children.[21] They shared that mix of names that characterised slave plantations: African names (Quashe, Cudjoe, Quahseba), names from classical antiquity (Nero, Plato, Hannibal), and a scattering of more traditional Christian and English names. The naming of slaves was intended to uproot them from their African past and then to recast them in a dependent role shaped by their owners.[22]

Even in times of high sugar prices, Egypt had too many disadvantages to become a really prosperous estate. Only about three hundred of the plantation's 1,500 acres were in use, and the sugar-cane fields were small and scattered. The factory machinery was inadequate and the labour force was too small for the tasks demanded of it. On top of all this, the new owner, John Cope, was badly in debt, and had little of the financial leeway necessary for running an estate. Even at the best of times, planters needed financial flexibility, not least because the entire sugar industry was dominated by incalculability. It was hard to plan ahead.

The markets were months away from the point of production, and planters had no idea what price their sugar and rum would bring when they finally arrived in Britain. They did not know when new Africans might arrive, or how much they might cost. There were, in addition, the uncertainties of the weather in the islands, the persistent dangers at sea, and the more or less permanent problems posed by international warfare throughout much of the eighteenth century. Yet men like Thistlewood and Cope clung to the dream of sugar-based wealth and prosperity.

John Newton (1725–1807):
slave trader turned abolitionist.

Scenes from below deck on a slaver.

SLAVES PACKED BELOW AND ON DECK.

African
insurrection
on board a
slave ship,
1794.

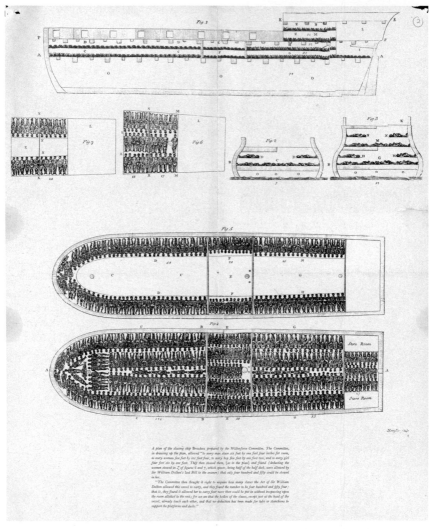

The slave ship *Brookes*: the most famous of all abolitionist images.

Granville Sharp (1735–1813):
pioneer of British abolition and
defender of black rights.

Thomas Clarkson
(1760–1846):
foot soldier of the
abolition move-
ment, with African
goods he used to
promote normal
trade with Africa.

William
Wilberforce
(1759–1833):
parliamentary
leader of the
abolition
campaign.

Caribbean sugar plantation: enslaved labourers marshalled in gangs to plant the cane.

Slave gangs preparing the ground for planting sugar cane.

Slaves working at a sugar mill.

Inside a sugar plantation's boiling house.

A caricature of West Indian whites and the luxury they enjoyed.

The Jamaican
Maroon leader,
Leonard Parkinson,
1796.

Poor blacks leaving London for Sierra Leone, 1787.

Black and white social life in poor London.

Grave of Scipio Africanus, 1720: a black servant buried in St Mary's churchyard, Henbury.

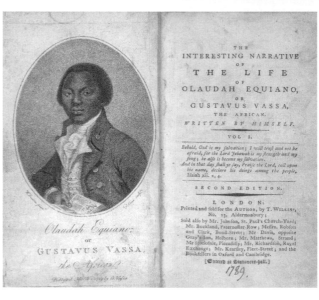

Olaudah Equiano (c.1745–97), the black voice of abolition: frontispiece and title page of his autobiography of 1789.

9 Sugar and Slaves

Few slaves were spared the rigours of labour on sugar plantations. The old and the young, the sick and the marginal, all were marshalled into suitable jobs for their age and condition. On a sugar property, the enslaved people endured the harshest of conditions, especially in the crop time between the new year and midsummer, when they were exposed to sun, heat, tropical downpours – all good for sugar, but hard on the labour force. Egypt's difficult terrain and swampy surrounds, infested with mosquitoes, made daily life and work taxing in the extreme. Sugar cultivation was the most gruelling of labours, a fact reflected in the demography of sugar slavery. Human suffering was at its worst on the sugar plantations: life expectancy, infant mortality, low fertility and sickness formed part of a persistent pattern indicating that sugar slaves fared worse than slaves in other industries and occupations.

The fittest and strongest formed the heavy labour battalions, thrown at the harsh work of harvesting the cane, and planting and manuring the next crops. It was unpleasant and arduous work. Whites had developed numerous methods of persuading slaves to work, including a number of incentives, but the ultimate tools were threats and punishment. Often, even they were not enough. Thomas Thistlewood was to become an imaginative innovator of new and excruciating methods of punishment, persuasion and control.

To keep slaves at this back-breaking, laborious work, overseers applied a tough, unbending regime. In the words of Trevor Burnard, 'Managing a sugar estate was hard work and required a hard man.'[1] Thomas Thistlewood was to prove himself adept in the ways of slave management and brought to the task a distinctive personal style which, even in the repulsive annals of sugar slavery, sometimes stretches credulity. But even he had to follow the established conventions of allowing slaves a number of rewards – free time at high days and holidays, extra rations for celebrations and festivals, cash for special efforts – though they soon came to know him best for his brutality. He was never reluctant to whip slaves: for running away, for being noisy, for impudence, for fighting and – the greatest of all ironies – for sexual transgressions.

Each day Thistlewood recorded the humdrum details of a working property: food, supplies and goods imported, crops exported, down the canals and river to the nearest port. The slave gangs were moved around from this task to that, shifting from field to field, preparing the land, planting the cane, cultivating the food – all in preparation for the heavy work of cane cutting. Then they advanced like a slow-moving army, hacking away at the sea of high-waving sugar plants, cutting the bamboo-like cane close to the ground, stripping off the surplus foliage and leaving the stalks for collection. A second gang of slaves bundled the stripped cane into manageable bunches, loaded it into carts, and mules or oxen then dragged it to the factory for crushing, boiling and distilling into crude sugar and rum.

Though relatively small, Egypt, like other sugar plantations, was a complex social and economic system. To get the best out of the land, Thistlewood needed the help of those slaves who were able and willing to supervise different aspects of plantation work. Experienced and trusted slaves, the drivers, were put in charge of the field gangs; skilled slaves took up positions in the factory, knowing how and when to turn the cane juice into raw sugar. Others, experienced cattlemen, transported cane and processed sugar between the fields, the factory and the boats waiting to ship the barrels for storage at the water-front.

Field slaves were equipped with a great variety of tools and equipment: hoes and bills, cutlasses and saws, each and every artefact of agricultural labour.[2] It seems amazing that Thomas Thistlewood lived in the midst of dozens of truculent and often hostile slaves, yet equipped them with implements needed for the field labour, which they could easily have turned into weaponry. Soon, many had good reasons to dislike Thsitlewood, but few rose in anger against him.

At Vineyard Pen Thistlewood had learned the lesson of his dependence on the enslaved labour force. But he brought to his new post at Egypt his own distinctive whims and peculiarities. Egypt's slaves had to cope with his anger, frustration and irritation — to say nothing of cold brutality — all of which flared on a regular basis. The enslaved labour force had to find out how to avoid the worst of his violence towards them; his stick and his whip were always close to hand in the daily business of running Egypt. He broke an English oak stick when beating one slave. He fought with another, who ran away to a neighbouring property (only to be rewarded by a whipping when he got there).[3] In fact, Thistlewood whipped slaves for any number of 'misdemeanours'. Like slaves everywhere, Thistlewood's new charges devised their own stratagems for coping with their master. They dragged their feet, pleaded ignorance and feigned misunderstanding. They also ran away, or wandered off for a short while, invariably returning to a beating. Yet how could Thistlewood possibly know what was going on among all of the eighty-nine slaves under his supervision? It was a demanding job which required ceaseless scrutiny of labour, land and machinery to ensure that all came together in a carefully choreographed exercise in cultivation and manufacture.

Even under the best of management, there were inevitable disruptions. Bad weather, animals wandering into the bush, equipment breaking down, accidents and slave sickness, all upset Thistlewood's plans. European doctors were hired to keep the labour force fit for work and often they were assisted by slaves' traditional folk medicines.

During his first year as overseer, Thistlewood's diary became in effect a plantation ledger, and by mid-April 1752 it shows that the crop was complete. Thistlewood reckoned the property had produced more than twenty-seven hogsheads of sugar in a harvest that had occupied the slaves for sixty-three days. Thistlewood rewarded the slaves for their work with extra food and drink. But their efforts were not enough to please the owner, John Cope, who decided to convert Egypt into a pen and to move the slaves to one of his other properties. This shuffling of workers from place to place was a common feature of Jamaican slavery, adding further insecurity and uncertainty to their lives. By the end of April, they were moved to a new plantation. The fit walked, the many sick were taken by boat along the waterways. As soon as they all arrived, they were once more set to work, this time building new homes for themselves.

The land they settled on was known as 'Paradise' – an irony that was not lost on Thistlewood. For the slaves, there were more urgent problems to worry about than the bizarre names chosen by their masters (only those with a biblical learning might have spotted the significance of Egypt), since Paradise proved to be a hellhole for its enslaved inhabitants. Throughout the second half of 1752 the slaves from Egypt worked alongside other slaves from Salt River, building huts and generally engaged in the preparation of the sugar harvest. At weekends, some slaves trekked back to Egypt, where they had family and where they cultivated their own plots. Throughout this period, Thistlewood supervised both Egypt and Paradise, assisted by other white men. He was becoming ever more familiar with the peculiarities of slave management. His slaves were also even more familiar with his style of control.

Like slave masters throughout the colonies, Thistlewood went about his working day with a whip or a stick in his hand, though at times even that was not enough. He generally delegated the task of thrashing a slave to someone else, mainly a slave driver. In his second year at Egypt, Thistlewood suspected that a number of his slaves plotted to kill him. Whites regularly imagined plots among their workers; often they were right, but sometimes it was merely the neurosis which afflicted all elites in slave societies – part of the mentality of the besieged. Despite the risks, there were times when Thistlewood's slaves could tolerate no more of his aggression: they fought back, cursed him, struck out, ran off. Towards the end of 1753, his slave driver Quashe Egypt, warned him 'That I should not eat much more meat here! I, asking him if he meant to poison or murder me, after a pause he replied, neither, but he intended to invent some great lie and go and tell his master, to get me turned away . . .'

Thistlewood needed Quashe, but also had to remain wary of him. He had been given instructions by the owner to ensure that the slave drivers did not harm the slaves. In late May 1753 Quashe badly whipped another slave and in his turn he received a hundred lashes and was put under lock and key.[4]

Quashe was only one of many threats. When he chanced upon Congo Sam, a runaway, in the bush, Sam attacked Thistlewood with a bill, shouting, 'I will kill you, I will kill you now . . .' Thistlewood cried out for help, but no other slave came to his aid. He successfully defended himself, grabbing the bill and dragging Sam to the road, where Sam clearly warned off other slaves ('He spoke to them in his language . . .'). Other slaves walked past, refusing to intervene, until one finally assisted Thistlewood, along with two passing white men, securing the runaway and finally locking him in irons. Congo Sam was sent to Savanna la Mar for trial and the slaves who had refused to help were liberally lashed. Sam's trial, however, failed because London, the slave who had helped Thistlewood and who was the key witness, simply would not testify; perhaps he was frightened of slave reprisals. We do not know why Thistlewood's word alone was not sufficient to condemn the accused.

Like other whites in the slave colonies, Thistlewood was the arbiter of local stability and order: the person who saw to it that the conventions and customs of slave society were enforced. At every level, those conventions relied on violence. Labour discipline and personal and collective obedience was secured by the lash, and an uneasy social accord between black and white was ultimately maintained by the threat and by the frequent reality of physical pain. At times it took on horrifying forms and extremes. In August 1753 a number of slaves belonging to Thistlewood's employer were punished for theft from the stores. One was hanged and two others had their ears cropped, nostrils slit and cheeks branded. The law authorised the most savage of slave punishments, but the white overseers on the plantations administered their own justice. When one slave badly beat another slave,

Thistlewood whipped the offender; when he caught slaves eating sugar cane at a time of food shortages, he had them flogged.[5]

In 1756 he devised a degraded form of retribution that is hard to explain. At the time food was scarce and the slaves were foraging for survival. Hot weather had parched the land, and crops withered in the ground. Thistlewood had to buy in food to feed his slaves but this still was not enough and the slaves wandered the neighbourhood looking for scraps. If Thistlewood caught them, he whipped them. One particular slave, Derby, tested Thistlewood more than others. He ate the sugar cane, ran away, was locked in the stocks (the 'bilboes') and was whipped, but he did not seem to care. When on 26 May 1756 Derby was again discovered eating sugar cane, Thistlewood 'Had him well flogged and pickled, then made Hector shit in his mouth'. Later that summer, a different slave suffered the same fate. Port Royal ran away, and when recaptured Thistlewood 'Gave him a moderate whipping, pickled him well, made Hector shit in his mouth, immediately put in a gag whilst his mouth was full & made him wear it 4 or 5 hours'.[6] In the next week, the same punishment was twice inflicted on a female slave, Phillis, and on 30 July he flogged two erring slaves, Punch and Quacoo, 'and then washed and rubbed in salt pickle, lime juice and bird pepper; also whipped Hector for losing his hoe, made New Negro Joe piss in his eyes & mouth etc'.[7] A day later he clamped another runaway in the bilboes, 'gagged him: locked his hands together; rubbed him with molasses & exposed him naked to the flies all days, and to the mosquitoes all night, without fire'.[8] This litany of violence and cruelty continued throughout the summer of 1756. Then, quite suddenly, in October 1756, Thistlewood put an end to this monstrous regime. Thereafter, erring slaves could expect only the usual violations.

What are we to make of this period of extraordinary

and perverted violence, rare even in the world of Caribbean slavery? Had Thistlewood lost control? How could he imagine that such treatment would do anything but revolt and alienate the people he needed for his every task? After all, white men were killed and harmed in all the slave colonies, many for having done much less than Thistlewood. Henry McCormick who worked for Thistlewood at Egypt, and who seemed especially debauched, was killed by a tree that was being felled by slaves; those same slaves claimed he had 'meddled' with their women.

Beating and whipping slaves was commonplace in all the slave colonies, but Thistlewood provides an altogether different story; we would be hard pressed to find comparable examples of such extreme punishments elsewhere in the Caribbean. Is this because Thistlewood kept a detailed diary which survived, and we therefore know about it? How many other men indulged in such bestialities but kept it secret? Was Thistlewood unusual only in writing about it?

Modern readers might wonder why Thistlewood's slaves tolerated such brutal and extreme maltreatment. Most likely they were frightened. They heard and saw what the law could do to erring slaves. The protracted torture, execution, burning and dismembering of slaves was part of the law's tyranny over the slave labour force; few slaves could have wanted to incur such excruciating suffering. In October 1766 Thistlewood recorded '2 of the Rebel Negroes were tried yesterday and one of them burnt with slow fire (alive) near the gallows at Savanna la Mar . . .' Two years later, on 2 July 1768, 'Hear Stompe, the Mial Man, was burnt alive this evening, and his wife (Dr Frazier's Polly, a mulatto) hanged.'[9] Slaves everywhere realised that slave violence would prompt violent retribution, and most were unprepared to take the risk.

Eventually this culture of violence was to help bring

down the whole system of Atlantic slavery, when, in the early nineteenth century, a transformed sensibility in Britain began to look on the slave islands in horror. If the slave system could only be kept in place with such levels of state-sanctioned violence, was it worth it? How could the British justify maintaining so fundamentally violent a system simply to satisfy the taste for sugar and other tropical staples?

Throughout his time at Egypt Thistlewood was wrestling with a difficult plantation. In addition to its natural disadvantages, Egypt was plagued by hot weather, drought and food shortages. Compounding his difficulties was the dangerous uncertainty posed by the Seven Years War (1756–63). War in the Atlantic and Americas not only threatened the supply lines to and from Britain, but planters in Jamaica frequently worried about the danger of a French or Spanish invasion of the island. On 16 February 1757, for example, Thistlewood 'Heard great guns fired out at sea'.[10] Most worrying of all perhaps was the effect international conflict had on the slaves. Rumours of war, garbled information about the frailty of defences, all were quickly absorbed by the workers and blended into a brew of unsettling gossip and tittle-tattle. Defeat by European rivals, however temporary, might expose a chink in the slave owners' armour. The real threat to the white settlers, however, was posed not by invaders but by the slaves, and the small-scale, individual, ad hoc acts of resistance and violence which were part of the normal life in the islands.

In midsummer 1757 Thistlewood quit Egypt to become overseer of Kendall, another estate, for £100 a year and other material benefits. He had quarrelled endlessly with Cope, his employer, mainly about wages and about Cope's endless interference. John Parkinson, the owner of Kendall offered him better prospects, so he headed the few miles north, taking with him the sixteen-year-old Ibo slave, Lincoln, who he had bought for himself the year before.[11] But he left behind Phibbah, who had become his common-law wife in 1754 and the separation distressed both Thistlewood and Phibbah: 'Phibbah grieves much, and last night I could not sleep, but vastly uneasy etc.'[12] He begged Phibbah's owner, Mrs Cope, to sell the woman to him, but she refused. The night before Thistlewood quit Egypt for his new position, he recorded that 'Phibbah gave me a gold ring, to keep for her sake.'[13]

This was surely a remarkable incident: a slave women giving her white lover a gold ring. Though it is tempting to define plantation life by the stark extremes of dispossessed blacks and all-powerful whites, the reality was often more complex. Slaves owned things: some white people, at the bottom of the white pecking order, had nothing. Thistlewood's pages occasionally report of poor white workmen who had fewer material items than Phibbah. There were many other slaves like Phibbah, whose skills, industry and good fortune enabled them to make the most of what seems a forbidding environment.

Thistlewood was greatly troubled when he left Phibbah behind in the summer of 1757. They frequently exchanged gifts, carried both ways by the young Lincoln. Phibbah even rode over to Kendall, in the company of Egypt's new overseer, to try to lure Thistlewood back to Egypt. When the time came for her to return home, he was left disconsolate: 'I wish they would sell her to me. Tonight very lonely and melancholy again.'[14] As he settled into what proved a rather lonely post at Kendall, Thistlewood looked forward to the regular weekend visits from Phibbah. When she could not make the journey, gifts and messages passed back and forth between Kendall and Egypt. A powerful emotional attachment had sprung up between the two. Was this just another relationship between a dominant white man and a slave woman, or was it love? It was clearly not simply just another of Thistlewood's many sexual adventures; it was a relationship which was to survive for thirty years. Phibbah bore him a son and when Thistlewood died in 1785 his will requested her manumission and set aside money to enable her to buy land and hence secure her independence.

The slaves shuttling back and forth between Egypt and Kendall, bringing messages and gifts, were just a few among many. On any day large numbers of slaves could be found on the move: walking, riding, herding beasts, driving carts, carrying goods and messages, delivering imports, transporting produce to market and to the ships. In fact, the slave system could only function on the back of slave mobility: from ports and quaysides to plantations, between the homes of white people and their neighbours or local stores, towns and ships, from the slave cabins to the fields. They travelled by boat along the rivers and along the coastline, and through the swamps. In addition, slaves set off to see each other, travelling on their days of rest to see a loved one: a husband, wife, child, relative or friend. Often they struck out without permission.

Whites and their social arrangements could not survive without travelling slaves, and Thistlewood's story illustrates this perfectly. The main slave love of his life regularly came at weekends, and when she could not make the trip, sent gifts and food to brighten up his life.[15]

Thistlewood had now proved his worth and a number of plantation owners in and around Savanna la Mar were keen to employ him. He was also offered various business opportunities, but was pondering how best to branch out on his own. His first step was to purchase three slaves of his own early in 1758; they were promptly hired out to work for others. Gangs of jobbing slaves were common: hiring slaves for specific tasks by the day avoided all the fixed costs of slave-owning. But through all this, he kept his eye on Egypt, despite bickering endlessly with Cope about pay and conditions, and reciting old grievances and irritations. By the end of June 1758 they struck a deal, and a little more than a year after he had quit for Kendall, Thistlewood returned to Egypt as overseer.

Thistlewood had by now become an ambitious agriculturist, and was keen to learn more about the theory and practice of tropical agriculture. He borrowed books from local planters, and gradually built up a considerable library of his own. He was just one among legions of people, on both sides of the Atlantic, enjoying and benefiting from the massive proliferation of the printed word in the course of the eighteenth century. Newspapers, tracts, periodicals and, above all, books came of age in that century of ever widening enlightenment.

Thistlewood had kept a journal from the age of nine in Lincolnshire, and throughout his youth he bought a steady supply of books each year – classical texts, poetry, periodicals. He arrived in Jamaica with two boxes of books, which included Chaucer, Milton, Pope and Addison, as well as the Bible and the Book of Common Prayer. He kept in touch with events in Britain through subscriptions to periodicals, bought publications about contemporary travel and exploration, and he acquired important reference books, notably the *Encyclopaedia Britannica*. He also owned an important collection of books on agriculture and horticulture, with volumes describing experiments and innovation in animal and crop husbandry and land use, both in the Americas and in Britain. Thistlewood was particularly attracted to practical reading, to science, mathematics and botany. For a man who never rose beyond modest material success, Thistlewood's library was a very impressive collection.

Thomas Thistlewood was not the only book collector in the district. He regularly borrowed books from neighbours and friends, in return lending out his own volumes.

Books formed an important lifeline for educated whites in the African world of western Jamaica. Living in stark isolation, books reminded them of a world they had left behind on the far side of the Atlantic, and formed a vital ingredient in the social life of white people.[16] Many of the books Thistlewood and his friends discussed together were volumes which were to have an enduring impact on intellectual life; Thistlewood borrowed or owned major works by contemporary Enlightenment writers such as David Hume, Adam Smith, Adam Ferguson and Edward Gibbon. Moreover, he read these books as soon after publication as transatlantic communications would allow. In brief, Thistlewood was a man of enlightened sensibilities, a devotee of the printed word anxious to keep himself informed about the latest intellectual trends in London and Edinburgh.

This life of the mind stood in sharp contrast to the brutality of everyday life. Thistlewood the reader and writer, keeping his journal, arranging his impressive library, placing transatlantic orders with his London bookseller, was also Thistlewood the brute and rapist, the architect of unimaginable torments. Perhaps it is not so extraordinary: intellectual refinement and educated pedigree are no guarantee that the same person is humane or kind. After all, the horrors of Nazi Germany were devised and implemented by large numbers of well-educated and cultured men. Still, it will strike many readers as odd that Thistlewood the brute was also Thistlewood the enlightened book lover.

In December 1758 back at Egypt, Thistlewood resumed old routines of plantation life and prepared for the next crop. Day after day, he recorded the mundane details of his own domestic life with Phibbah, the pleasure they found in each other's company, though often spiced with domestic discord: they argued, she stormed out, stayed away, he damned her for her cheek. Yet all the time he thought about her, wrote about her, wanted her back. But when she was not around, he had no qualms about turning to the nearest or most available slave woman. And he always recorded his sexual couplings in detail – in bed, on the ground, in the field or curing house. Nevertheless he always returned to Phibbah. By October 1759, she was pregnant. Their child, Thistlewood's son, 'Mulatto John', was born on 29 April 1760.

The year 1760 began quite normally, with slaves preparing for the next sugar harvest. Equipment was tried and tested, paths cleared, animals and their fodder tended, and the slaves performed an endless parade of duties and tasks. Before the year was over, however, the tyranny of Jamaica's slave system was on the brink of blowing up.

10 Tacky's Revolt

The Jamaican slave rebellion – known as Tacky's Revolt – threatened to bring down the whole edifice of plantation slavery. It erupted at Easter in St Mary's parish on the north-east coast of Jamaica, in an area of heavy concentrations of African slaves (notably Coromantines) with few resident whites. With mountainous forest and valleys close by, at first many thought that the rebels simply wanted to follow the example of the Maroon communities and escape into the inaccessible interior. But others feared that there was an even grander plan at work. In his *History of Jamaica*, published in 1774, Edward Long claimed that the aim was the 'entire extirpation of the white inhabitants, the enslaving of all such Negroes as might refuse to join them, and the partition of the island into small principalities in the African mode; to be distributed among their leaders and head men'.[1]

On 7 April 1760, Easter Day, more than one hundred slaves, under the leadership of Tacky, a handsome young African slave, swept down from their estates to Port Maria on the coast, where they raided the gun store. They then moved rapidly south-east, burning and killing and gathering recruits until they were four hundred strong. Local militia did what they could to stall the rebellious slaves until trained regulars rushed from the other side of the island, but even their arrival did little to quell the revolt. Rebellion now flared like bushfire on other parts of the island, in the far east of Jamaica and in the central valleys. Rumour had it that even Kingston was threatened.

Alarmed white people saw signs and symbols of African unrest everywhere: insignia and tokens of war, rumours of slave ceremonies, stories about overheard slave conversations. Many of the suspected plots reflected the permanent neurosis among whites, but even when a district remained untouched, they had only to look a few miles away to see bloodshed and destruction.

On 25 May a group of slaves killed some whites on Captain Forrest's plantation in Westmoreland. The slaves had been imported as captives after the recent fighting on the French island of Guadeloupe and these Africans had military experience. Estate owners panicked, and some armed their slaves as defenders, only to watch them run away to join the insurgents. Hastily assembled militia were repulsed by the rebels, prompting more slaves to join their ranks, which by now numbered perhaps a thousand. This swirl of rumour, panic and disastrous news inevitably reached Egypt.

Only a few months earlier Thistlewood had sold a hunting gun to one of his slaves.[2] He must have regretted his action when, in late May, he heard rumours of a planned rebellion of three thousand slaves in neighbouring Hanover parish. At the same time, Tacky led his force to attack frontier estates at Port Maria, and on 26 May 1760 four of Thistlewood's neighbours arrived in panic, barely dressed, to report the murder of an overseer and savage assaults on other whites. Thistlewood kept a close watch on his property, posting trusted slaves as armed guards and making sure that the military, traversing his land to confront the rebels, were well supplied with grog. Egypt was in effect a staging post, with the military and militia resting and feeding at Thistlewood's table and expense.

The local slaves seemed hostile and ready to follow the rebels' example. Reports reached Thistlewood of subversive mutterings and a defiant mood among them. Breathless slaves arrived with tales of nearby skirmishes, of rebels suddenly appearing with guns before melting back into the bush and the swamps. Like rural whites everywhere on the island, Thistlewood ultimately had to rely on his own slaves, employing those he trusted as his own eyes and ears, posting them as guards and hoping they would indeed defend him. Here, again, we see the ultimate dependence of whites on their slaves: they were, at one and the same time, both a threat and a safety net.

The slaves had their own difficult choices to make. To join the revolt, even to speak openly in favour of it, was to run the risk of a terrible vengeance. There was no doubt about what would happen to them if their rebellion failed. Apart from their instinct for self-preservation, most of them had loved ones to consider. Many slaves also had some stake, however small, in the system: they had acquired small items of property and personal possessions. Thistlewood's slaves could see and hear the rebellion, and the panic all around them. The Great House on a neighbouring property had been destroyed, and the sight of distant land and buildings in flames, the shouts and confusion of men marching past, at night, to confront the rebels, all helped to convey a sense of real anxiety, and showed that whites could barely hold the line against a rising tide of unrest.

The military made great use of loyal Maroons, led by Cudjoe, who could surpass the rebellious slaves in bush craft. The irony was that the slave system was secured in part by ex-slaves; Tacky himself was tracked down and killed by a Maroon. Tacky had been shot dead but other rebels were killed more slowly. One, condemned to be burned alive, 'was made to sit on the ground, and his body being chained to an iron stake, the fire was applied to his feet. He uttered not a groan, and saw his legs reduced to ashes with the utmost firmness and composure, after which, one of his arms by some means getting loose, he snatched a brand from the fire that was consuming him, and flung it in the face of the executioner.' Two others were hanged on a gibbet in Kingston, one surviving seven days, the other nine.[3] Thistlewood himself went to see the execution of local rebels. Goliath, a slave from Captain Forrest's estate, was gibbeted, but died within a few hours, and avoided the fate of being removed from the gibbet and burned. So too did Wager, 'King of the rebels' on Forrest's property.[4]

The impenetrable terrain made it difficult to snuff out the slave trouble completely and the revolt was not officially ended until October 1761. By then some sixty whites and as many free 'coloureds' and freed slaves had been killed. Slave casualties were much higher: between three and four hundred had been killed, a hundred executed and about five hundred were transported, largely to the Mosquito Coast.[5]

The past year had been a profound shock both to the Jamaican whites and to the broader imperial system. The most prized of British islands, the island which disgorged prosperity and trade on a staggering scale for the imperial metropolis, had come close to total collapse. The slaves, so basic to European strength and power in the tropical Americas, had almost overwhelmed the white elite. Tacky's revolt confirmed whites in their deep-seated suspicion that slaves were not to be trusted, forcing them back to an even stricter reliance on power, violence and intimidation. Slavery could only survive, and deliver its economic benefits, via the smack of firm government. And few were firmer than Thomas Thistlewood.

Looking back over the tumults of 1760, Thistlewood

recognised many of the telltale signs of ferment among his own slaves. Some had been known, or related to, rebels; others had adopted the shaven head, the motif of rebellious slaves. On some nights, panic had almost taken over; on others, Egypt had been a resting place for military contingents and their supporting slaves, free blacks and Maroons, camping out on the land overnight, sometimes sleeping in Thistlewood's house. But Thistlewood did not lose his nerve: throughout the rebellion he was resolute and devised a carefully thought-out defence of the property. Yet it was the loyalty of a small band of his slaves, and the reluctance of the majority to throw in their lot with the rebels, that seems to have saved the day.

The immediate outcome of Tacky's revolt was a new colonial act tightening still further the control over the island's slaves. Their movements were restricted, they were denied access to firearms, and the practice of *obeah* (slave 'sorcery' and belief with African origins) was punishable by death. Anyone who was not white, but who claimed to be free, had to register and carry a certificate to prove their freedom when they travelled. Whites, in their turn, were obliged to exercise a closer scrutiny over their slaves, mainly by remaining on their properties on Sundays and holidays. Slaves who had helped suppress the rebellion were rewarded, a few were freed and given a medal. But just in case they might not be so reliable the next time round, the island's military preparations and infrastructure were improved.[6] Such measures did not reassure large numbers of white people about their long-term security: there were rumours of one thousand people leaving Jamaica for a safer life elsewhere. The simple truth was that whites would never be secure as long as slavery survived; yet they could not envisage a world without it.

By the end of 1760 Thistlewood's life at Egypt had returned to normal. The fact that he had emerged from the ordeal more or less unscathed seemed to justify the way he managed his land and his slaves. He ended the year describing the slaves' preparations for the crop, his own venereal problems and, most tellingly, 'Mr Crawford's Jackie condemned, and burnt, by a slow fire'.[7]

11 An Independent Man

The Jamaican slave system was badly shaken by the 1760 revolt, but Thomas Thistlewood was not deflected from his ambition of moving on to better things and to become an independent man. At Egypt, he was employed by the plantation's owner, Mr Cope, but he also sold produce locally, exported his own share of sugar and rum, and hired out his own slaves. Thistlewood had become a remarkable mix of agriculturist, labour manager, merchant and higgler. After a decade in Jamaica, he had shown his ability to ride out local difficulties and to make the most of the varied commercial openings which came his way. To make further progress, he needed more slaves.

A majority of all Africans shipped across the Atlantic were male. Though the preference for male slaves was not as pronounced as historians once claimed, it was still the case that men and boys outnumbered women and girls on the slave ships.[1] Slave owners made no real distinction about gender when they turned out their slaves to work in the fields. Their demands were simple: they wanted people who were strong enough to undertake the task in hand. The heaviest field work was done by men and women working side by side. When it came to buying new slaves, each master or planter had particular preferences, though, and after a decade on the island, Thomas Thistlewood too had his own ideas about what sort of slave yielded the best returns.

Early in 1761 Thistlewood began to cast around the district for new slaves. He was looking for a particular specimen, 'none exceeding 16 or 18 years old, as full grown men and women seldom turn out well'. The problem, facing all potential buyers, was spotting the tricks which slave traders got up to when selling their imported Africans. The slave ships were filled with people who had endured a terrible ordeal; many were sick after spending months in the seaborne filth of the slave decks. The last task of the crew of the slave ship was to prepare the assembled Africans for sale in the Americas, to clean them and add those cosmetic touches which might make them appear younger and healthier. In late May 1753, as his Liverpool-based ship the *African* closed on the West Indies, John Newton ordered his men to wash the Africans and then, a day later, to shave their foreheads.[2] Seven years later Thistlewood was clearly alert to this ploy, 'they shave the men so close & gloss them over so much that a person cannot be certain he does not buy old Negroes'.

Thistlewood did not want certain physiques.'Those Negroes that have big bellies, ill shaped legs. & great feet, are commonly dull and sluggish & not often Good.' Better, he thought, were those 'who have a good calf to their leg and a small moderate size foot' for they tended to be 'nimble, active Negroes'. He preferred not to buy Africans who were 'fat and sleek' because they 'soon fall away much in a plantation'. On the other hand, those 'which are in a moderate condition hold their flesh better and are commonly hardier. Those whose lips are pale, or whites of their eyes yellowish, seldom healthy.'[3]

Whites treated Africans like animals: when they inspected them for purchase from the ships, when they traded slaves within the islands, when they treated their ailments and problems. Whites scrutinised them time and again, at every turn of a slave's life. Thistlewood felt no qualms about inspecting female slaves in the most personal manner, examining their private parts for disease or injury. Discretion and privacy were not a consideration. For the Africans Thistlewood examined in Jamaica in 1761, such intrusions continued their physical humiliations which had begun on the African coast and had continued across the Atlantic on the slave ships. Thistlewood, like all other slave owners, wanted to know what he was buying.

In December 1761 he bought six freshly landed African slaves for the sum of £312, promptly branding them on their right shoulder with the letters *TT* and renaming them. He carefully calculated the best (and cheapest) ways of feeding them, and within two weeks they were put to work in the fields. A few months later he bought a young Congolese girl, and had her trained as a seamstress. Thistlewood now had thirteen slaves to his name.

In February 1764 Thistlewood's nephew, John, arrived from England to join his uncle at Egypt. He promptly took up with Little Member, despite Thistlewood's firm warnings, and despite her marriage to a slave named Johnnie. Thistlewood tried to break up his nephew's liaison, by punishing the wretched woman. At the end of March 1765, a year after landing in Jamaica, John set off in a canoe, equipped with a gun, and was later found dead in the water. He was buried only yards from Thistlewood's house. A few nights later, Thistlewood heard a shell blowing, guns firing and loud 'Huzzaa' echoing from the slave quarters: '. . . for joy that my Kinsman is dead, I imagine. Strange impudence.'[4] By now, Thistlewood was too experienced a Jamaica hand not to spot the significance of the slaves' pleasure: one of the enemy had fallen, and it brought nothing but merriment to the slave quarters. Their rejoicing is hardly surprising, given the regime of sadistic violence Thistlewood imposed on his slaves. Only months after his nephew's death, he punished a female slave, Cubbah, for wandering off the property, by having her 'picketed' on 'a quart bottle neck till she begged hard'.

At the end of April 1765 Thistlewood bought ten more Africans – two men, two 'men boys', two women, three girls and one boy for a total £535. Again, all were renamed, branded *TT* on the right shoulder and listed: their heights, their scars, country marks (facial markings) and personal characteristics. A month later Thistlewood rounded off his investments by paying £550 for three hundred acres of land, close to Egypt, bordering the Carabitta River and the road to Savanna la Mar. In two months he had invested more than £1,000 in slaves and property. For the next year he and the slaves continued to work at Egypt, but spent as much time as possible preparing for the move to his own pen, Paradise Pen, which had been renamed Breadnut Island Pen. Gradually supplies were moved there, buildings constructed and slaves moved in to clear the land and to guard the initial, flimsy settlement. As the slaves did the heavy work, Thistlewood began to plant his garden.

Throughout this time, he regularly punished his slaves for a variety of infractions. He flogged, chained and 'pickled' Lincoln for having savagely beaten a female slave; he flogged others for allowing raucous singing in the slave houses, and some were beaten for 'meddling' with Thistlewood's possessions, and for sexual infidelities. Slave ailments had to be attended to: the clap was commonplace, so too was the yaws; one female seemed to be losing her mind; women fell pregnant and gave birth (thus adding another slave to Thistlewood's material possessions). But slave sickness rarely got in the way of Thistlewood's drive to bring order and profitable cultivation to his new investment, and, bit by bit, Breadnut began to take shape.

The slaves and Thistlewood were carving out a new piece of land in a small, remote and apparently unyielding corner of the island. The bedrock of local white society consisted of English, Scots and Irish, and all of them socialised with transient Europeans and Americans, especially the captains and crews of visiting ships docking from London, West Africa and North America. The bulk of the population was of course African, or born of African parents, occasionally augmented by new arrivals from Africa. But the slave population was more varied than might be imagined at first glance. Of the twenty-seven slaves Thistlewood purchased, we know the origins of sixteen: three were from Biafra, four from the Gold Coast, three from Congo, one from Sierra Leone, three from the Bight of Benin and two were Creole.[5]

This group of people, in a remote location, formed the tiniest of close-knit communities on Britain's vast, global map of empire. Yet it was also a remarkable crossroads of culture and peoples, all of whom had traversed great distances (most of them unwillingly) at great danger, and who found themselves bound together in a common enterprise. They had very little in common, but circumstances drove them into each other's company and into a mutual dependence. They formed a community which was, at once, parochial and international.

The thirty-six-year-old Englishman from Lincolnshire who commanded this small outpost of empire finally moved to Breadnut Island in September 1767. He took the greatest care with the transfer of his books and his office equipment, followed by other important personal effects; his pistols, guns and whip, as well as his household furnishings, all travelled by canoe or were carried on slaves' heads. He left the running of Egypt in the hands of John Hartnole, a white driver, telling the slaves there 'that I hoped they would behave well & I did not doubt but he would use them well . . .' The slaves, however, did not share his optimism: they called Hartnole 'Crakka Juba' ('Crazy

Somebody'). The slaves may have moved location, but they were in no doubt about what the future held for them.

At Breadnut, Thistlewood was now his own man – the owner of all he surveyed. Though not sugar plantations in the classic mode, pens like Breadnut were vital to the broader island economy, providing livestock, foodstuffs and casual slave labour to enable the major export producers to concentrate on their prime crops. Thistlewood owned sixty-six acres of workable land all worked by twenty-seven mainly young slaves. Over the years his slave-labour force would grow mainly by natural increase; at his death, twenty years later, he would own thirty-four slaves. On so small a property, it was difficult for the slaves to escape from a master who maintained a close personal watch over everyone. Not only did he observe their daily work, noticing their slacking or lack of productivity, but he was alert to their personal and intimate lives. He knew who was sleeping with whom, which slave was visiting another, which slaves quarrelled or fought, who had been drunk, who stole what from whom. He heard them curse, and he complained that he could even hear them fart. Thistlewood scrutinised and recorded their every move. For the women, there was the added risk of his insatiable sexual appetite. They were rarely safe from his spur-of-the-moment lust. Thistlewood had sex with female slaves, young and old, wherever and whenever the mood took him: in the fields, in their cabins, on the pathways, by the riverside, in different rooms in his home and outbuildings. In his first few months at Breadnut, for example, he recorded sex with Mirtilla in another slave's house, and in a field by the riverside, and with Franke under a cotton tree. The slaves knew about Thistlewood's sexual activities; he took women at any time of the day, not choosing to cloak his lust by darkness or by seclusion. Thistlewood's sexual behaviour was one element in the commonplace venereal infections which seeped through the Breadnut community and which occupied so much grim space in Thistlewood's diary.[6]

What is extraordinary is the detailed record, in schoolboy Latin, which Thistlewood produced of his sex life. He may occasionally have failed to record a particular encounter but his diary tells an amazing story. He lived in Jamaica for thirty-seven years and by his own account had intercourse on 3,852 occasions. In a typical year he took fourteen different partners, and had sex 108 times, though the intensity of his sex life faded as he grew older. There seems little point trying to make comparisons with modern sexual behaviour, but what made Thistlewood's sexual activity possible was his domination over slaves. On rare occasions Thistlewood had sex with white prostitutes, but the overwhelming majority of his sexual partners in Jamaica were slaves he owned or had close domination over. Sometimes he had willing partners, though their willingness stemmed from a variety of factors, not least that he tended to pay or reward them for their sexual services. There is no reason to feel that most of Thistlewood's sexual approaches were anything other than unwelcome. Slave women had no choice in the matter. We know that Thistlewood's male friends and neighbours behaved much as he did. They took slaves as common-law wives and lovers, but also imposed themselves on other slave women when they felt like it. White men invariably held sway over black women, and this dominion of white superiority and black subservience was the essence of the slave system. If we set Thistlewood's predatory sexuality alongside his other habit, of physically violating slaves in so capricious (and sometimes perverted) a fashion, it is surprising that his slaves did not hurt or kill him. Most had very good reason to hate him and wish him harm. It should have been no surprise when he heard the slaves celebrating the accidental death of his nephew: it was a small comfort to those who had little to look forward to

but the likelihood of further misery at Thistlewood's
hands.

At Breadnut, his young African house servant, Jimmy, was
Thistlewood's shadow both in the house and when he travelled. He was entrusted with money, and with the sale of
farm produce. But even he suffered his master's wrath: one
day he was collared for lying, at another time he was put
in the stocks overnight. As he grew older, he would occasionally provoke Thistlewood's anger and he was flogged
for drunkenness, for 'impudence, laziness, carelessness,
lying, etc etc'. Later in life, his impudence was more
pronounced; in a revealing phrase, he told Thistlewood,
'If this is living he did not care whether he lived or died
. . .' The young reliable houseboy became, by turns, a truculent adolescent and later a defiant and aggressive adult.
Time and again he was punished: whipped, pickled,
collared, deprived, relegated to the fields. It was a litany
of defiance, desperation and suffering.

Jimmy was not alone in his hopelessness. Slave misery
flitted in and out of Thistlewood's journal and it normally
prompted his anger or violence. Occasionally slaves told
him to his face that they despaired of life and he could
not help but notice their periods of misery. Their difficulties were not just caused by their master. When slaves
wandered off the property they ran the risk of attack from
lawless elements in rural Jamaica: from runaway slaves
answerable to no one, from whites who might simply take
advantage of a chance encounter with a slave, or from
other slaves who stole from vulnerable travellers.

For women, of course, there was the additional threat
of sexual assault: from Thistlewood at home, and from
men they encountered elsewhere. But even when a female
slave had been brutally violated by another, she could not
rely on Thistlewood for sympathy. Women he knew to be
suffering from venereal infections and yaws – suppurating

open sores which were hard to cure – were nonetheless pressed into sexual services for their master. Sometimes, slaves simply did not tell Thistlewood of their ailments. When he discovered that Phoebe's leg was again ulcerated, early in 1772, he 'Had her flogged and put in the bilboes'.[7] This ailment recurred throughout her twenties, but neither that, nor the presence of a slave husband, nor the death of a number of babies, deterred Thistlewood's regular sexual interest in her. She was also flogged 'for wishing she was dead already'. When Damsel, a nineteen-year-old African woman, was badly bitten by a dog in 1771, she concealed the wound from her master. When it was discovered, Thistlewood had it dressed – then flogged her and put her in the stocks.[8] Handing out a whipping never prevented Thistlewood from returning to the same woman for sex; having chastised them physically, he punished them sexually.

Thistlewood was at once slave owner, driver and doctor. He monitored their health and conditions, examining them intimately and recorded their symptoms and problems in fine detail. He examined their urine and their stools, he scrutinised their private parts, commenting on whatever imperfections he discovered. He personally removed slaves' intestinal worms, pulling the intruder from the slave's anus. Slaves were his property, and Thistlewood felt no compunction about examining, probing, feeling and handling slaves in the most personal of fashions. We can only speculate how all this grotesque, intrusive physical violation affected the slaves. It is so delicate a topic, it has rarely been discussed by historians, yet it was the fate of every single slave.

Not surprisingly, many of the babies born to Thistlewood's slaves were stillborn, or survived only for a short time. Their deaths evoked the briefest of comments from Thistlewood. In 1775, when Fanny's baby of a few months died, Thistlewood recorded that 'Had it buried'.[9]

It, not she; not her name, Patty. In the accountancy of slavery, the slave was an object.

Some slaves responded to these miseries by running away. Some had lovers and friends to head for, but many, like Sally, a sick young African who could hardly walk and could not escape Thistlewood's sexual demands, limped off time and again. She was flogged and collared endlessly, but each punishment was followed by another escape, retrieval and further misery heaped on her head. Other slaves took refuge in drink. Thistlewood regularly reported incidents of drunken slaves, and their consequent injuries — falling over, burning themselves, fighting — followed by his own retribution.

It is not surprising that so many of Thistlewood's slaves were disheartened and reacted with outbursts of anger, desperation and running away. They fought the system when they could and they evolved stratagems to cope with the woes which came their way. But at times, the slaves were simply overwhelmed, bowed down by forces beyond their control. Slavery was a regime to test the spirits and the physical resolve of the toughest men and women: Thomas Thistlewood's version of it was as taxing as any.

12 *A Refined and Prospering Man*

There were many sides to Thomas Thistlewood. He was an ordinary man capable of extraordinary brutality.[1] He would be much easier to comprehend if he were consistently cruel or barbarous, but it is his contradictions that are troubling.

Thistlewood was a bookish man who took delight and pleasure in the printed word. When he arrived in Jamaica his luggage contained seventy-five books which were to form the core of his Jamaican library. In the course of the eighteenth century, England experienced a remarkable increase in book ownership, in both town and country, which formed part of the broader development of a material culture that changed the social and domestic face of English life.[2] But Thistlewood now lived on the very edge of the British Empire, in the farthest corner of Jamaica, where he and his fellow whites maintained only a precarious grip over their slaves and land. Yet he and his neighbouring bookworms indulged their sophisticated pleasure of reading – and book ownership:[3] they educated themselves, argued, debated and improved their knowledge. They were people for whom the world of print was a defining feature which at once elevated their sense of self-worth, and distanced them still further from the slaves around them. They thought themselves cultured and learned; their enslaved slave force they viewed as uncivilised, barbarous and untutored.

Thistlewood read widely in the classics, disliked contemporary novels, but was quick to follow the literary fashions of London and Edinburgh, plunging into the thirty volumes of the *Edinburgh Review* borrowed from a friend in 1778.[4] He was particularly interested in books that provided instruction and help in his work and in understanding the natural world he struggled to bring to profitable cultivation. Such works tumbled from the British presses in profusion, including books describing the more exotic reaches of the world which had recently been 'discovered' by European explorers and scientists. The eighteenth-century revolution in print and learning made available to Thistlewood a huge body of knowledge. Obviously, Thistlewood had learned on the job: by watching others, he saw what worked and what did not, and he served his own trial-and-error apprenticeship on the Jamaican land. But in addition, his books enabled him to consult other authorities.

The Caribbean islands were a veritable cornucopia, home to some of the most lush and varied of vegetation, and able to absorb and transform almost anything that the white colonisers transplanted from the far ends of the earth; after all, sugar cane was an alien import. Jamaica had a remarkable range of climatic and geophysical qualities: plenty of sun and water, lush alluvial plains and coastlines, while the altitude of its mountains and hills brought coolness for more temperate cultivation. A huge African labour force worked this fruitful environment to produce exotic goods which had established themselves at the heart of Western life. Like many around him, Thistlewood was keen to see how far he could push the process.

The growing preoccupation with rationalisation and beautification of the land in the tropical colonies also had a strategic drive. The global wars of the eighteenth century prompted a metropolitan reappraisal of the empire's potential – and its limitations. The risk of losing portions of the world to their enemies encouraged the British to look more critically at the territory they held. It was a good time to see how their possessions could be used more productively, and to explore what else might be cultivated on the fertile lands of the West Indies. Products from Africa and Asia, for example, might be acquired more easily, and more profitably, by being transplanted and cultivated in the Caribbean. Captain Bligh, for instance, was dispatched on the *Bounty* to the South Pacific on his infamous voyage in 1787 in order to find plants and foodstuffs that could be transplanted to the slave islands. He was successful on his next voyage in 1793, returning with breadfruit which was promptly transplanted to the Caribbean, thereafter establishing itself as a basic ingredient in the local diet. Bligh also brought a new strain of sugar from Tahiti, which by the end of the century was being cultivated throughout the Caribbean.[5]

Across the English-speaking world, from India to North America, from London to the Caribbean, and by the end of the century even in Australia, this process of exploitation and experimentation was aided and pushed forward by the printed word. Thomas Thistlewood, perched at one edge of this global system, absorbed what he read and set out to put it into practice. The results could be seen in his garden.

Thistlewood was one of nature's compilers, recording his daily experiences and observations in tabulated data in his diary. For more than thirty years he kept a regular account of the weather in all its tropical variety, but perhaps his most impressive achievement was to be found in his 'showpiece' garden at Breadnut Island Pen.[6] As with his books, Thistlewood bought, borrowed and exchanged plants, seeds, cuttings and bulbs from Jamaican neighbours; he placed orders with merchants in London and imported items from North America, Central America and even from as far afield as Peru and India. Between 1765 and 1768 he imported 139 varieties of flora from England.

This welter of horticultural transactions not only served the purpose of botanical self-improvement but also produced additional income. Produce from Breadnut's gardens was sold by his slaves at local markets and found its way into kitchens across the region. When in March 1772 the governor, Sir William Trelawny, dined with his neighbour, Mr Cope, Thistlewood dispatched a slave carrying 'a teal, a whistling duck & 2 Spanish snipes, 10 large broccoli, about 3 quarts of English peas in the pods, and a large calabash full of asparagus; also 4 ripe figs, 3 sweet limes, and flowers'.[7]

Helped by a gardener from Hexham, Thistlewood seems to have been the first to cultivate asparagus in the island. Not all his experiments succeeded of course, but when his imported seeds or plants failed, he tried to find out why, and to explain the failure to interested parties. By 1770 he had imported more than two hundred items for the garden, though only 136 had taken. By 1775, there were more than three hundred species growing in his garden and in the grounds: sixty from England, twenty-five from North America and the rest from around Jamaica.[8]

Not surprisingly, then, Thistlewood developed a considerable local reputation as an innovative and successful horticulturist: his skills brought him money, pleasure and social esteem – although he would clearly have loved to move higher and join the men of greater wealth and standing.

Whenever Thistlewood visited fellow gardeners he invariably took seeds, shoots, plants and bulbs, or samples of fruits and vegetables from his garden, returning home

with similar gifts from his hosts. Although they were all
self-taught amateurs, learning from each other, and from
the literature which passed from hand to hand, they
belonged to the refined men of the mid-eighteenth-
century Enlightenment. Yet all of them – doctors,
planters, managers, merchants, manufacturers – were
closely tied to the slave economy.

Thistlewood's diary bears witness to a host of contradictions. Entries about books, ideas, cultured commentary
and intellectual give-and-take, all sit side by side with slave
sufferings and anguish, harsh punishments, cruel executions and torture. Passionate about ideas and gardening,
Thistlewood writes of his slaves with a cold detachment:
they drift in and out of his journal like inanimate beings,
devoid of humanity and stripped, by Thistlewood's words,
of that complexity of emotions and feelings which shaped
their real lives.

Thistlewood personifies the general dilemma facing
everyone trying to understand the world of Atlantic
slavery: how are we to locate this brutal system of
slavery in a Western world which took increasing pride
in its intellectual attainments? The most powerful,
sophisticated and, in many respects, highly cultured societies, on both sides of the Atlantic, emerged in close
harmony with African slavery. Indeed, to a marked
degree their development as progressive societies was
dependent on slavery. Thistlewood had emerged from
humble English circumstances to enjoy a degree of colonial prosperity which, in turn, enabled him to relish the
expensive habits of learning, and made possible the
pursuit of cultured enthusiasms. None of this would
have come about without slavery, yet his claims to refinement stopped at his dealings with his African slaves.
Perhaps this is the nature of the slave owner everywhere, from the Roman patrician to the Jamaican planter.
Like them Thistlewood regarded and treated his slaves

as deeply inferior beings, beyond the pale of normal civilised treatment and behaviour.

Twenty years after he first landed in Jamaica, Thomas Thistlewood had prospered. Though he did not belong to the elite of planters, he had come a long way from the uncertain prospects of his early years in the island. For all that time Thistlewood had led a very parochial life, pinned to the west of the island, but by the 1770s had carved out a niche for himself. He enjoyed a decent material well-being, had established a reputation for his intellectual and horticultural interests, and occupied a humble rank in the government of the region. From 1770, as a member of the militia, he was charged with drilling junior officers and soldiers in the fort at Savanna la Mar, and in 1775 he became a justice of the peace. But perhaps the most important aspect of his life in this period was the development of something approaching a normal family life.

For all his sexual philandering, Thistlewood had made Phibbah his common-law wife, and she came to occupy a dominant role in his private life in a relationship that was to last more than thirty years. She had two children (one stillborn) before her son John was born to Thomas Thistlewood in 1760. Throughout his diaries, Thistlewood described his son as 'Mulatto John'.

Of a similar age, Phibbah had been the chief domestic slave at Egypt when she met Thistlewood, and in his early days he turned to her for much more than sexual comfort. He borrowed money from her, and was the regular recipient of a wide range of gifts and favours. In return he safeguarded her considerable cash savings, which she had made by buying and selling foodstuffs and animals. She unquestionably benefited from her attachment to Thistlewood, but the real explanation for her remarkable success lay in her personal qualities. Phibbah was an industrious and enterprising woman, blessed with an ability to make the most of the small opportunities which came her way. Her own family associations and a coterie of trusted slave partners in business formed a network, helping and caring for each other, providing support and comfort in times of need, working for each other, and always promoting their mutual economic interests.

Although Thistlewood was a solitary white man surrounded by unfriendly slaves, he had also 'married' into a slave network: he acquired a common-law wife who came with her own family and intimates. It seems that Phibbah had a 'civilising' influence on Thistlewood. He never relinquished his habit of fierce punishment for what he deemed slave transgressions, nor did he completely lose his sexual interest in other slave women, but the worst of his sadistic penalties declined. His brutality faded as he settled for a permanent relationship with Phibbah and her relatives.

This diminution of Thistlewood's cruelty might tell us something about a fundamental process at work across the slave colonies: slaves influenced whites just as Europeans imagined they influenced the Africans. Too often, the slave colonies have been seen as a crucible in which an African majority adapted to the cultural norms of the dominant whites. It is true that, in time, they came to speak the master's language, adopted his religions and, later, took on the trappings of his political and social systems. But it was a two-way process. Throughout the classic years of plantation slavery, whites were greatly influenced by the enslaved African majority. And few examples illustrate that process better than the life of Thomas Thistlewood. By the 1770s, when his relationship with Phibbah had lasted twenty years, Thomas Thistlewood had, after a fashion, been civilised by his slaves: civilised though not completely restrained.

Phibbah's daughter, Coobah (renamed Jenny), was a servant to a local white family, and she spent a year in

England, as an enslaved domestic to their son. Jenny's grandparents were African, her mother an industrious and commercially minded common-law wife of a white man, while Jenny herself possessed the necessary social and domestic skills for working in England. 'Mulatto John' was emancipated in 1762 two years after his birth, educated at a local school, given a formal apprenticeship and joined the local coloured militia. He was destined to become part of that distinctive free, coloured class of Jamaicans, offspring of black and white, who created their own niche in the emerging social system of Jamaica. His mother clearly adored him, lavishing him with fondness and attention often to his father's irritation. John passed through a variety of teenage troubles – skipping work, telling lies and generally not applying himself. Equally disappointing, the boy took no interest in his father's books.

In early September 1780, the twenty-year-old Mulatto John was taken ill with a fever, and despite the attention of local doctors and his distressed mother he died on 7 September. He was buried that same evening in a ceremony attended by his former workmates, the slave friends of his mother and the friends of his father: a cross section of the whole of Jamaican life gathered round his grave. Thomas Thistlewood suspected that his son had been poisoned by Port Royal, a local coachman, but the doctor thought otherwise.[9] It was in many ways a classic case of death in a slave society: sudden, unexpected and inexplicable.

Thistlewood's assets grew steadily. It was his luck to be making his way in Jamaica at a time of rising slave values. In the 1770s he paid twice the price of the 1750s for comparable slaves, and towards the end of his life average slave prices had edged up to more than £100 per head. Though Thistlewood made regular investments in new slaves, he had moved to Breadnut with a core of Africans who, purchased when prices were lower, provided him with a young labour force. Their children added to the master's assets, and their overall value rapidly appreciated. The durable and physically resilient labourers he acquired proved to be a hardy group of people who profited their owner year after year: seventeen of them worked for him for twenty years.

In the thirty years to his death in 1786, Thistlewood is calculated to have made around £5,000 from his slaves. He rarely sold them, though he sometimes got rid of troublesome slaves, generally at a profit. Thistlewood made his money not so much from his land or from the sale of produce, but from hiring out his slaves to neighbouring planters. His methodical annual accounts confirm that his prosperity flowed directly from his slaves.[10]

Thistlewood was very careful and attentive to his finances because he faced a systemic financial problem, and his prudence saved him from the indebtedness which was the blight of so many in the sugar industry. Planters and landowners depended on a range of imported items – most obviously of course the slaves – all of which had to be bought long before any income materialised.[11] Time and again, they built up major debts to their suppliers, and those merchants in turn could often only secure payment by offering loans and mortgages on the planters' properties and slaves. When times were hard, planters had to sell up or consign their properties to their financiers, and in this way, a number of prominent West Indian merchants were transformed into planters. Perhaps the most spectacular example was the transformation of the Lascelles family, from Yorkshire, first into West Indian merchants, then into bankers, and finally into West Indian planters on a grand scale. Their conversion was completed when their wealth eased their passage into the English aristocracy, their affluence and rank confirmed by the construction of their fabulous home, Harewood House in Yorkshire.[12]

While many of his local planter friends were weighed down by debt, Thistlewood remained amazingly solvent throughout his life. To a degree he was lucky: he bought slaves and land at the right time, and he made the right judgement in selecting his labour force. But Thistlewood resolved to avoid debt. His policy was not to overspend, to restrict his debts, and resolutely to pursue money owed to him. His daily financial management, however, was much more painstaking than these general principles might suggest. He accounted for *everything* that was spent or dispensed, right down to an individual fish given to a slave, and how much small change – 'bits' – he gave to slave women for sex. Thistlewood spent part of each day accounting for his possessions and his outgoings: counting money, supplies, clothing and produce from the fields. The end result was that he was never really troubled financially. At his death his only debt was £18 which he paid annually to Mr Cope for Phibbah, whom his employer refused to sell him.[13]

Although Thistlewood continued to prosper at Breadnut Pen, he was always exposed to the fickle circumstance of international politics, and the revolt in the northern American colonies in 1776 sent ripples of discontent through the islands. Once again, Thistlewood found himself close to the latest outburst of slave discontent, this time in the neighbouring parish of Hanover. At its centre were not the Africans, but the Creole, skilled and privileged slaves who were better rewarded than the rank-and-file field labourers. Thistlewood had his own distinctive explanation for the revolt. It was, he claimed, 'owing to the foolish indulgence of the Negroes ...' His was the classic slave owner's reaction: give them an inch, and they'll take a mile.

The local militia and planters marshalled, troops arrived at the nearest port, and there was a general harassment of slaves throughout the region. Thistlewood reported the killing of innocent slaves by nervous or drunken whites; sometimes whites even shot each other.[14] Whites saw dangers all around them: American privateers, French threats from St Domingue, but most immediate and most troubling, endless rumours about insurrectionary Maroons, and plots and sabotage among local slaves. Again, slaves were executed, transported, burned alive and gibbeted.[15]

But the real threat to Thistlewood's life and fortunes came in 1780 when a devastating hurricane swept across western Jamaica.[16] It was the first, and worst, of five hurricanes between 1780 and 1786. The damage to life and property was enormous. Buildings and trees were flattened, crops and equipment blown away. An estimated thousand slaves died, though many died after the hurricane, from the food shortages caused by the devastation. Thistlewood and Phibbah had barely recovered from the death of their son when, days later, the hurricane passed over Breadnut Pen. As the storm gathered intensity, Thistlewood corralled his slaves into his hall, the safest room on the property. The slave cabins were blown apart, along with the cookhouse, storehouse and stables, even the 'necessary house'. Finally Thistlewood's house also disintegrated, and the whole of Breadnut's population, black and white, huddled in terror against surviving walls and rooms, exposed to lacerating rain 'which came like small shot'.[17]

When it was over, the land presented a scene of utter devastation: the ground blasted, trees uprooted or denuded, crops vanished, animals dead. Water was undrinkable, the air stank of death and decay, and roads were impassable. Many of Thistlewood's white friends had been killed, and the military was called out to offer protection against possible slave reprisals.[18] But the danger to white security passed. In fact, unsurprisingly, the slaves had been battered most seriously of all, their flimsy material possessions among the first items to be blown away; they too had suffered death and injury among their friends and loved ones. Once again, however, they were seen not so much as fellow victims of a natural disaster, but as a threat.

13 The End to It All

In 1780 the lush landscape of western Jamaica had been replaced by a blasted and bleak panorama which reminded Thistlewood of an English winter. He had suffered huge damage to his worldly goods, from the crops on his land to the precious books in his library (he had to throw away a large number). The garden he had tended so lovingly for years had simply vanished. His first task was to supervise emergency salvage and repairs, and the bruised slave force set about retrieving what they could, constructing temporary shelter from the debris, rounding up the surviving animals and restoring food cultivation. By the year's end, normality had slowly returned. But the hurricane seems to have disheartened Thistlewood. In February 1781 he advertised the sale of Breadnut Pen, all 160 acres along with its '26 or 28 Negroes', twenty-five cattle and sixty sheep. The advertisement claimed he was leaving on health grounds, but he must have known that in the immediate wake of a natural disaster he was unlikely to find a buyer. There were no offers and in the event he was to stay at Breadnut until his death six years later.

Thistlewood no longer enjoyed robust health. His diary had recorded in graphic detail his each and every ailment and symptom, especially his venereal infections, but 1781 heralded a marked physical deterioration. Henceforth he was plagued by ill health, unable to shake off a string of complaints: he suffered rheumatic pains, had deafness in his right ear and a dimming of his vision. He even found riding his horse too tiring. He had bouts of itching, outbursts of boils, swellings in his groin, and deep-seated pains and temperatures. By early 1784 he had developed a shaking and numbing of his hand, which at times prevented him from writing, and there were periods when he could hardly walk.[1] For the first time since his arrival on the island three decades earlier, Thistlewood began to attend church. He was becoming very aware of his own mortality and by 1785 a local doctor was a regular visitor to Breadnut. This deteriorating physical condition was inevitably reflected in his fading sexual appetite and the ritual tabulation and accounts of his sexual encounters became more and more infrequent.

A second, less powerful, hurricane in 1781 quickened Thistlewood's resolve to build a stronger Great House for himself, a costly investment at a time when he had little produce to sell from Breadnut. Over the next two years, however, he managed to get Breadnut back into profitable cultivation and by New Year 1784 he had plenty of hard cash in his coffers, from his farm produce and timber sales, and from hiring out his slaves.

Thistlewood continued to rule his slaves with his customary severity, lashing them for every conceivable shortcoming, yet he was also forced to hand out cash to enable them to leave the property in search for food, which was difficult to come by after the hurricanes of 1780–1. In Thistlewood's words, 'I never saw such a scarce time before, that is certain. Nothing to be had for money.'[2] Needless to say, the burden of these privations were felt by the slaves. Thistlewood, meanwhile, continued to wine and dine prominent guests in grand style. In August 1786 he entertained one of the island's grandees, the planter William Beckford. Over a civilised conversation they dined on 'stewed & fried mudfish, stewed crabs & boiled crabs, a plate of shrimps, a leg of boiled mutton & caper sauce, turnips, broccoli, asparagus, a roast whistling duck, a semolina pudding, cheese, water melon, pine, shaddock, punch, brandy, gin, Madeira wine, porter, Taunton ale'.[3]

But the master's physical decline was visible to all around him. He, who was privy to the most personal physical details of all his slaves, now found himself the object of scrutiny, and doubtless the subject of discussion in the slave cabins. Thistlewood's workers witnessed his shakes, his inability to ride, his failure to see or hear properly. Thomas Thistlewood, whose status and dominance depended on a very physical presence, had become an old man.

The summer of 1786 unfolded with Thistlewood's usual routines of planting and gardening, of socialising locally, all intermingled with his regular floggings of his slaves. By the autumn his physical weakness began to get the better of him. Most telling of all, he began to neglect his diary. The evidence he had traditionally recorded in his journal dried up when he could no longer patrol his house, property and slaves. He admitted, at the end of October 1786, 'Am quite confused, don't know how things go on.'[4] Dr Bell paid daily visits and the drugs he took, especially laudanum, induced wild dreams.

Thistlewood wrote his last diary entry on 14 November 1786; two weeks later he made his final will. He died on 30 November, and was buried in the Anglican cemetery the day after. He was sixty-five years old.

Typically, perhaps, his last entry in the diary was very businesslike, detailing of what Lincoln had bagged on a shoot; 'Lincoln shot 9 teal. Sent Mr Wilson a pr. Sold 2 pr for them rec'd 6 bitts = 1,785 bitts.' His last written words described how much cash he had in hand.[5]

Thistlewood's will, and the inventory of his belongings, listed his worldly goods. There, in black and white, lay the nucleus of his possessions, and the foundation of his wealth. The single most valuable item he owned was his labour force. He possessed thirty-five people whose total value amounted to more than £1,500. (By comparison, the 160 acres of Breadnut fetched £600 in 1789.) For all their physical imperfections, their ailments, disabilities – and their unswerving truculence – this group of people had created all the wealth and prosperity which Thistlewood enjoyed. In return, their own lives were meagre, deprived and often miserable beyond words.

Lincoln was the first slave Thistlewood had bought, in 1756, and he was the last one mentioned in his diaries. He had paid £43 for the sixteen-year-old; thirty years later Lincoln was valued at £50. Except for Phibbah, Lincoln knew his master better than any other person. He was at his daily beck and call for practically the whole of Thistlewood's life in Jamaica. He had undertaken almost every form of work possible: from field hand to driver, from gardener to messenger. He was clearly his master's favourite, certainly the most trusted, though Thistlewood regularly denounced him as a deceitful liar and a thief, beating and whipping him when angered.

Ten years after Thistlewood's death, Lincoln was a runaway, by now in his mid-fifties, working as a fisherman in Savanna la Mar. He presumably still bore the brand marks on each cheek which Thistlewood had ordered when Lincoln was still in his teens.[6] The slave had been invaluable to the master, and his access to goods and favours doubtless brought produce and foodstuffs into the slave quarters. Thistlewood had been angered by Lincoln's apparent interest in other men's wives, and Lincoln finally settled into a childless marriage with Sukey (who at Thistlewood's death was worth £20 more than her older husband). Needless to say Sukey too had been one of Thistlewood's sexual partners.

Phibbah must surely have mourned Thistlewood's passing. She had shared his life more closely than any other person, notwithstanding his sexual meanderings. She had been his common-law wife, although, despite many attempts, Thistlewood had been unable to free her (it was common for Jamaican slave owners, when they died, to free their enslaved lovers – and their mutual offspring). She was already an old woman when Thistlewood died but had to wait another six years before her owners, the Copes, freed her in 1792.[7]

What of the others? What of the thirty-five men and women, plus the fifteen children, he had owned who were put up for sale, along with the land and the equipment, alongside the livestock and all other artefacts on Breadnut Pen? Thistlewood's slaves had turned the unpromising piece of land once known as Paradise into a 'show piece property'. Its survival was remarkable: droughts, storms, warfare, rebellious slaves, all had periodically visited Breadnut in almost biblical fashion. Yet when Thistlewood died in 1786, it was a thriving commercial enterprise which continued to profit from the abundance of its land and waters – and from the sweat of its slaves.

They now found themselves put up for sale and their fate offers a cameo of the lives of millions. However well settled in one place, rooted with family and friends in a small village, with links to loved ones and friends throughout a wide community, slaves often found themselves uprooted, separated and dispatched elsewhere. Along with the land and the livestock, slaves were simply redistributed on their owner's death. The fact that Thistlewood's slaves lived alongside him for many years did not, at his death, make their lives any more secure or certain. When they first joined him, and at his death, Thistlewood's slaves did not know what tomorrow might bring.

In his declining months, Thistlewood seemed unaware that the world he had helped to shape, and which he had clung to so tenaciously for more than thirty years, was under serious threat. It was endangered by some of the very forces Thistlewood had sought to recreate in western Jamaica: the intellectual debate of the transatlantic world. The Africans had of course always opposed and resisted slavery, but by the 1780s, the slaves' resistance was joined by a rising tide of religious and ethical sensibility both in London and the Americas. Thistlewood did not live to see what were to prove the first seismic upheavals against slavery. They began effectively in the revolutionary ideology of the American Revolution, with its grand assertions of universal rights, and were advanced further by the French Revolution's 'Declaration of the Rights of Man', though the most devastating onslaught against slavery was to be the massive slave uprising in Haiti in 1791. Within a year of his death, people determined to put an end to Thistlewood's world came together to form the London-based Society for the Abolition of the Slave Trade.

Today, all traces of Breadnut Pen have vanished. The garden which was the envy of many returned to the anonymous scrub it had been before. It is as if Thistlewood and his slaves had never been there. What survives, however, is the remarkable record Thistlewood kept throughout his life: his diaries. That we know so much about this one man and his slaves derives almost entirely from this compulsive habit. He may have been no worse, no more violent or predatory, than many other whites who masterminded the slave societies of the Americas; what distinguished Thistlewood from the thousands of other men like him was the simple fact that he kept a diary.

His diary reveals Thistlewood to be a cruel, sometimes sadistic man. From the first, he realised that he had joined a society which functioned through brute force and intimidation. It was dangerous, possibly even fatal, for a slave master to be faint-hearted. We also know that most of Thistlewood's white neighbours all worked and lived on the same principle and ruled their slaves with an unremitting harshness. They feared that if they dropped their guard for a moment they would be overwhelmed by sullen ranks of Africans who wished them harm and longed for revenge and freedom. Thistlewood described in fine detail the punishment and severity he deemed necessary to prevent this, and to get the best out of his labour force. He did some appalling things to his slaves, and wrote them up in his diary, but at the same time he was a man of some culture and sophistication.

Thistlewood was a book lover, a successful amateur scientist and botanist, and a man always eager to improve himself. He was clearly part the world of the late eighteenth-century Enlightenment, albeit in a distant corner of the empire. But the learning and vicious brutality seem so obviously contradictory, that it is hard to reconcile them in the same person. But if we step back, to take a broader historical view, this problem seems less intractable. The history of the twentieth century, for instance, is teeming with similar contradictions; men of erudition and intellectual sophistication who set aside, say, their love of music, books, science and the arts to impose unimaginable cruelties on other people. Nazi Germany is perhaps the most obvious example that springs to mind, but there are many others. Equally, we know of myriad cases of ordinary people – unremarkable, mundane men, undistinguished in any way – who were transformed into brutes and killers. Unimpeachable men (and also women) sometimes commit terrible and wicked acts in wartime.[8] Thomas Thistlewood of course was not at war, nor did he live in fear of having to obey immoral orders. But he did live in more or less permanent fear. And here perhaps lies the explanation to Thistlewood's story.

He was, in most respects, a typical slave owner, using the harsh tools of slave management to extract labour and compliance from an African labour force which was permanently truculent, often rebellious and always untrustworthy. Thistlewood went about his daily work clutching his whip, symbol and instrument of his power, status and style. But there were times when he felt he needed more than the whip: at such moments he turned to bizarre and sadistic punishments. When Thistlewood was struggling to maintain his dominance using normal methods of punishment and control, he resorted to tactics which were the product of a mind under enormous stress.

Like most slave owners, Thomas Thistlewood feared his slaves. Throughout his thirty-six years in Jamaica he lived in an isolated position, miles from supportive white neighbours, surrounded at close quarters by an overwhelming majority of sullen Africans. Most of those enslaved men and women had deep personal grievances against him. He needed to be permanently alert to the manifold dangers posed by the ranks of disaffected Africans. He knew what might happen if his attention slipped. In Tacky's revolt in 1760 people he knew were slaughtered by rebellious slaves. For their part, the Africans also knew what would happen to them if a slave revolt failed. Both sides then, black and white, lived in a climate of mutual suspicion and fear; each side needed the other, but each was also aware of the dangers posed by the other. So there were times when Thistlewood felt unable to hold the line and when he slid into periods of desperate behaviour. It was at such moments that he devised his own improvised brutalities.

Thistlewood died at the very moment when unease

began to surface in Britain about the Atlantic slave system. It was an unease which made great play of the experiences of men who had seen slavery at close quarters, on the slave ships, in the slave auctions and on the plantations. The criticism of slavery, however, had intellectual and theological roots in Enlightenment writings which Thistlewood had read: the literate culture of which he was so avid a participant was to prove corrosive of slavery itself. When ever more people read about slavery, they turned away in revulsion, and within a year of Thistlewood's death, tens of thousands of men and women in Britain were demanding an end to the slave trade.

The rise of the abolition movement was also strengthened by the fact that it represented both black and white. The words of black spokesmen who knew at first hand the hell of the slave ships, and the remorseless oppression of plantation labour, became a critical ingredient in its appeal. Abolition thus quickly established itself not only as a popular movement with intellectual dimensions, but it also embraced black experience and ambitions. In fact Thistlewood's diary, filled with details about the struggle of his own slaves against their bondage, was itself testimony to black opposition, although Thistlewood would not have seen it as such.

After 1787 help for the slaves seemed at last to be on hand, in the form of an abolitionist campaign, five thousand miles away in England. And among those keen to bring slavery to an end was an African, living in London, who knew better than most the sufferings of the enslaved people of the Americas. Thistlewood died precisely when Olaudah Equiano was about to make a name for himself.

PART THREE

The Slave

Olaudah Equiano (1745–1797)

14 An African in England

In December 1754, Thomas Thistlewood was dragooning the slaves on Egypt in preparation of the next Jamaican sugar harvest, and John Newton was trawling for slaves on board the *African* on the Windward coast. In faraway Cornwall, that month marked the beginning of an exceptionally cold winter. In the small village of Ludgvan, north-east of Penzance, the vicar and amateur meteorologist William Borlase recorded the heaviest, snowiest winter in twenty years.[1]

The snow caught the attention of a young African arriving in England for the first time. He had been on board the *Industrious Bee* for the past thirteen weeks, as it swung a slow, laborious arc from Virginia, heading north towards Newfoundland before tracking east across the Atlantic. As the vessel approached the Cornwall coast, the African, when he clambered up from below one morning, was amazed to find overnight snow covering the deck: 'I had never seen any thing of the kind before, I thought it was salt.' Rushing back down he told the mate 'to come and see how somebody in the night had thrown salt all over the deck'. The mate corrected him: it was snow, made, he said, by 'a great man in the heavens, called God'. The

179

African was as mystified by this explanation as he was by the snow. When they docked, everything he saw was startling and unusual: 'I was very much struck with the buildings and the pavements of streets in Falmouth: and indeed, any object I saw filled me with new surprise.'[2] The African boy, aged somewhere between nine and twelve years old, had sailed into an alien world.

His story was not that unusual by the mid-eighteenth century: tens of thousands of Africans had been uprooted from their homelands and cast ashore on the far side of the Atlantic. But the boy belonged to a small band of Africans whose displacement was even more spectacular: it had taken them from Africa to the Americas and thence to Europe.

Like millions of others, this young man was a slave, and like many before and after, he must have been puzzled about precisely who he was. When he arrived in England, he was as confused about his name as he was mystified about the snow and the local deity. As the *Industrious Bee* crossed the Atlantic, the boy's owner, Captain Michael Henry Pascal, had given him the name Gustavus Vassa, though the boy insisted on being called Jacob. Yet even that name was not his own, for it had been given to him in the Americas by a white man. To add to the confusion, previously, on board another ship, he had been called Michael.[3] His initial refusal to accept the name Gustavus Vassa prompted 'many a cuff', but he 'at length submitted'; in 1789, he said it was the name 'by which I have been known ever since'.[4] History, however, has come to know him as Olaudah Equiano.

A person's name seems a straightforward matter, but it was very different for the millions of Africans loaded on to the Atlantic slave ships. Bought and sold, traded and exchanged as items of business, they were consigned below decks as objects, given a number in the ship's papers, then given new names in the Americas. At sea, they were reduced to mere figures, transformed into crude ciphers as the ships' crews tabulated and described their human cargo. This process is captured in the medical log kept by Christopher Bowes, surgeon on the *Lord Stanley*, which was trading for slaves on the African coast in 1792. On 15 June 1792 he recorded:

> The man slave No. 8 not much pain . . .
> The man No. 4 the same as yesterday . . .
> The man No. 5 rather worse . . .
> The girl No. 2 rather better . . .
> The boy No. 3 not relieved . . .

And so it continued, page after page, day after day, as his African patients headed to the Americas. Some of course did not make it. 'A girl No. 4 yesterday complained of a pain in the head for which she had no medicine as she did not seem to be otherwise ill, this morning at 3 a.m. she was seized with delirium, a few hours afterwards convulsions came on and at 8 a.m. she died.' There is nothing exceptional in this bleak medical log; it is a typical slave-trading document. Throughout this listing of human misery, we never *once* encounter an African name. We know the slaves, and remember them, by their numbers.[5] The confusion about Equiano's name was, then, not exceptional.

When he came ashore in England in December 1754, the young African bore two defining characteristics imposed on him by others: his name and his status. Gustavus Vassa stepped on to English soil a slave. There had been ancient forms of indigenous English slavery for centuries, but it had effectively died away until it was re-introduced by the Atlantic system. The Atlantic slave system was a major maritime enterprise, and for more than three centuries, thousands of slave ships ploughed their way along a complex network of routes linking Europe, Africa and the Americas. In the process, Africans inevitably found themselves cast ashore in all corners of the known world. The prime purpose of the system was to deliver Africans to the plantations of the Americas, but in time ever more Africans were moved on, settling on the very edges of European colonisation: along the ragged edges of the American frontier, in the most distant parts of Asia, on the rim of the Arctic, and even in the penal colonies of Australia after the arrival of the First Fleet in 1787. But one of the most striking group of displaced Africans were those who formed the black community in England.

Unlike slavery in the Americas, there was no real economic need for African labour in England. Instead, Africans settled in the company of returning masters and owners, arriving as slaves to sailors on the home-bound slave ships, as enslaved servants of ex-planters and military, or merely as exotic personal attendants to those who were keen to cut a swagger in fashionable circles. Or, like Equiano, they arrived as servants to a master who had acquired them when trading and travelling in the Americas.

Africans had made their first impact in the sixteenth century. The slave Jack Francis had been employed as a diver to locate the armaments on the sunken *Mary Rose* in the 1540s and, a decade later, the direct maritime links between England and Africa saw Africans shipped to England as slaves. The piratical voyages of John Hawkins in the 1560s yielded huge material bounty for himself and his backers in the City, the court and the West Country; appropriately Hawkins's coat of arms contained an image of a black woman in chains. By the last years of her reign, Elizabeth I expressed her disquiet about the numbers of blacks settling in England: 'There are lately blackamoores brought into this realm, of which kind there are already too many.' In 1601 she licensed a Lübeck merchant, Casper van Senden, to ship England's blacks to Iberia. Shakespeare's *Othello*, written in 1604, spoke to audiences familiar with black people in the capital city, but it was the settlement of the British colonies in North America and the Caribbean which led to the reappearance and expansion of the black population in England. Equiano arrived in 1754 from the two colonies which had driven forward the slave economy: Barbados and Virginia.

From the early days of this new English slavery, the English courts would wrestle with the complex legal issues involved. The core question – was slavery legal in England? – was asked in a number of cases, though the issue was normally addressed indirectly. One recurring problem was whether it was legal to return Africans to the American slave colonies, against their wishes. In the 1720s the West India lobby, that powerful federation of planters and merchants, alarmed that an unfavourable English legal decision might undermine their business, invited a legal judgement from the Attorney and Solicitor Generals. Both obliged, denying in 1729 the widely held belief that a slave landing in England was freed merely by stepping ashore, or by being baptised. They also decided that 'The master may legally compel him to return again to the plantations'.[6]

And despite contradictory decisions about slavery from a number of English courts, the practice of buying and selling Africans had also taken root in England. Blacks were offered at auctions, owners advertised for their runaway slaves, and slaves were put up for sale alongside a range of other items. Newspapers in the major slave ports of London, Bristol and Liverpool frequently published slave advertisements. In 1765 for example a slave was auctioned in Liverpool: 'To be sold by Auction at George's Coffee-house, betwixt the hours of six and eight o'clock, a very fine Negro girl about eight years of age, very healthy, and hath been some time from the coast.' In 1757, three years after Equiano had arrived in England, the following advertisement appeared in a London paper:

'For Sale immediately, ONE stout NEGRO young fellow, about 20 years of age, that has been employcd for 12 months on board a ship, and is a very serviceable hand. And a NEGRO BOY, about 12 years old, that has been used since Sept. last to wait at table, and is of a very good disposition, both warranted sound.'[7]

The presence of black slaves was evident everywhere. Church records listed black baptisms, marriages and burials; one Scipio Africanus was buried in St Mary's churchyard at Henbury in 1720. Contemporary portraits showed African servants to prosperous families and legal records and newspapers frequently mentioned black slaves. Of course, not all British blacks were slaves, but all had landed in England *because* of slavery. So when Equiano disembarked in Falmouth, that cold December of 1754, he was just the latest of many enslaved African arrivals. In time, however, he was to emerge as one of the most influential Africans in England in the era of slavery.

We know so much about Equiano because he published his autobiography in 1789 when he was in his forties. By then he had achieved a remarkable public fame, and his book, *The Interesting Narrative*, was written partly as a contribution to the rising mood of abolition sentiment, partly to describe one man's extraordinary rise from slavery to freedom in England, and partly as a portrayal of the author's spiritual journey. Perhaps one of the most curious questions about Equiano is his fluent literacy. How did an African, bought and sold as an item of trade, become literate? Equally, why should those who taught him require a literate slave? Africans were shipped across the Atlantic to work on the plantations, but as the colonies became sophisticated urban and rural communities, skilled slaves were put in charge of other areas of the economy, such as artisan work, transport or clerical tasks. The ever greater complexity and maturity of the slave economies, then, contributed to the spread of literacy among slaves. More than anything else, however, slave literacy emerged on the back of Christianity. Many owners of black domestics taught them to read and write so that they could study the Bible and become good Christians. It was a pattern which was repeated time and again in the Americas: Christian slaves became literate slaves.

In England, literacy had spread rapidly from the sixteenth century onwards, driven forward by the young Protestant Church and, above all, the translation of the Bible into English. The printed word soon became a cheap, everyday feature of Western life, through readily available newspapers, pamphlets and books. People reading a book or a newspaper, sitting in the corner of a coffee house, tavern or below deck on a ship, were a regular sight by the mid-eighteenth century.

As he crossed the Atlantic on the *Industrious Bee*, Equiano encountered a young man, Richard Baker, 'a native of America', who was four or five years older than the African boy.[8] They soon became close friends, and Baker, a well-educated youth, took great pleasure helping to educate the bemused African, who found himself confronted by one new mystery after another. And nothing seemed more mysterious than the art of reading. When he saw sailors reading, Equiano assumed they were talking to the text. He imitated them, picking up a book in the hope that he too could talk to it: 'I have often taken up a book, and have talked to it, and then put my ears to it, when alone, in hopes it would answer me; and I have been very much concerned when I found it remained silent.'[9] Soon, however, Equiano moved on from his initial bemused curiosity and began learning to read and write.

Equiano was bright, quick and eager to study. Even before he landed in England, he claimed, 'I could smatter a little imperfect English . . .'[10] He had willing teachers; apart from Richard Baker, 'the friend and instructor of one who was ignorant',[11] others also helped him too – ship-mates, employers, clerics. Three years after he arrived in England Equiano confessed that he 'could now speak English tolerably well, and I perfectly understood every thing that was said'. He made slower progress with his reading and writing: 'I had long wished to be able to read and write: and for that took every opportunity to gain instruction, but had made as yet very little progress.[12] The key to Equiano's literacy, and the event that transformed his life was his introduction to Christianity and to the Bible.

Equiano's first visit to England had only been brief and for the next three years he was caught up in a whirl of travel, sailing to the Channel Islands, back to England, on to Scotland and thence into naval combat in North American waters, before returning to England in 1757. Throughout this period he accompanied his English owner, Michael Henry Pascal, a sailor and trader. In London, Equiano met Pascal's cousins, the three Guerin sisters, who were impressed by the young African, and sent him to school. They also wished to have him baptised. At first Pascal refused to allow it, no doubt because he was concerned that baptism might lead to Equiano's freedom; after all this was the very question that had prompted the legal judgement from the Attorney and Solicitor Generals in 1729. For his part, Equiano was keen to be baptised, having been told that 'I could not go to heaven, unless I was baptised'.[13] Eventually Pascal gave his consent, and on 9 February 1759, Equiano was baptised in St Margaret's, Westminster. The parish register recorded him as 'Gustavus Vassa a Black born in Carolina'.[14]

Equiano's travelling years with Pascal had been spent mainly at sea, serving on board the warship *Namur*, a large vessel which had its own schoolmaster. These seaborne schoolteachers had clearly defined duties laid down by the Admiralty and they were expected to teach the young boys serving on the ship reading, writing, arithmetic and navigation, and to encourage draftsmanship that could be used for cartography. British warships traditionally had large complements of young boys of Equiano's age, little more than children really, sent to sea to be trained and reared up in the skills and rigours of life at sea. All the great naval heroes of the period had begun their naval careers as boys; Nelson entered the Royal Navy at the age of twelve, Rodney at thirteen, Hawke at fifteen. All had to be educated at sea, in a protracted transformation from children to young officers.

On the *Namur* Equiano improved both his reading and writing,[15] and when he was transferred to the much smaller *Aetna* in 1759, the young African was employed as the captain's steward, 'in which situation I was very happy, for I was extremely well treated by all on board, and I had the leisure to improve myself in reading and writing'.[16] Even without a formal schoolmaster on board, there were others on hand to help. His fellow mess mate, Daniel Quin (called Queen by Equiano) was a well-educated man of about forty who developed a great attachment for the African. Quin 'took very great pains to instruct me in many things. He taught me to shave and dress hair a little, and also to read in the Bible, explaining many passages to me which I did not comprehend.' Quin was a father figure, and as Equiano openly confessed, 'some even used to call me after his name'.[17]

Such relationships between boys and men were commonplace on board naval vessels, but what is of course different in this case is that a young black slave is taken under the wing of an older white man. The system of Atlantic slavery hinged on the dehumanisation of the African, and it was conceived, nurtured and honed through acts of individual and communal violence. Yet we know of deep affection between black and white: close, abiding friendships and love clearly cut across the barriers of colour and class created by slavery.* Equiano provides a good example of all these varied, contradictory relationships enjoyed and endured by Africans in this era. He was enslaved and brutalised throughout much of his life at sea and in the Americas. Yet he was also the object of great kindness and affection: a man some whites were proud to have as a friend and whom some clearly loved. As Equiano developed into a young man of growing intellectual maturity and learning, he was driven forward not only by that personal drive for success and improvement, but he also thrived on the help and encouragement of many people around him. On board the *Aetna*, his friendship with Daniel Quin proved to be a major force in Equiano's life, not simply in his formal education, but in prompting his intellectual curiosity, about his past and about the world he found himself thrust into.

During his formative years on British warships, Equiano developed two interests which were to remain with him for the rest of his life: he became a serious student of theology and the Bible, and he developed a passion for books. The cleric who baptised Equiano in 1759 gave him his first text, Thomas Wilson's *An Essay towards an Instruction for the Indians*, published in 1740. It was the beginning of a lifetime's attachment to books and reading.

Life aboard ship was a curious mix of violence and self-improvement, and Equiano later recalled the contrast between the mayhem and bloodshed of naval battles, and the humdrum periods of reading and reflection. Like others around him, Equiano always managed to find a corner, even on a small, crowded ship, where he could read and, later, write.

* Another example is the relationship of Dr Johnson with his black servant, Francis (Frank) Barber. On his death, Johnson left Barber the bulk of his estate, but more significantly, Barber inherited the wedding ring of Dr Johnson's wife – surely the clearest sign of deep and abiding affection from master to servant.

When the *Aetna* returned to Deptford in late 1762, the young Equiano, although still a slave, was ready to step ashore and strike out on a new life. Life at sea had provided training in a number of useful skills: he was an experienced sailor, a good hairdresser and he proved to be a competent servant. Indeed, Equiano possessed many of those skills which masters and mistresses valued in domestic staff. In addition, his blackness would be attractive to employers in fashionable society. But Equiano landed with more than just hopes and expectations. He now owned a sea chest filled with clothes and books, and no less than nine guineas which he had accumulated during his voyages: he had won money at games of chance, charged for shaving and haircutting, and had saved his wages.

Equiano believed that he would be freed when he and his master returned to England, but to his astonishment and dismay, Captain Pascal refused to allow him ashore as a free man. Instead, he traded him to another ship, the *Charming Sally*, bound for the West Indies. Equiano's bold assertion to Pascal that 'I was free, and he could not by law serve me so' merely enraged his master, reinforcing his decision to hand him over to Captain Doran, master of the *Charming Sally*. Doran for his part clearly did not like Equiano's articulate assertiveness, nor his plea that baptism had conferred his freedom. The African also argued that throughout his time at sea he had been a faithful servant to Captain Pascal. But his arguments failed to impress Captain Doran, whose answer was uncompromising: 'You are now my slave.' Equiano's sea chest had been left behind on his previous ship. Having lost all his savings and possessions, and his 'heart ready to burst with sorrow and anguish',[18] Equiano was back where his Atlantic story had started all those years ago; a slave aboard a ship.

15 Kidnapped

When the *Charming Sally* left English waters in December 1762 heading for Montserrat, Equiano had effectively been kidnapped and sold – not on the coast of Africa, but on a British ship and in British waters. He was forced to return to the slave colonies against his wishes and had been robbed of all his worldly possessions.

Equiano believed that he had the law – and certainly moral right – on his side but the problem of slavery in England was more complex than he imagined. English courts and legal officials had swung back and forth on the subject. The judgement of 1729 had been that slavery was not automatically removed by baptism, and that a master was entitled to remove a slave from England back to the plantations. Parish registers show that many black slaves were baptised in England; we do not know whether all baptised Africans regarded their new faith as heralding full social freedom, but many had become aware of the link between baptism and freedom.

The expanding black community in England, notably that based in London, had developed its own informal networks in the course of the eighteenth century. Blacks socialised with each other and with new arrivals from the Atlantic ships who brought news from the Americas and from the African coast. Rumour, tittle-tattle and hard news from the colonies blended with conversations overheard and gleaned in homes, coffee houses and taverns, provided the black community with a potent brew of information. In addition, pamphlets were widely circulated and their contents passed on by word of mouth, thence below deck of the Atlantic ships before emerging in the slave colonies weeks later. Thus the black communities on both sides of the Atlantic were well informed and discussed slavery and freedom, emancipation and baptism.

Although weighty legal conversations about slavery in England were the preserve of specialised circles, the simple issues at the heart of those debates inevitably seeped out into a much broader community, both black and white. And it did so not least because there were growing numbers of black people in England for whom the question was no mere legal abstraction. It mattered to ever more black people in England to know if they were free, or whether they, like Equiano in 1762, might find themselves kidnapped and dispatched, against their wishes, to the horrors of the plantations. Ironically, the latest legal decision favouring British blacks came from the Lord Chancellor, Lord Henley, in 1762, in a complex case involving a baptised slave. Henley concluded, 'As soon as a man sets foot on English ground he is free: a Negro may maintain an action against his master for ill usage, and may have a *Habeas Corpus* if restrained of his liberty.'[1] Yet the decision was not much comfort to Equiano, distraught on board the *Charming Sally*. It was simply unenforceable on the deck of a departing ship.

Perhaps more relevant for Equiano, in 1758 the Admiralty had pondered the complex legal case of William Castillo, a Barbadian slave brought to England by his master in 1752. Despite being baptised in Plymouth in

1758, Castillo found himself in irons and a metal collar, on board a Royal Naval warship, the *Neptune*, waiting to be transferred 'on Board the first Ship Bound to Barbados to Be sold'. Remarkably, Castillo managed to send a petition, written in his own hand, to the Prime Minister, William Pitt, who passed it on to the Admiralty for scrutiny. The case proved more complicated than Castillo suggested, his master claiming that the man was apprenticed to him and had broken the term of an agreement by seeking freedom, but the Admiralty took a dim view of chains and collar on a Royal Naval ship. On Christmas Day 1758 it made its judgement known to Admiral Holburne, the harbourmaster at Portsmouth: 'Acquaint Admiral Holburne that the Laws of this Country admit of no badge of Slavery, therefore the Lords hope and expect whenever he discovers any attempt of this kind he should prevent it.'² Despite its obvious relevance to Equiano, what could he, and others like him, do when they found themselves unexpectedly manhandled from one merchant ship to another?

But in the ten years between Equiano's kidnapping in 1762 and the famous Somerset case of 1772, the issue of enforced repatriation to the slave colonies became a source of growing legal friction, and the occasion for growing public outrage. It was a critical decade in the story of British slavery, which laid the foundations for the abolitionist campaigns of the last twenty years of the century.

On 30 December, the *Charming Sally* set sail, 'and, before any of my friends had an opportunity to come off to my relief, to my inexpressible anguish, our ship had got underway'. Seven weeks later, on 13 February 1763, they sighted Montserrat. Although he had previously spent only a short time in the Caribbean, he knew that what awaited him was unlike anything he had experienced in England or at sea.

Since the 1720s, the tiny volcanic island of Montserrat was home to a small number of big plantations. By the end of the eighteenth century, 7,500 Africans toiled there and for all he knew Equiano might never again leave the island. His time in Montserrat coincided with that island's apogee as a sugar colony, and through the spring and early summer of 1763, the *Charming Sally* slowly filled with the sugar and rum from the island's plantations. Initially, Equiano had to load the hogsheads of sugar and rum from the dockside into the tender, and thence, after a precarious trip out to deeper water, into the ship's belly. 'I now knew what it was to work hard,' he wrote in his autobiography. He realised that his best chance of freedom lay in a swift return to England, but Captain Doran knew that 'He could not venture to take me to London, for he was very sure that when I came there I would leave him'.

By the 1760s, only the most optimistic slave holder could hope to maintain a tight grip on any slave they might ship back to England, and Equiano made it abundantly clear to all around him that he wanted freedom. Doran decided to sell the difficult African. It is hard to calculate how many times Equiano had been bought and sold, but what made this latest move unusual was that in 1763 Equiano found himself sold to a Quaker.

Quakers had long been a voice in the wilderness, one of the few groups to have raised their voice in protest against enslavement. As early as 1671 the founder of the movement, George Fox, had urged slave owners on a visit to Barbados to convert and train up their slaves 'in the fear of God'. But these early strictures warning against participation in slavery soon caused problems. In the eighteenth century, Quakers were at the forefront of a range of entrepreneurial activities and slavery offered huge scope for commercial enterprise. However, it was increasingly difficult for Quaker merchants, manufacturers and traders to draw a line between their commercial opportunities and their ethical revulsion.

The iron industry of the 1750s, for example, was dominated by Quakers, yet great demand for metal goods came from the slave system: guns to be traded in Africa, armaments on Atlantic warships, metal goods to be bartered for Africans on the coast, chains and shackles to anchor enslaved Africans on the slave decks.[3] Slavery had become so intrusive, so pervasive, that few areas of the Atlantic economy remained immune to it. Even the prototype local corner shop, run by energetic and enterprising Quakers throughout Britain, relied for their trade on slave-grown produce: on sugar, and those two other commodities it was mixed with, tea and coffee, and on tobacco. However much Quakers disliked slavery, it was hard for them to avoid commercial involvement with it, if only indirectly. But this was quite different from actually owning slaves.

Captain Doran sold Equiano to a local man, Robert King, 'the very best master in the whole island'. King assured Equiano he had bought him 'on account of my good character' adding that the African 'should be very well off with him'.[4]

King was based in Philadelphia, from where he traded to and from the West Indies, and Equiano was relieved to hear that his new owner planned to make the most of his literate and numerate skills and to train him as a clerk at his home in Philadelphia. Equiano was already far too valuable and far too skilled a man to be thrown into the fields or to other forms of hard physical labour. The prospects of a clerical position, and further education, in Philadelphia were encouraging, but Equiano took leave of his shipmates on the *Charming Sally* 'with a very wishful and aching heart, and followed her with my eyes until she was totally out of sight. I was so bowed down with grief that I could not hold up my head for many months.'[5] Once again, Equiano had to say farewell to the friends he had made and had lived close to in the crowded intimacy below decks.

Initially, working for King was not without its physical exertions. Equiano was charged with the heavy work of loading and unloading the smaller boats to and from the bigger ship anchored offshore. At the height of the sugar season, the first six months of the year, when the cane was harvested and processed into crude, barrelled sugar and rum, Equiano did this for sixteen hours a day. At other times he travelled to inland plantations collecting produce. King gave Equiano fifteen pence a day for living expenses, and seems to have been a humane employer who tried to treat his enslaved labourers decently, ensuring that they had enough to eat.

At first sight this variant of jobbing slave labour might seem to be less harsh than traditional field labour. Yet as he worked side by side with other slaves, Equiano heard a litany of complaints: of wages and debts unpaid, of personal property stolen by whites, of random and persistent violence and, inevitably, of more favourable working conditions afforded to white working men. Slaves were beaten merely for asking for their wages. King was clearly different from most of his fellow slave owners on Montserrat, sometimes arbitrating between aggrieved slaves and their masters, feeding a hungry slave or otherwise making good the shortcomings of other whites. We must wonder: who was the more typical slave owner – Robert King or Thomas Thistlewood?

Being paid in cash brought opportunities denied to other slaves: careful, industrious slaves might, with luck, be able to save money. Equiano had saved money in his early years at sea and slaves everywhere scraped together meagre savings from their long hours of labour. As we have already seen, money, material possessions and the habit of self-improvement were features of slave societies everywhere. Crops and foodstuffs cultivated on plots and gardens, animals reared and sold for slaughter, domestic skills such as sewing, cooking, joinery and childcare, singing, playing musical instruments, and knowledge of African medicine and traditions, all and more yielded profits for slaves. Some were able to clothe themselves in extraordinary finery for special occasions. The simplicity of slave cabins and huts was augmented by decoration, and by 'luxuries' which were often hand-me-downs from the master's home and table: chipped crockery, damaged cutlery, cast-off shoes or clothing. It rarely amounted to very much, but it meant a great deal to people who had stepped off the slave ships in conditions of extreme distress and wretchedness. This largely informal slave economy, in cash and in kind, generally operated out of view and has eluded historians until quite recently. It grew on the back of the broader local economy, but it was made possible by the enterprise, energy and initiative of the slaves themselves. And few became more adept at its practice than Equiano.

Equiano worked for King as a clerk, tallying the imports and exports and looking after the stores, as well as serving him as a domestic servant, tending to his hair, caring for his horse and, all the while ferrying goods to and from the incoming and departing vessels. King acknowledged that compared with the more elevated wages of free white clerks in his employment, Equiano saved him at least one hundred pounds a year. In his autobiography Equiano put great emphasis on this fact in an effort to counter the argument advanced by the pro-slave lobby that slave labour never repaid the outlay required for its purchase. It seems an odd, implausible argument: would the slave trade have persisted for more than four centuries if Africans had been an unprofitable investment?

One of Equiano's important tasks in Montserrat was working on board newly arrived slave ships: 'I used frequently to have different cargoes of new Negroes in my care for sale . . .' Again, he was ideally suited. Who better to talk to them, to reassure them, to explain matters to them, than a young African who understood their language and who had passed through a very similar experience? Moreover, British ships carried the overwhelming bulk of their enslaved Africans from the Bight of Biafra,[6] the region of Equiano's own family background.[7] But were they comforted by the presence and words of another African, stepping aboard the slave ships in the Americas? After all, they had passed through the hands of other Africans in West Africa: the traders and merchants on the coast who had sold them to the European slave ships.

Whatever the difficulties, Equiano was a valuable go-between. There is no sense in his recollections that he had any qualms about his work on board the slave ships; Equiano never suggests that he felt his work inappropriate or wrong. In any case, he was as much a victim of the system as the newly arrived Africans. Like many others, Equiano had managed to find a place for himself in a hostile and dangerous world. Indeed, this was to be his most amazing trait throughout his life. Not only was he a survivor, but he was able to find a route towards security and material comfort in the most unlikely circumstances. He was a lucky slave, but he made his own luck and he appreciated his relative good fortune when he saw what terrible lives many of his fellow slaves were forced to endure in the Caribbean.

16 In Miserable Slavery

Equiano avoided work as a field hand in the tropics, but he bore witness to the daily sufferings of slaves in the Americas. At the heart of the abolition campaign launched in 1787, lay revelations about the sufferings of Africans, on the slave ships and in the plantations. From the first, abolitionists consciously paraded the cruelties of slavery before the British reading public. In lectures, tracts, sermons and books, in parliamentary speeches and in evidence before a string of parliamentary hearings, in pictures, cartoons, caricatures and paintings, it was the cruelties of slavery which surfaced, time and again, as a central theme.[1] Slavery stood condemned because it was cruel. To a public which, from the late eighteenth century onwards, began to object to cruelty against children, animals, women, even against criminals, such abuse came to be seen as the ultimate denunciation of slavery. Yet the puzzling question remains: why was slavery regarded as cruel in the 1780s, whereas its brutalities had gone unnoticed and unremarked for centuries before? Was this apparent change of heart and mind simply a result of powerful abolitionist propaganda; or did the campaign play upon fundamental social changes, and changes in national sensibilities, which spurned the older attachment to cruelties in all corners of British life?

When Equiano wrote his autobiography in 1788–9, he followed a well-established literary convention describing slave sufferings. The focus initially had been on the Middle Passage, the Atlantic crossing: the descriptions and images of life on the slave ships – the overcrowding, the squalor, the death and suffering – could hardly fail to create outrage and revulsion among readers. The attack on the slave trade after 1787 emerged as a long, protracted, national campaign to describe the unimaginable.[2]

While most accounts and eyewitnesses found the sexual violation of enslaved women too delicate a subject to describe in detail, Equiano confronted it head-on. As he helped to process the newly arrived Africans in Montserrat, Equiano recorded regular incidents of sexual attacks on African women. It was, he wrote, 'almost a constant practice with our clerks, and other whites, to commit violent depredations on the chastity of the female slaves'. He could do nothing to stop them. When the Africans were shipped to other islands or to North America, Equiano testified that sailors would 'commit these acts most shamefully, to the disgrace, not of Christians only, but of men. I have even known them gratify their brutal passion with females not ten years old.' At times, the sexual violence was so extreme that the ship's captain discharged the men involved.[3] Equiano's account was designed to shock but it was no mere propaganda. There are plenty of other sources, not published at the time, and not designed to horrify the reading public, which tell the same tale.

As we have seen, John Newton recorded the rape of an African woman on board the *African* in his log in 1753. Newton never forgot the horrors visited upon African women on the slave ships. In his 'Thoughts Upon the African Slave Trade' of 1788, he described how, as the women and girls were loaded on board, frightened, naked and exhausted, they were eyed by the crew: 'In imagination, the prey is divided, upon the spot, and only reserved till opportunity offers. Where resistance or refusal, would be utterly in vain, even the solicitation of consent is seldom thought of.' He concluded that 'the enormities frequently committed in an African ship . . . are little known *here*, and are considered *there*, only as matters of course'.[4] Equiano told his own account of sexual violence towards slave women, on board slave ships at Montserrat and elsewhere in the Caribbean. Both slave trader and slave told the same story.

Time and again writers and witnesses described what they had seen on the ships and on the plantations. Parliamentary committees were regaled with detailed and irrefutable evidence about the sadistic brutality which underpinned the slave system. Abolitionists also offered an array of graphic images of the brutalities suffered by slaves. The implements of torture (chains, neck and head restraints, whips and thumbscrews), pictures of slaves beaten, whipped and impaled, dead and dying, dangling from trees, broken on a wheel and branded – all and more affronted the public. What was presented was not so much supporting evidence that slaves were cruelly treated, but a sustained and shocking argument that slavery itself was a human violation; an institution that was barbaric to the core and stood condemned for its fundamental inhumanity, whatever profits it might deliver. The abolitionist movement quickly secured the moral high ground and the slave lobby found it impossible to respond.* It seemed

* It was true, as Marcus Wood has shown, that the iconography of slave suffering was rooted in, and drew upon, a much older, Western tradition of representations of pain and punishment, most notably the flagellations, crucifixion and death of Christ. In the process, abolition was able to elevate slave sufferings to the level of Christ on the Cross.

unacceptable that such suffering should be endured merely to sweeten European and American food and drink, and provide men with the happiness of a smoke.

Equiano's eyewitness account was, then, just one contribution to a major campaign, but what gave his story an added edge and poignancy was that he had suffered the cruelties of slavery at first hand. Although he was not a field slave and his more privileged position, his higher status within the slave hierarchy, had insulated him from some of the worst threats and torments, he nonetheless confessed that 'I was often a witness to cruelty of every kind, which were exercised on my unhappy slaves.'[5]

Equiano blamed the worst violations in the Americas on the overseers of the plantations, who dealt with slaves face to face on a daily basis. 'These overseers are indeed for the most part persons of the worst character of any denomination of men in the West Indies. [They] cut and mangle the slaves in a shocking manner on the most trifling occasions, and altogether treat them in every respect like brutes. They pay no regard to the situation of pregnant women.'[6] In St Kitts, Equiano reported that most of the slaves were branded with their owners' initials. What added insult to these terrible injuries was that they were doled out for the most inconsequential of incidents. Equiano told of a slave beaten till his bones were broken 'for only letting a pot boil over'.[7]

Again, it is difficult to know how typical such extreme incidents were, but in precisely the same years that Equiano witnessed such outrages in Montserrat and St Kitts, Thomas Thistlewood was recording his own sadistic punishments of his slaves in western Jamaica. Yet it is very unlikely that Thistlewood's diaries could have been published in the late eighteenth century: the refined and religious sensibilities of the main leaders of abolition would have recoiled at the publication of such obscene detail. Even in the drive to discredit slavery, there were limits to what abolitionists felt they could reveal.

Slaves needed no one to tell them about the cruelties of slavery: it formed the warp and weft of their lives. But they quickly learned of outrages against other Africans thanks to the remarkable network of news and information at all points of the Atlantic compass. News sped as fast as ships travelled between Africa, the Americas and Europe. Wherever Africans gathered together for friendship, comfort and social life, helping and entertaining each other, they swapped tales, keeping abreast of news from all corners of the ocean.[8] And although white abolitionists, their readers and audiences, may have been hesitant or restrained in what they told or learned about the cruelties of slaves, Africans themselves had no such inhibitions.

Not surprisingly, the sufferings inflicted on the slaves often led to suicide. Equiano asked the obvious question: 'Is it surprising that usage like this should drive the poor creatures to despair, and to make them seek a refuge in death from those evils which render their lives intolerable.'[9] Europeans noticed mental despair among Africans as soon as they were brought on board the slave ships on the African coast. Dr Trotter, a Royal Naval surgeon, had spent ten months on the slave coast in 1783. Later, in giving evidence to a parliamentary select committee, he told how the slaves showed 'extreme distress and despair, from a feeling of their situation, and regret at being torn from their friends and connections; many retain those impressions for a long time'. At night, his ship echoed to the 'howling, melancholy noise' of slave anguish. Trotter found many of the women 'in hysterical fits'. One of Trotter's slaves slashed his throat, then ripped open the doctor's stitches declaring 'he never would go with white men'. He died a few days later.[10]

Dr Alexander Falconbridge, perhaps the most influential

and best remembered medical witness before Parliament, reported that many Africans simply refused to eat and had to be force-fed. One of his female patients 'was dejected from the moment she came on board, and refused both food and medicine'. She told the interpreter she wanted only to die: 'and she did die. Many other slaves expressed the same wish.'

Slave ships were designed to prevent suicides, with nets rigged to stop slaves throwing themselves overboard, but dejected Africans still managed to drown themselves. In the Americas, too, distressed slaves sought relief from life's miseries by killing themselves. Thomas Thistlewood's diaries report suicides among his slaves in western Jamaica: Moll drowned herself in 1756; Mocho Jimmy tried to hang himself in 1780.[11]

Some responded to their misery by stoic resilience, others by fury, or by violent defiance. Others, however, slid into catatonic gloom which ended in self-destruction. Equiano concluded that, by 1789, 'The small account in which the life of a Negro is held in the West Indies is so universally known' that the suffering of West Indian slaves cannot 'afford novelty to recite them: and they are too shocking to yield delight either to the writer or the reader'. But no historian's account of those cruelties can hope to come close to the reality visited upon the millions of Africans by the slave systems of the Americas.

Equiano argued that benevolent slave management was in the owners' best interests: decent treatment, good food and lodging would help create a healthy slave population. And a healthy slave population reproduced itself. Equiano pointed to plantations in both Montserrat and Barbados where planters 'from such judicious treatment, need no fresh stock of Negroes at any time'.[12] The inability of slave populations to increase was characteristic of many of the Caribbean islands – though less so of Barbados – and of the colonies in North America. As long as the enslaved population declined, planters needed to buy new Africans. To abolitionists it seemed that the problem was largely a matter of treatment and intent. If a planter determined to treat his slaves better, the results were self-evident.

In fact, the matter was much more complex than Equiano and others realised. There were basic demographic problems on many of the islands, which unbalanced the populations and made it difficult for them to increase naturally. Too many men, the wrong age structure, ailments imported from Africa and/or compounded by the Atlantic crossing, bad health through hard work in the sugar fields – all had damaging effects on the slaves' ability to conceive and reproduce. In addition there was widespread venereal disease, made worse by the predatory sexuality of white men towards slave women.[13] There were fundamental problems that could not be solved by benevolent or compassionate slave management. In fact, it was not until long after the abolition of the slave trade in 1807 that the overall populations of the British colonies in the Caribbean first levelled out and then started a process of natural growth.

When Equiano argued that better treatment was the key to improved health and well-being for slaves in the colonies, it was only part of the story. The miseries of the slaves were rooted in much deeper – and much less visible – causes. Yet he, and other slaves, knew from bitter experience that it was the *system* that was at fault. Slavery was flawed, not in this or that particular, not in the benevolence or viciousness of individual slave owners, but in its entirety. It was both ethically rotten and economically irrational. Equiano and other slaves tried to persuade the rest of the world what they knew from personal experience.

17 Prospering in Slavery

It is tempting to assume that slavery in the Americas consisted of stark alternatives – white freedom on the one side, black servitude on the other. In many cases this was true, but often, it was not. There were, for example, large numbers of poor slave owners – many whites simply assuming that they required the help of slaves. Slaves were also owned by 'people of colour' (to use that unattractive phrase, devised in order to categorise mankind into ranks and shades of colour). In a culture spawned by slavery, ever more people were born from relations between black and white. Those favoured by their white fathers, and provided with freedom and property, often became slave owners themselves.[1]

On the other side, there were all sorts and conditions of slaves. They ranged from those whose lives were spent toiling in the fields, undertaking the simplest but most physically demanding of tasks, through to the most privileged of slaves, those who lived close to the owner, often sharing his bed and raising his offspring, and who were often able to insulate themselves from the worst of degradations. Equiano's story was not unique, but he himself was extraordinary. Few others left us such an abundant account of slavery, and few of his peers enjoyed or endured such a range of personal experiences. Equiano stood out among his contemporaries, and he did so by dint of his own efforts and mental resilience. He elevated himself, slowly and laboriously, and he rebounded time and again from the most crushing of reverses. Nothing illustrates this better than his progress from slave to free man in Montserrat between 1763 and 1766.

Robert King, Equiano's Quaker master, owned a number of ships trading between the Caribbean islands. One of them, ferrying passengers between the islands, was commanded by Captain Thomas Farmer, who spotted Equiano's potential. When King hesitated to release Equiano to work on Farmer's sixty-ton sloop, the two white men began competing for Equiano's services. Farmer sometimes refused to sail unless he had the African on board, claiming 'that I was better to him on board than any three white men he had'. King finally gave way and released the African from his storekeeping. Equiano, for his part, spotted the opportunities offered by the new job: '... I immediately thought I might in time stand a chance by being on board to get a little money, or possibly make my escape if I should be used ill.' He threw himself into his new work. 'I did all I could to deserve his favour, and in return I received better treatment from him than any other I believe ever met with in the West Indies in my situation.' Life at sea, with the frequent calls at ports throughout the Caribbean, offered a host of other opportunities: 'I at length endeavoured to try my luck and commence merchant.' With the investment of one half-bitt – the equivalent of three pence – Equiano launched into his new sideline as private dealer and vendor.[2] When he was kidnapped in 1762, Equiano had lost nine guineas and all the personal possessions he had accumulated during his years at sea.[3] Now, with his base in Montserrat, he started all over again.

His trading life began with a single transaction: a tumbler bought for half a bitt in St Eustatius and sold for twice that sum in Montserrat. Equiano frequently visited St Eustatius, a thriving entrepôt where he bought goods unavailable on other islands. At the end of six weeks, his initial investment of a half-bitt had grown to one dollar. 'I blessed the Lord that I was so rich.' He didn't allow his money to lie idle, and reinvested it on the next voyage, 'especially when we went to Guadaloupe, Grenada, and the rest of the French islands'. For four years, Equiano crisscrossed the eastern Caribbean, 'ever trading as I went'.

Inevitably his journeys brought more than their share of problems. Time and again Equiano, and others around him, fell victim to what he called 'ill usage' in dealings with whites. Even when simply relaxing and enjoying themselves, Equiano and his fellow slaves found themselves 'without cause molested and insulted'. When he traded, and when he had both cash and goods on his person, Equiano was especially vulnerable to capricious and violent meddling – and blatant theft – by local whites. When he and a friend landed at Santa Cruz with two bags of fresh oranges and limes to sell on the island, a couple of whites simply seized their bags. The two victims followed the thieves, begging for their goods to be returned, but instead were simply threatened with 'if we did not immediately depart, they would flog us as well'. The theft meant that everything Equiano had saved and accumulated was gone at a stroke, much as it was when he had been kidnapped.[4] Eventually, the thieves relented and handed back one of Equiano's bags, but his companion was less fortunate and returned empty-handed and in tears. Equiano shared his fruits and they managed to sell what they had at an unexpectedly high profit. The African put his good luck down to divine intervention.[5] Having accumulated some money, one of Equiano's first purchases was a Bible, available in St Kitts but hard to come by on other islands.

Equiano felt the fears and pressures of life in the Caribbean more than most because he had 'seen many better days, and been, as it were, in a state of freedom and plenty'. Other places he visited as a sailor 'seemed to me a paradise in comparison of the West-Indies'.[6] He was driven, throughout, by hopes of freedom, and prayed 'to God for my liberty' but knew that he would have to secure it for himself.

Captain Farmer was critical of Equiano's ambitions, partly as the African had become indispensable to Farmer's work up and down the islands. Equiano was a competent sailor, an honest clerk and an industrious working man. Such men were hard to find, both among the slaves and among the free white sailors. But Equiano had become worried about the dangers of a seafaring life, especially where it was a tough, strenuous and dangerous existence that seemed to compound Equiano's thwarted ambitions of freedom. The regular threat of drowning seemed a poor reward for all his industry and application. He was also troubled when he saw, or heard of, free blacks kidnapped and transported against their wishes into slavery elsewhere. He reported such kidnappings in St Kitts, in Jamaica and other islands; he even heard of two cases in Philadelphia. These outrages served to persuade him not only that slavery was an abomination, but being a free black in a world of slavery hardly seemed much better.

The experience of his kidnapping weighed heavily on Equiano. He knew that he needed fully *documented* – i.e. provable – freedom which could only come through formal emancipation, granted and legally sanctioned by his master, Mr King. Equiano was determined 'To make every exertion to obtain my freedom, and to return to Old England'.[7] He even played with the idea, if he was further abused, of commandeering a fast sailing sloop, using his navigational experience to head for Britain, along with whichever fellow slaves might be prepared to join him. He set out to learn navigation from the mate of his current vessel, and agreed to pay him $24, but when Captain Farmer learned of the arrangement he put a stop to it. Modest chances of escape regularly presented themselves – he was very tempted in Guadeloupe to join a fleet heading for France – though by now Equiano had developed a loyalty to Captain Farmer and Mr King. It seems strange that he should opt for loyalty to his owner and employer rather than strike out towards possible freedom, but Equiano had to make a delicate calculation: the prospects of a *qualified* freedom in Europe versus the risks of working towards *formal* freedom in the West Indies.

Late in 1764 Equiano joined his master's new ship, a sloop of about eighty tons, under Captain Farmer's command, on its first voyage to ship a cargo of African slaves to Georgia and Charleston. Georgia was a newly settled region and, like its neighbours, inevitably turned to Africans to work its tobacco fields; Charleston on the other hand had long been the major port of entry for Africans destined for the rice plantations of the low-lying, steamy coastal region. There, and elsewhere in North America, Africans often arrived via the Caribbean. Once again, Equiano assisted in the painful processing, transportation and settlement of new arrivals from the slave ships.

Carolina had close links to the West Indies. It had first been pioneered by settlers from Barbados, a fact reflected in a number of architectural styles which survive to this day in South Carolina. More important perhaps, the Barbadians also brought their slaves. Local economic practice and, later, legal custom transplanted the vital elements of plantation slavery from England's first colony in the West Indies into its latest in North America. Growing rice in Carolina was a punitive form of slave labour, and its harsh physical conditions looked remarkably like the slave labour in the Caribbean sugar fields. Carolina's port, Charleston, like Bridgetown before it, was a bustling seaport and commercial hub, with Africans arriving by the boatload, both direct from Africa and via the West Indies, and with its produce, mainly rice and indigo, leaving for Britain, it soon grew into an elegant town of eight thousand people.

In Charleston, Equiano had to be permanently alert to the tricks and threats of customers who knew they could walk away with money or goods without worrying about legal or social punishment for cheating black traders. When he sold his goods to a group of white men, they bought his wares 'with smooth promises and fair words, giving me, however, but very indifferent payment... There was one gentlemen particularly who bought a puncheon of Rum of me, which gave me a great deal of trouble... being a negro man, I could not oblige him to pay me.'[8] Equiano was so angry that he missed Sunday worship, instead gathering together a group of black friends to set off in search of his debts. After a great deal of argument, the man reluctantly paid, though even then some of his money was worthless. It was an old, familiar story: 'he took advantage of my being a Negro man ...'[9]

Being cheated and robbed was often the least of his worries. Blacks everywhere were exposed to casual and capricious threats of violence and drunken aggression. In Savannah Equiano was badly beaten up by a doctor and his companion. He was taken to the local jail in a mangled state before Captain Farmer found him and took him to his own lodgings. He was bedridden for more than two weeks, carefully tended by his captain, and it was a full month before he could return to work on the ship. It had been a severe physical attack, prompted by little more than a drunken man's anger at finding strange blacks in his yard.[10]

Incidentally, it was at exactly the same time that a

similar act of brutality proved to be a major turning point in the story of British slavery. In 1765 a young, London-based black, Jonathan Strong, was savagely beaten about the head with a pistol by his owner, David Lisle. He was cared for by Dr William Sharp at his surgery in Mincing Lane, London, and later at St Bart's Hospital. Dr Sharp's brother, Granville Sharp, was outraged by the incident and the subsequent legal case; and what he learned about slavery in England – and by extension about slavery in the colonies – led to a one-man campaign against the practice. He became the defender of blacks in England and, in the process, the man who laid down the basis for the movement against the slave trade later in the century.

Up and down the islands, and between the islands and North America, Equiano continued to trade. His master, Mr King, even encouraged him to trade in sugar and rum on credit on his own behalf when the ship docked in Philadelphia; it was perhaps King's way of securing Equiano's loyalty. Nonetheless, it was a remarkable fact that a slave owner gave valuable goods to a slave so that the African could profit on his own behalf.

King had agreed to free Equiano for the amount he had paid initially. 'I might depend upon it that he would let me have it for forty pounds sterling money, which was only the same price he gave for me.' Everywhere he landed, Equiano was dealing and trading, to accumulate cash towards his own purchase price. It was an unusual story: an African, barely out of his teens, working as hard as he could to save cash to buy his own freedom.*

Freedom was getting closer when Equiano was given the chance in 1766 to join King's new sloop, the *Nancy*.

* When full freedom came for all slaves in the British slave empire in 1834–8 it too came at a price. The British effectively bought the slaves, buying off their owners, at a staggering cost of £20 million. Every man had his price.

It was 'the largest I had ever seen' and, best of all, it provided Equiano with 'more room, and could carry a large quantity of goods with me'. He bought four barrels of pork in Charleston, laying in 'as large a cargo as I could, trusting to God's Providence to prosper my undertaking'. It worked. The voyage 'made nearly three hundred percent' when he sold his goods in Philadelphia, mainly to Quakers.[11] From their early days as a small but vociferous sect in seventeenth-century England, the Quakers had established a reputation for plain and straightforward trading and dealing. They bought and sold at a fair price, took pains to manufacture decent products, and they were unimpeachably honest in their financial dealings. Equiano was only the latest customer to be struck by their commercial and personal virtues: 'They always appeared to be very honest discreet sort of people, and never attempted to impose on me; I therefore liked them, and ever after chose to deal with them in preference to any others.'[12]

In the summer of 1766, back in Montserrat, Equiano counted his savings: he had accumulated enough money to secure his promised freedom. But now King seemed unwilling to go through with his promise. When Equiano arrived at his master's breakfast table, clutching the necessary cash for freedom, King's response was disheartening. '"What!", said he "give you your freedom? Why, where did you get the money; Have you got forty pounds sterling?"' When Equiano showed the cash, King asked: 'How did you get it?' The reply was simple: 'Very honestly.'

Equiano's industry and frugality were confirmed by Captain Farmer, who was also at the breakfast table, but King still hesitated, 'and said he would not have made the promise he did if he thought I should have got money so soon'. Fortunately for Equiano, Captain Farmer supported him. 'Come, come, come Robert . . . I think you must let him have his freedom; – you have laid your money out very well; you have received good interest for it all this time, and here now is the principal at last.'

He pointed out that Equiano had earned King more than one hundred pounds a year for the past three years, and the initial outlay was about to be repaid: 'Come, Robert, take the money.' King finally agreed, took the money and 'told me to go to the Secretary at the Register Office, and get my manumission.' These words struck Equiano 'like a voice from heaven'. He burst into tears, thanked both men and dashed off to complete the transaction.[13] A few minutes later Equiano had secured his certificate of freedom. He was to remain emancipated until the day he died, thirty-one years later.

18 *A Free Man*

For the first time in many years Equiano was a free man. 'My feet scarcely touched the ground, for they were winged with joy . . . Every one I met I told of my happiness, and blazed about the virtue of my amiable master and captain . . . I who had been a slave in the morning, trembling at the will of another, now became my own master, and completely free. I thought this was the happiest day I had ever experienced . . .'[1]

When he wrote his *Narrative* in 1789, Equiano reproduced his freedom pass in full. For the previous twenty years he had waved it under the noses of doubters whenever his freedom was endangered. Written in that formal manner of any late eighteenth-century legal document, Equiano's certificate of freedom is worth reprinting in full.

Montserrat – To all men unto whom these presents shall come: I Robert King, of the parish of St Anthony, in the said island, merchant, send greeting: Know ye, that I the aforesaid Robert King, for, and in consideration of the sum of seventy pounds current money of the said island to me in hand paid, and to the intent that a negro man slave, named Gustavus Vassa, shall and may become free, have manumitted, emancipated, enfranchised, and set free, and by these presents do manumit, emancipate, enfranchise, and set free, the aforesaid negro man-slave, named Gustavus Vasa, for ever, hereby giving, granting, and releasing unto him, the said Gustavus Vasa, all right, title, dominion, sovereignty, and property, which, as lord and master over the aforesaid Gustavus Vasa, I have had, or which I now have, or by any means whatsoever I may or can hereafter possibly have over him the aforesaid Negro, for ever. In witness whereof, I the abovesaid Robert King, have unto these presents set my hand and seal, this tenth day of July, in the year of our Lord one thousand seven hundred and sixty-six.

ROBERT KING

Signed, sealed, and delivered in the presence of Terry Legay.

Montserrat,
Registered the within manumission, at full length, this eleventh day of July, 1766, in liber D. TERRY LEGAY, Register.

Equiano organised dances for friends to celebrate his freedom, sporting a new blue suit which he had bought in Savannah, much to the approval of local women, 'who formerly stood aloof, [but] now began to relax, and appear less coy'. Equiano was intent on returning to London, despite what had happened to him on his last trip. For the time being, however, he agreed to serve King and Farmer 'as an able-bodied sailor, at thirty-six shillings per month', adding – significantly – 'besides what perquisites I could make'. He wanted to make a couple of voyages and then, in a year's time, head for England in the hope of finding Pascal, the man who had condemned him to American slavery.

A Free Man

Only a month after he had purchased his freedom, Equiano was again confronted by the inescapable dangers facing black people everywhere. When on another voyage to Georgia, the *Nancy* docked in Savannah and Equiano found himself in a dispute with a slave: 'I lost all temper, and fell on him and beat him soundly.' The beaten man's master promptly arrived, demanding that Equiano be flogged in town. 'I was astonished and frightened at this, and thought I had better keep where I was, than go ashore and be flogged round the town, without judge or jury.' He knew that the defences of being a 'free Negro' were paper-thin and that some whites took the news of a black man's freedom as a positive incentive to goad and threaten. Equiano eventually escaped punishment, but his first taste of freedom had proved a complex saga of hide-and-seek, of constables' warrants, of deceptions and secret efforts by his captain to protect him.

On the return voyage to Montserrat, Captain Farmer fell sick and died. Distressed at the death of his friend and protector, Equiano was now determined to return to England 'where my heart had always been'. He nonetheless agreed to undertake one last voyage for Mr King – again to St Eustatius and Georgia – but this time under the command of William Phillips. It proved disastrous.

Refitted, and with a cargo of slaves, Captain Phillips sailed the *Nancy* to St Eustatius and then, on 30 January 1767, on to Georgia. On the second leg of the voyage, despite Equiano's repeated warnings, the captain sailed the vessel on to some rocks. They were all in great peril. Compounding his negligence, the captain was fearful that the twenty slaves below decks would overpower the crew and threatened to entomb them by nailing down the hatches on the holds. Equiano openly denounced Captain Phillips, accusing him of putting them in mortal danger, and threatening, in turn, to unite the rest of the crew against him. The crew and the slaves then evacuated the

vessel in the rowing boat, Equiano making five trips to a
nearby island and ferrying everyone on board to safety.
He rowed alongside 'three black men and a Dutch Creole
sailor . . .' Instead of helping, the white sailors 'lay about
the deck like swine' in a drunken fit, and had to be manhandled into the rescue boat. After a hard day's toil, all thirty-
two people aboard the *Nancy* were on dry land and safe.[2]
They found themselves on one of the hundreds of tiny
small Bahama islands, and what now unfolded was a
Robinson Crusoe-like adventure. The men spent eleven
days repairing their damaged boat before Equiano, the
captain and five others struck out to find their way to New
Providence and seek help for those left behind. It was yet
another risky venture, but just when they feared again for
their lives, they were sighted by a hoy, a wrecker in search
of salvage. Two days later, they took on board the other
survivors of the *Nancy*.

On the last leg of their journey to Providence the rescue
hoy was endangered by a storm, and again Equiano
claimed to have exercised a decisive role in steering the
vessel to safety. In his autobiography he was quick to
dismiss the other men's efforts and pointed out their failings and professional shortcomings. It was a theme which
ran throughout his story, persuading readers that he was
a man of remarkable decisiveness and resolution,
succeeding where lesser mortals failed. There is no reason
to doubt what he said, but we need to be aware that he
was advertising his own virtues to a sympathetic readership.

It had been a gruelling, dangerous three weeks, and
having survived the latest string of terrible ordeals,
Equiano rejoined Captain Phillips in his hired sloop
heading for their original destination of Georgia. Once
again, luck was against them when the ship sailed on to
rocks and had to limp back for repairs. Such a run of bad
luck needed some explanation – despite the most obvious

being the nautical incompetence of the captain. Some thought that a spell had been cast on the voyage in Montserrat, others blamed the African slaves, claiming 'We had witches and wizards amongst the poor helpless slaves'. Equiano urged the crew to be steady, 'and swear not, but trust to God, and he will deliver us'. Eventually, seven days later, they arrived in Savannah.

But, again, Equiano was not safe. Just outside Savannah, he was 'beset by two white men, who meant to play their usual tricks with me in the way of kidnapping'. He warned them not to touch him: one of his aggressors thought 'that I talked too good English'. When threatened with a stick, the men left him in peace. Equiano now became ever more anxious 'to take a final farewell of the American quarter of the globe.' But before he could, he had to return to Montserrat to say his goodbyes.[3]

Equiano sailed on the *Speedwell*, filled with rice and destined for Martinique, hoping to get to Montserrat in time for the fleet leaving for England in July, ahead of the hurricane season. On 23 July 1767, six months after he had left, Equiano arrived back in Montserrat. King was happy to see his former slave and urged him not to head for London. He reassured Equiano that he was much respected and could prosper on the island. He might even be able 'in a short time [to] have land and slaves of my own'. But Equiano was not to be deflected by such flattery. Before leaving, however, he wanted King to give him a 'certificate of my behaviour'. Signed on 26 July 1767, the document read:

The bearer hereof, Gustavus Vasa, was my slave for upwards of three years, during which time he has always behaved himself well, and discharged his duties with honesty and assiduity.

ROBERT KING

Equiano now possessed two documents, one proving his freedom, the other confirming his exceptional qualities as an employee. Everything was now in place for returning to London. On 27 July 1767, Equiano boarded the *Andromache* bound, as a working sailor, for England.[4]

He was happy to leave: 'I bade adieu to the sound of the cruel whip, and all the other dreadful instruments of torture! Adieu to the offensive sight of the violated chastity of sable females ... adieu to oppressions (although to me less severe than to most of my countrymen!).' He knew that he had been a lucky slave. At precisely the time Equiano's vessel began its seven-week voyage to London, Thomas Thistlewood, in western Jamaica, jotted in his diary: 'flogged Lincoln & every one of the field Negroes for impudence and laziness, etc ...'[5] Equiano was very conscious of what he was leaving behind.

Seven weeks later, in early September, he stepped ashore at Cherry Garden stairs on the south bank of the Thames, a few miles east of the city centre. He collected his wages of seven guineas for the voyage – 'I never had earned seven guineas so quick in my life before.' He arrived back in London, after an absence of four years, with thirty-seven guineas to his name. He had left, against his wishes, robbed of everything he owned – and his emancipation. Now he returned as a free man. Equiano was clearly delighted to have turned his back on the slave islands. But in eighteenth-century England too, life for a black person, free or enslaved, was fraught with problems and dangers.

London in 1767 was home to a noticeable black community. It did not approach the size of more familiar, traditional immigrant communities (such as the Scots and the Irish), but it was striking, even in a city which was home to myriad migrant groups. Africans were also scattered across the face of England, serving their masters in the grandest of homes, and sometimes in the most remote and isolated of places. The very year Equiano returned to England, 'Peter, a black boy of Peter Hancock' was baptised in Twyning, Gloucestershire. So too was George William, 'a Negro' aged about eighteen, in Birchanger, Essex. A few years earlier, a young African, Charles Bacchus, was laid to rest in Culworth Churchyard, Northamptonshire.[6]

In the second half of the eighteenth century, the numbers of blacks in Britain had increased. As the slave trade expanded, and as more and more ships completed their Atlantic voyages, they discharged cargoes and passengers in ever greater volume. Planters and traders, merchants and soldiers, sailors and settlers all found their way 'home' to the mother country after their various sojourns in the Americas. With them arrived African sailors (free and enslaved), black domestics accompanying their masters and mistresses, and slaves imported for sale in Britain by sailors (who had acquired them as a bonus on a recent voyage). And it was on the streets of the capital, and especially in the dockside communities that were home to the transient population serving the naval and maritime trades, that blacks made their presence felt. In the summer of 1767, Equiano stepped ashore in a city familiar, though not always at ease, with a local black population.

His first task was to seek out his old friends: the Guerin sisters, who had concerned themselves with his welfare on his previous visit. Delighted to see him again, they were appalled to learn that their cousin, Captain Pascal, had been responsible for Equiano's re-enslavement. A few days later, Equiano met the man himself in Greenwich Park. There followed an understandably stiff exchange, though it is surprising that Equiano was not more hostile. Pascal, surprised to see him, showed no signs of remorse for what he had done. Later, at the Guerin sisters' house, the two men had a further dispute when Equiano demanded the prize money owing to him from his time spent with Pascal. The request was brushed aside and Equiano threatened to go to court to secure his money. Nothing seems to have come of this spat, but it shows the African's acute awareness of his rights and the legal options open to him. More pressing, however, was Equiano's need for employment. The Guerin sisters were unable to offer him a position as a domestic, but they recommended him to a barber in Coventry Court in the Haymarket, where he worked until February 1768.

Equiano was not a man to idle away his spare hours. He persuaded one of the neighbours, an accomplished musician, to teach him to play the French horn and quickly mastered the art.[7] Readers of Equiano's memoir would certainly approve of what they learned of the author: an industrious African who was rarely idle, and always keen, in his spare time, to enjoy himself by mastering refined pleasures. In eighteenth-century England, many employers encouraged their black domestics to play the French horn. A Bristol newspaper advertisement in 1757, for instance, sought 'A NEGRO LAD about 18 years of Age, near five Feet two inches high answers to the name Starling, and blows the French Horn very well'. In 1764, a social evening organised by blacks in a tavern in Fleet Street, attracted '57 of them, men and women, supper, drank, and entertained themselves with dancing and music, consisting of violins, French horns and other instruments ... No whites were allowed to be present for all the performers were Black.'[8]

In the Americas, slave owners and visitors regularly commented on the importance and universality of slave music-making in the colonies. Slaves made music in their spare time, on days of rest, at funerals and at weekend celebrations. Musical instruments appeared as if from nowhere, made from wood, skins, gourds, pans, anything that could be used to produce a distinctive sound. It was not surprising, then, that blacks were encouraged to play music in England to cater for the refined musical tastes of fashionable society. Soubise, the black servant to the Duchess of Queensbury, who in 1778 was dispatched to Madras over scandalous gossip about his familiarity with the Duchess, became an accomplished fencer, horseman and 'played upon the violin with considerable taste, composed several musical pieces in the Italian style, and sang them with a comic humour'.[9]

When not working or playing music Equiano attended evening classes in mathematics at a nearby academy, where he sought to improve his bookkeeping skills.[10] But his savings were disappearing fast, and his wages – £12 a year – were not enough to pay for all his activities, especially for his lessons. And then, the sea beckoned once more.

Sailing had become Equiano's real trade; he made much more money at sea than he could in London. In July 1768, only nine months after leaving his last ship, Equiano signed on again. The *Delaware*, captained by John Jolly, 'a neat, smart, good-humoured man', was destined for the eastern Mediterranean. Turkey fascinated Equiano, with its amazing mix of peoples, black, brown and white, slave and free, from all corners of the Ottoman Empire. On arrival in Smyrna, he was struck by the absence of women in public, and by the fact that the Greeks 'are, in some measure, kept under by the Turks, as the Negroes are in the West-Indies by white people'. Locals seemed 'fond of black people' and he was invited into people's homes, asked to stay, and, on a later visit, was even offered two wives, although he refused 'thinking one was as much as some could manage . . .'[11]

His next journey in 1771 took him to Grenada, and in 1772, as a steward on Captain David Watt's vessel *Jamaica*, he was bound for Nevis and Jamaica. Jamaica was now approaching the peak of its slave-based success and increasing numbers of Africans were toiling in the sugar fields. (By the time the slave trade ended, there were almost a third of a million slaves in the island.) When Equiano arrived in Kingston in 1772, the port was awash with newly arrived Africans, many from the Bight of Biafra,[12] serving the massive maritime trade from Africa, Europe and North America, working for town residents, or transporting goods to and from the inland plantations. Equiano was struck by what he saw: 'There were a vast number of Negroes here, whom I found, as usual exceedingly imposed upon by the white people . . .'

Whatever its daily brutalities, Jamaica provided Equiano with the usual opportunities to make money, which, as always, came with the usual risks. Again, he was cheated out of £25 by a white man and, again, he was forced to cut his losses. Equiano had arrived well prepared to trade, carrying whatever goods his captain allowed, in the sure knowledge that he would find a willing customer at a distant port. Whatever his formal role on board his ship, Equiano always seems to have travelled as a well-prepared and ever-optimistic small-scale merchant.

By August 1772, Equiano was back in London. A little more than a month earlier, a large crowd had gathered at Westminster Hall to hear the Lord Chief Justice pronounce on one of the most hotly debated cases of the time. The issue was simple: did the owner of the slave James Somerset have the legal right to ship the African from England, against his wishes, back to the slave colonies? Or, even more profoundly, was slavery to be declared illegal in England? Lord Mansfield's judgement, delivered on Monday 22 June 1772, was a simple assertion: Somerset's owner, the Boston customs official Charles Stewart, and Captain Knowles, charged with shipping Somerset back to the Americas, were not allowed, under the *Habeas Corpus* Act, to remove the African against his

wishes. It seemed a small, personal victory, but the consequences of the Somerset case were not lost on the black
delegation in the public gallery: '... after the judgment of
the Court was known, [they] bowed with profound respect
to the Judges, and shaking each other by the hand, congrat-
ulated themselves upon the recovery of the rights of
human nature, and their happy lot that permitted them
[to] breathe the free air of England.'

This report, in *The London Chronicle*, may have exag-
gerated the legal point, but it certainly captured the mood
of black London. A few days later, two hundred blacks
gathered 'At a public house in Westminster, to celebrate
their triumph which their brother Somerset had obtained
over Stewart his master. Lord Mansfield's health was
echoed round the room, and the evening was concluded
with a ball. The tickets to this Black assembly were 5s.'[13]

Equiano returned to London at the very moment when
the issue of legal black freedom had made its first major
impact. Somerset had been spared what Equiano had
endured, and the judgement marked a pivotal moment in
the history of blacks in Britain.

On his return, Equiano started to work for Dr Irving,
one of his customers when he worked as a barber in the
Haymarket. Irving experimented with desalination tech-
niques – or to use Equiano's quaint phraseology, 'reducing
old Neptune's dominions by purifying the briny element,
and making it fresh'.[14] Nine months later, in May 1773, in
Dr Irving's company, he embarked on what was to prove
the most extraordinary voyage of his life.

Europeans had long wondered how best to sail to Asia:
would it be possible to forge a passage northwards towards
the Pole, through the ice, and then drop south towards
India instead of the prolonged voyage round Africa? It
had been tried many times, often with disastrous consequences. If it could be achieved, it would cut weeks off
the usual itinerary, and significantly lower commercial

costs. But in 1773 there was much more than commercial gain in the mind of the Admiralty as it gathered a Royal Naval fleet to head north into the ice. It was an era of remarkable oceanic exploration and navigation, with the associated development of more detailed cartography of the world's coastlines. Geography, cartography, adventure, commercial and strategic benefits all came together in a heady intellectual and political brew throughout Europe, propelling different navies to dispatch a variety of fleets to all the world's uncharted waters and coastlines. Only five years earlier, in 1768, Lieutenant James Cook had been dispatched to the Pacific to observe the 'transit of Venus' and in 1772 he had been sent on his second voyage to the same ocean.[15] In all these adventures there was, as always, a remarkable degree of tentative fancy: of scientists blending findings with speculation, to create proposals which looked tempting to the necessary political and military backers. And so it was that in 1773 the Royal Society, the King and the Admiralty came together to support an expedition to seek the north-east passage to Asia.

The two-vessel convoy was led by Constantine John Phipps (later Lord Mulgrave), a twenty-seven-year-old naval officer. Phipps was a close friend of Joseph Banks, the great natural scientist of the era and, despite his youth, already had enormous naval experience, both in peace and war. Phipps captained the 350-ton *Racehorse* and Skeffington Lutwidge commanded the 300-ton *Carcass*, both ships specially fitted to deal with the ice. When the ships sailed from the Nore on 4 June 1773, Equiano was on board the *Racehorse* – and so too was the fourteen-year-old Horatio Nelson. Nelson was the youngest man on the convoy and had to pull every string available to sail with the Arctic expedition. The youthful Nelson and the African joined a remarkably international crew. Their crewmates came from the British Isles, Sweden, Holland, Italy, Pennsylvania and South Carolina – and alongside Equiano there were at least two other Africans on board.[16] The difficulties of manning British warships remained a permanent problem throughout the eighteenth century and captains were not choosy about their men's origins. Although Equiano was only one of many exotic sailors, in 1773 he was very unusual indeed: an African heading to the Arctic.

As the vessels sailed north, Equiano recorded the distinctive sights and experiences of life in northern latitudes: the endless daylight, the appearance of rare sea creatures, bears on the ice and plunging temperatures, all the time assisting Dr Irving to produce invaluable fresh water from the sea. There was a haunting beauty about this barren landscape, but the dangers were plain to see. The ice, as many had warned, put an end to the venture. By the middle of August the two ships were gripped by pack ice and the men 'were in very great apprehension of having the ships squeezed to pieces'. Officers tried to plot a route to open water, while the men sawed away at the encircling ice to free the threatened ships, and tried to drag them clear. Their prospects were bleak and, as was his habit, Equiano's thoughts turned to eternity. Even the men who had a reputation for cursing the Almighty 'began to call on the good God of heaven for his help'. Their prayers seemed to work. A change of weather, a fresh wind, and the ice began to break up creating open channels to the sea. Thirty hours later, the ships were in open water and able to hove to and refit. They made their storm-lashed way home, ending their four-month Arctic adventure 'to the no small joy of all on board'.[17] They had sailed further north than anyone before, but they had also fully proved the impracticality of finding a passage to India.

There had been any number of potential disasters in the expedition to the Arctic. One which Equiano reported in his *Narrative* was a near-serious accident of his own making. Both ships were heavily packed and afforded little spare room; hence Equiano had to sleep in Dr Irving's storeroom. It was there that he wrote his journal by candle-light. One evening, a spark from the candle ignited his clothing and the fire was only put out by fellow sailors using blankets and mattresses. Suitably reprimanded by his officers, Equiano abandoned his journal.

By now Equiano had visited dozens of places around the enslaved Atlantic. He had criss-crossed the Caribbean, made frequent visits to North America, had lived and worked in Britain, and explored the eastern Mediterranean. When he returned from the Arctic in 1773 he was not yet thirty.

19 Religion, Redemption and America

When Equiano returned to London in 1773 he continued to work with Dr Irving, but in the spring of 1774 he left to become, once again, a barber in the Haymarket. But he was in an altered mood: the Arctic experience had clearly shaken him. Life's dangers, 'particularly those of my last voyage', weighed on his mind, causing him, he admitted, 'to reflect deeply on my eternal state, and to seek the Lord with full purpose of heart ere it be too late. I rejoiced greatly; and thanked the Lord with full directing me to London, where I was determined to work out my own salvation.'

In search of this salvation, and like John Newton twenty years earlier, he consulted theologians about his religious worries and visited the churches in his neighbourhood. Equiano was initially drawn to the Quakers, whose distinctive faith he had experienced in Philadelphia, but he found their ethos baffling 'and I remained as much in the dark as ever'.[1] Trying to fathom the meaning of Roman Catholicism, Equiano found himself 'not in the least edified', before turning to the Jews 'which availed me nothing'. He was in despair: 'The fear of eternity daily harassed my mind and I knew not where to seek shelter from the wrath to come.'

Equiano had been baptised in February 1759, yet fifteen years later he was still searching for a meaningful faith. It was during this time that he encountered 'an old seafaring man, who experienced much of the love of God shed abroad in the heart . . .' The man was now a silk-weaver, living with his wife in Holborn, and it was in their home that he was introduced to the Methodist faith. Methodism attracted large numbers of humble folk for whom the Anglican Church was socially too remote and often irrelevant. John Wesley taught that everyone could be saved, however wretched or modest their station in life.

Invited by a Methodist preacher to a local chapel, Equiano found himself with fellow worshippers speaking openly of their spiritual experiences, many of them similar to his own. Stunned by the Methodists' resolute belief in their sure salvation, secured by faith and not good works, Equiano was, after a four-hour service, won over. He resolved to renounce worldly pleasure and weaknesses, all the time studying the Bible. But his spiritual turmoil continued when he returned to sea in the autumn of 1774, and it was there, on a voyage to Cadiz, that it became apparent to him that his whole life had been guided by the Lord:

> Now every leading providential circumstance that happened to me, from the day I was taken from my parents to that hour, was then, in my view, as if it but just then occurred. I was sensible of the invisible hand of God, which guided and protected me, when in truth I knew it not . . . When I considered my poor wretched state, I wept, seeing what a great debtor I was to sovereign free grace. Now, the Ethiopian was willing to be saved by Jesus Christ.[2]

On his return to London in December 1774, Equiano was admitted to the Methodist Chapel in the New Way, at Westminster.[3]

The former slave's autobiography was as much an account of his spiritual journey, through life's hardships and dangers, towards truth and salvation, as about hard facts. It was a familiar genre, and the best-known and most influential example was John Bunyan's *Pilgrim's Progress* (1678 and 1684), the allegorical classic of seventeenth-century Puritan literature. But Equiano's account also resembled a book describing the personal and spiritual journey of another African writer. Ukawsaw Gronniosaw, born in modern-day Nigeria, was shipped as a slave to Barbados, and later to New York, before serving as a British soldier in the Caribbean. Discharged and migrating to London, Gronniosaw, who now called himself James Albert, married Betty, a poor weaver. Poverty and personal disaster stalked their lives, and his story was one of extreme family privation. Published in Bath in 1770, his *Narrative* helped to create the literary genre of slave narratives that would become popular in the nineteenth century.

Equiano's *Narrative* presented the British readership with an epic and adventurous saga of physical and spiritual redemption. Here was a man who had dragged himself up from the squalor of slavery to emerge as a Christian gentleman whose Bible was always close to hand. The African was the kind of person that British readers would recognise as one of their own: a man they could trust and believe. In fact, Equiano demonstrated what could be achieved if slavery were removed.

For the next two years, 1774–1776, Equiano returned to life at sea, trading between London and Spain, and towards the end of 1775 he joined Dr Irving on a speculative venture to establish a new plantation on the Mosquito Coast. Again, he decided to return to the region which had seen his greatest sufferings, and where he had learned that being a free black guaranteed little security or protection. Even more surprising perhaps was the nature of the work he embarked on. Dr Irving wanted Equiano as a companion and 'he would trust me with his estate in preference to any one'. Equiano must have known that slaves were vital to the whole undertaking: no new settlement could hope to survive, let alone prosper, without slave labour. He 'accepted of the offer, knowing that the harvest was fully ripe in those parts, and I hoped to be an instrument, under God, of bringing some poor sinner to my well-beloved master, Jesus Christ'.[4] It is a sign of Equiano's evangelical piety that he felt ready to embark upon missionary work among African slaves and indigenous Indians in the Americas.

In mid-November 1775 their ship, the *Morning Star*, left Gravesend for Jamaica and the Central American coast. Among the passengers were four Mosquito Indian chiefs who had spent the past year in London to protest about the English administration of the region. The 500-plus-mile coast of modern Honduras and Nicaragua had long been disputed between Spain and England. The harsh habitat, disease, insects and Indians had, between them, prevented much European settlement, although the region yielded good logwood (for dye) and some of the world's best mahogany. Dr Irving's venture was just the latest British effort to stake a more durable claim in the region. The local Indian population was caught up in the conflicts between the European powers and began to decline under the onslaught of alien diseases. It was a familiar pattern which had been played out across the Americas.

As the *Morning Star* headed towards Jamaica, Equiano embarked on his missionary activity, trying to convert the Mosquito Indians on board. Much to his disgust, no one had bothered to take the Indians to church during their stay in London, and Equiano had just enough time to take them on a visit before they sailed. At sea, the Indians were unable to escape the evangelical attention of the zealous African. The eighteen-year-old 'Prince George' was especially responsive and he was taught both the alphabet and some rudimentary Christianity, but Equiano's good work was undermined by the ridicule and mockery of other passengers. They must have found the whole scene bizarre: an African, himself freshly converted to evangelical Christianity, locked in theological debate with an Indian youth, somewhere in the middle of the Atlantic. The mockery sadly affected Prince George: 'it depressed his spirits much; and he became ever after, during the passage, fond of being alone'. It seemed to Equiano that 'Satan at last got the upper hand'.[5]

On 14 January the *Morning Star* arrived in Jamaica, the island that served as an entrepôt for Africans shipped to the Americas. In preparation for the next leg of Dr Irving's venture, Equiano accompanied his employer to buy slaves. 'I went with the Doctor on board a Guinea-man to purchase some slaves to carry with us, and cultivate a plantation; and I chose them all of my own countrymen.'[6] He had worked with African slaves before, especially in Montserrat, and on voyages between the islands and North America, but his role in 1776 was different. By selecting a new batch of imported Africans, Equiano was a voluntary and willing partner in Dr Irving's enterprise.

On 18 February, six days after leaving Jamaica, the *Morning Star* arrived on the Mosquito Coast. Having discharged the Indians, the expedition began to look for a suitable spot to establish a plantation. The pioneer settlers constructed shelter, planted foodstuffs, and struggled against the elements and local wildlife. They traded with the local Indians, who were, like Indians across the Americas, reluctant to work for the settlers.

Equiano found some Indian characteristics very attractive. Men, women and children all worked, and they seemed monogamous and rarely swore.[7] But Equiano was unhappy to discover that they appeared to have no religion. They also shared the African appetite for strong liquor (which they distilled from pineapples), and social and trading meetings had a tendency to turn into drunken brawls. This was made worse by imported European drinks, in this case rum, and the settlers' alcohol proved corrosive of Indian social stability and health.

Equiano's personal hopes for the expedition and settlement were soon dashed. He was as much disappointed by the behaviour of the settlers – blasphemous, Sabbath-breaking and generally irreligious – as he was by the Indians, and consequently decided to quit Irving's expedition and strike out on his own. He told the Africans, who 'were very sorry, as I had always treated them with care and affection, and did every thing I could to comfort the poor creatures, and render their condition easy',[8] and there he left the matter. (In his *Narrative* he would be quiet about the moral ambiguities of his role in the Mosquito Coast venture.) Taking a tearful farewell from Dr Irving, Equiano joined a vessel for Jamaica, but again he was soon in trouble: the ship's duplicitous co-owner tied and beat him, threatening to sell him back into slavery. Equiano managed to escape by canoe – with the help of local Indians – and found another ship bound for Jamaica, but he was to be thwarted once more when the captain decided to return to the Mosquito Coast.

Equiano finally managed to join a vessel bound for Jamaica as a crew member. By chance Dr Irving was on board, travelling back to the island to buy more slaves. Equiano learned that the Africans he had selected had all drowned in an escape attempt soon after his departure.[9] In November 1776 he joined a ship bound for England and on 7 January 1777 he arrived at Plymouth, 'happy once more to tread upon English ground...'

When Equiano returned to London early in 1777 he was 'heartily disgusted with the seafaring life' and resolved to settle in England for good. The sea had been part of his life for almost twenty years, and he had been luckier than many; he had come through combat unscathed, and had avoided death and injury from shipwreck, crushing Arctic ice and the terror of mid-Atlantic storms.

Turning his back on the sea, Equiano found a position in domestic service and for the next seven years, until 1784, his life was to be as stolid and steady as it had previously been risky and uncertain. His employer was Matthias Macnamara, the former British governor of James Island, and his home became a new outlet for the African's evangelicalism: 'I used to ask frequently other servants to join me in family prayer; but this only excited their mockery.'[10] Macnamara, however, was more impressed. After quizzing Equiano about his faith, he suggested that 'I might be of service in converting my countrymen to the Gospel-faith', and return to Africa as a missionary.

In March 1779, Equiano wrote to Robert Lowth, Bishop of London, petitioning for ordination:

To the Right Reverend Father in God, Robert, Lord Bishop of London.
THE MEMORIAL OF GUSTAVUS VASSA, SHEWETH THAT your memorialist is a native of Africa, and has a knowledge of the manners and customs of the inhabitants of that country.

That your memorialist has resided in different parts of Europe for twenty-two years last past, and embraced the Christian faith in the year 1759.

That your memorialist is desirous of returning to Africa as a missionary, if encouraged by your Lordship, in hopes of being able to prevail upon his countrymen to become Christians; and your memorialist is the more induced to undertake the same, from the success that has attended the like undertakings when encouraged by the Portuguese through their different settlements on the coast of Africa, and also by the Dutch; both governments encouraged the blacks, who by their education are qualified to undertake the same, and are found more proper than European clergymen, unacquainted with the language and customs of the country.

Your memorialist's only motive for soliciting the office of a missionary is, that he may be a means, under God, for reforming his countrymen and persuading them to embrace the Christian religion. Therefore your memorialist humbly prays your Lordship's encouragement and support in the undertaking.

GUSTAVUS VASSA

Bishop Lowth received Equiano with great courtesy, listened carefully, but declined to ordain him.[11] Lowth had every reason to be hesitant. Earlier attempts to send missionaries to the Cape coast had proved unsuccessful. Moreover, sending an African preacher into a slave society was a dangerous enterprise.[12] Equiano's ambition to become a missionary had no real prospects of success. Despite his genuine faith and his biblical learning, it was unlikely that his roots would qualify him to preach and convert success-fully in Africa. Why should Africans abandon timeless beliefs and worship simply because another black man spoke eloquently of Christianity?[13] But, Equiano's religious zeal raised his profile among the good and the great in London society. And it did so at a time of great political upheaval.

The American breakaway from British colonial control in 1776 was a defining moment in the history of the Western world. It established the first modern republic, soon to be followed by the French, and it laid the foundations for modern democratic debate and practice. The language of the revolution – of inalienable rights, of equality and elected representation – and the rejection of everything the British imperial presence stood for, created the vision of a new world order. This vision did not, however, include black citizens, whose labours, in the tobacco and rice fields of Chesapeake and Carolina, had brought such material well-being to the rebellious colonies. True, a number of the revolutionary leaders had expressed doubts about slavery and the slave trade, most notably Thomas Jefferson, but the revolutionary generation had no intention of including their black neighbours as equals in whatever democratic polity they could salvage from the war against the British.

The confusion of the war allowed many North American slaves to escape. Some were enticed by the offer of freedom in return for joining the opposition. But those who fought alongside the British Army ended up on the defeated side. In 1783 the retreating forces were faced with the problem of what to do with all those men huddled close to the British flag. There were thousands of ex-slaves, freed blacks and former soldiers, many with families, and they all understandably rejected a return to their former owners and the inevitability of bondage for themselves and their offspring.

Here we witness a profound irony. The American breakaway and the emerging republic established the basis and vernacular of modern democratic politics, yet it was rooted in slave-holding and the material benefits which flowed from it. The British, on the other hand, had shipped more than three million Africans across the Atlantic in the course of the past century, yet here they were, in 1783, providing a refuge, and the promise of freedom, to blacks fleeing from American slavery.

Some estimates suggest that one-fifth of the total black population had worked their way to the British forces in the course of the war. Thomas Jefferson thought that his own state, Virginia, had lost 30,000 slaves. As both sides negotiated the terms of surrender, the fate of the ex-slaves became a bone of contention. George Washington demanded that they return to their former owners; Sir Guy Carleton, the British commander-in-chief, insisted that all slaves who wished to be evacuated with the British should be allowed to board the retreating fleet. In the end, the blacks clambered aboard British ships, all of them logged in Carleton's 'Book of Negroes'. By the time the fleet sailed down the Hudson, carrying the ex-slaves to a new life in Nova Scotia, he had logged 3,000 of them. Many others had departed from other American ports. A large group had fled from Boston as early as 1776, others left at the end of the war from Savannah and Charleston, first to East Florida, later to Nova Scotia;[14] others quit North America for Britain.

Nova Scotia soon proved unsuitable as a refuge for people accustomed to life in tropical and subtropical regions, and the British were forced to launch another resettlement, this time to Sierra Leone. In 1792, after an epic storm-tossed Atlantic crossing, the ex-slaves finally arrived on the African coast.[15] Those who settled in London were spared the extreme conditions of a Nova Scotia winter, but the distress of being isolated and with few prospects in London was little better. It seemed that the blacks who had rallied to the British in the recent war, hoping to find freedom and security, had traded bondage for miseries they could barely have imagined.

But the upheavals caused by American independence were not limited to the confused migration of former slaves. The revolution provided slaves with a new vernacular, about freedom, rights and liberation from oppressors. It is all the more curious that Equiano made no mention of these tumultuous events, despite having been in the Americas in the early years of the revolution.

Instead, he preferred to regale his reader with details of his rather mundane experiences in England. These years formed the most uneventful period of Equiano's life so far. In 1779 he became a servant for George Pitt, commander of a regiment of the Dorset militia, and for a while was bivouacked in Kent. It was a time of heightened national danger – both the French and Spanish had become allies of the Americans in 1778 – and there was real fear of invasion.[16] Equiano's encampment was part of the defences of the capital's southern flank against invaders.

In 1784 Equiano decided to go back to sea and he took a job as a steward, sailing for New York on the *London*.[17] Three months after returning to England, he left again for Philadelphia. Equiano had fond memories of Philadelphia and he was especially pleased to see local Quakers actively working to free and comfort 'many of my oppressed African brethren'.[18] His visit to the city was to prove another turning point for Equiano.

Philadelphia was a thriving port, the focal point for the recent revolution, and also the home of a free black community. By the time of Equiano's visit in 1785 only about 13 per cent of the city's black population was enslaved. With thriving black churches and schools, Philadelphia presented an inspiring example to Equiano of what might be achieved once slaves were freed. He also noticed that the black schools and churches took pride in the word 'African'. Two years later, in 1787, two ex-slaves, Richard Allen and Absalom Jones, founded the Free African Society in Philadelphia. When Equiano published his memoirs in 1789 he would adopt an African name (Equiano) and relegate the name Gustavus Vassa, which he had used for thirty years. He would describe himself as 'Equiano the African'.

He also renewed his contact with the Quakers of Philadelphia. During the War of Independence, the Quakers had found it hard to insist on principles which might seem to be harming the American cause, and appear unpatriotic, but peace in 1783 allowed them to return to active opposition to slavery. Equiano wrote that it 'rejoiced my heart when one of these friendly people took me to see a free-school they had erected for every denomination of black people, whose minds are cultivated here, and forwarded to virtue; and thus they are made useful members of the community'.

On 21 October 1785, after his return to London, Equiano and seven other Africans presented a letter to a London Quaker meeting.[19] Describing themselves as 'part of the poor, oppressed, needy, and much degraded Negroes', they thanked the Quakers for their 'benevolence, unwearied labour, and kind interposition, towards breaking the yoke of slavery . . .' In return, the Quakers promised to continue 'to exert themselves on behalf of the oppressed Africans'.[20] Equiano and his African friends were particularly pleased with the London publication of Benezet's hugely influential anti-slavery tract, *A Caution to Great Britain and her Colonies* . . . first published in Philadelphia, and then in London by the Quaker printer James Phillips.

In the summer of 1786, Equiano heard of a scheme to deal with the problem of London's black poor, whose numbers had greatly increased since the end of the American war. The government planned 'to send the Africans from hence to their native quarter, and that some vessel were then engaged to carry them to Sierra Leona'.[21] Equiano's involvement in the scheme would transform his life completely. Within months, he would become a prominent public figure.

20 *Africa, Abolition and the Book*

I n the summer of 1786 it was hard to avoid the groups of black beggars in London, especially in the dockside communities of the East End and Rotherhithe. They were refugees who had lost everything by their decision to join the British side in North America. Many were free people, others were slaves, or had been servants to British soldiers. But all had decided to flee from American bondage. 'Prince William' had been freed but tricked back into slavery before escaping to the British. Newton Prince, a pastry cook and shopkeeper from Boston, had been marked out by revolutionaries as 'an Obnoxious Person' because he gave information to the British; Benjamin Whitecuff had been a spy and only narrowly escaped hanging by the Americans.[1] Some found work in England, but many did not, and had appealed to the British authorities both for the loss of possessions in America, and for means to survive in England.

John Provey testified that he had been a slave in North Carolina, but had served in the Black Pioneers during the war. Now, in England, he found himself 'an entire Stranger in this country illiterate and unacquainted with the Laws thereof'. The official response was that he should feel grateful to be in 'a much better Country where he may with Industry get his Bread & where he can never more be a Slave'. Peter Anderson had been a woodcutter in Virginia and, threatened with execution, he had escaped to the British lines, leaving behind a wife and children. Now he was destitute in England: 'I endeavor'd to get Work but cannot get Any I am Thirty nine Years of Age & am ready & Willing to serve His britanack Majesty While I am Able But I am realy starving about the Streets, Having Nobody to give me A morsel of bread & dare not go home to my Own Country again.' The government commissioners assessing these cases needed proof of what the blacks claimed and, almost by definition, these refugees could not provide such evidence. The commissioners simply did not believe Anderson's story until it was confirmed by Lord Dunmore, the former governor of Virginia.[2]

It was not surprising that some black refugees were caught up in crime, and their stories surface in the criminal justice records; some were even sent to Botany Bay. We know that by 1786 at least 1,144 blacks were living penniless in London.

The broader debate about London's black population ebbed and flowed for more than a decade, especially since the fierce controversy around the Somerset case in 1772. The prospect that Lord Mansfield's verdict might free all blacks in England prompted the West India lobby to pick up their pens in defence of their slaving interest. Part of their argument focused on the black people living in England, and a number of their tracts sought to alarm readers by exaggerating the size of the British black community. Edward Long, one of Jamaica's foremost planters, drafted an especially splenetic attack, hurling a string of hateful comments at this community and inflating the numbers: his initial guess of 3,000 rose, in a postscript, to 15,000. As the argument spread, the numbers rose further, until it was claimed that 30,000 blacks lived in England. There was – and is – no factual basis for such figures.[3]

Whatever the demographic reality, in the summer of 1786 the problem of the black poor was evident and made an impression on people of conscience. It was widely accepted that these were no ordinary poor people. The black poor, argued one writer in the *Public Advertiser*, 'have served Britain, fought under her colours, and after having quitted the service of their American masters, depending on the promise of protection held out to them by British Governors and commanders, are now left to perish by famine and cold, in the sight of that people for whom they have hazarded their lives'. Should they, he asked, 'be left to the agonies of want and despair, because they are unfriended and unknown?'

As a result, early in 1786 the Committee for the Relief of the Black Poor was set up to help, raising funds through a public appeal and distributing food and clothes to the needy. By April they had given relief to 460 people, and by September that number had risen to 1,000. The aid effort had cost an estimated £20,000, but only £890 had come from private funds, the rest had been paid for by the government.[4] By the autumn the government had effectively taken over the funding of the relief programme, but it soon became obvious that poor relief was not solving the basic problem. Why not seek a permanent solution by finding a new home for the black poor?

Africa seemed the obvious destination, and Henry Smeathman, who had just returned from West Africa, presented a plan to the committee to resettle the black poor in Sierra Leone – all for a mere £14 a head. Despite the evidence accumulated by more than a century of slave trading on the coast, with its roll-call of death and disease among sailors, traders and slaves, Smeathman's fanciful prospects seemed to offer a solution for the benefactors of

London's blacks. The committee consisted overwhelmingly of abolitionists and this benevolent scheme, which would give the black poor the chance to found a new community of independent agriculturists, appealed to them. There were many who shared Granville Sharp's hope that Sierra Leone would become the 'Province of Freedom' – although the black poor themselves seemed less than enthusiastic about the prospect of returning to one of the centres of the West African slave trade.

Equiano returned to London in midsummer 1786, and later in the year the organising committee asked him to help with the recruitments and the preparations for departure. Equiano had reservations, however, and so did his friend Ottobah Cogoano, another prominent African writer in London's black community, who wrote: 'For can it be readily conceived that government would establish a free colony for them nearly to the spot, while it supports its forts and garrisons, to ensnare, merchandize, and to carry others into captivity and slavery?'⁵ Equiano told the committee about the obvious dangers: 'I pointed out to them many objections to my going; and particularly expressed some difficulties on the account of the slave traders.' Despite these objections, in November 1786 Equiano was formally appointed commissary to the expedition, and in January 1787 he joined the crew on the two waiting vessels, the *Atlantic* and the *Belisarius*. He had most of the qualifications the organisers needed: he was a very experienced sailor, had worked extensively as a dockside and shipboard clerk, and was a prominent member of London's black community.

In the new year of 1787, the two ships weighed anchor for Spithead, where they were joined by a third vessel, the *Vernon*. But Equiano was unhappy about the management of the ships' supplies and soon clashed with the superintendent, Joseph Irwin, who had been chosen by the blacks themselves. After complaining to the Admiralty, Equiano was dismissed in March 1787, accused of fermenting discontent and destabilising the entire enterprise. It seems that both men, Equiano and Irwin, were at fault, but Equiano felt deeply aggrieved.

The expedition left England in April 1787 and arrived in Sierra Leone the following month, just in time for the rainy season. The disaster many had feared rapidly ensued. Of the four hundred people who sailed away from England, fifty died at sea and fifty-two more within a month of arrival. To add to the weather and disease, a local African ruler destroyed the first settlement of Granville Town. Life in the 'Province of Freedom' quickly degenerated into a struggle for survival. Only sixty of the original settlers were alive four years later.

In London, Equiano was furious at his dismissal and busy bombarding the press and friends with letters justifying his behaviour. But soon he himself was under attack: 'Let us hear no more of those *black* reports which have been so industriously propagated: for if they are continued, it is rather more than probable that most of the *dark* transactions of a *Black* will be brought to light.' Another letter spoke of 'the cloven hoof of the author'.[6] Equiano eventually received full payment of everything the Admiralty owed him. His last words on the whole affair were that he was delighted to receive a 'sum [which] is more than a free Negro would have had in the western colonies !!!'[7]

In the summer of 1787 Equiano was thus very much in the public eye. He was uniquely well placed to speak with authority on black issues and to speak on a topic which had, quite suddenly, become a major social and political issue. Who better to agitate against the slave trade than the ex-slave Olaudah Equiano?

The campaign against the slave trade was formally launched in May 1787 with the founding of the London Abolition Committee. Intent on campaigning and disseminating information 'as may tend to the Abolition of the Slave Trade', the committee, and their subsequent campaign, had emerged from the earlier Quaker initiative. Abolition now became a topic of national political attention.

In the first major upsurge of abolition sentiment, which ebbed back and forth across Britain in 1787–8, abolitionist petitions descended on Parliament in their hundreds. On 21 March 1788, signing himself Gustavus Vassa, Equiano himself presented a petition 'on behalf of my fellow African brethren' to Queen Charlotte, wife of George III. It was much more than a request to end the slave trade, asking instead that the Queen should 'supplicate your Majesty's compassion for millions of my African countrymen, who groan under the lash of tyranny in the West Indies'. Equiano's petition asked that the slaves 'may be raised from the condition of brutes, to which they are at present degraded, to the rights and situation of men, and be permitted to partake of the blessings of your majesty's happy government'. Speaking of 'the rights of men' after the loss of the American colonies to revolutionaries who had flung similar phrases in the face of George III must have appeared unusually audacious.[8]

If the abolitionist cause needed an authentic voice of the slave experience, if they wanted someone to tell the story of slavery in a way no white observer could hope to achieve, Equiano was the obvious candidate. It was not surprising then that, when he began to write his life story, he was greatly encouraged by his friends within the abolition movement. It was equally predictable that Equiano would want to profit from his writing, and he therefore decided to publish the book himself.

The Interesting Narrative, in two volumes, was published in 1789. To finance his autobiography, Equiano raised subscriptions among his friends and contacts across Britain. The book was designed both to be his personal contribution towards the burgeoning abolition campaign and to make money for the author. But it also established his historical reputation: we remember Equiano, above all else, because of his *Narrative.* The book asserted his recently acquired African name – Olaudah Equiano. Previously, he had used, and was known as, Gustavus Vassa. Now, for the first time, he described himself as Equiano 'the African'.

The timing of publication was perfect. With Parliament scrutinising the slave trade, Equiano added a unique voice to the debate. The book was an immediate success and the author was able to attract more subscribers for subsequent editions, which would run to nine in his lifetime. His subscribers included the good and great, radicals and abolitionists, peers and clerics, and men and women of sensibility. It is hard to think of another contemporary black capable of rallying such a body of support.

Over the next five years, with his tome in hand, Equiano embarked on a series of promotional tours, staying with friends and connections wherever he spoke. He was also a good salesman, peddling the book much as he traded goods earlier in the Americas; and because he held his own copyright, he pocketed generous profits: he may have made more than £1,000 from the nine editions he masterminded.[9]

The book was available at a dozen bookshops across London, and by the mid-1790s had been published in Dublin, Edinburgh and Norwich. It was translated into Dutch, German and Russian, and also appeared in North America. *The Narrative* was an early example of a literary genre that was to become popular in the nineteenth century – the autobiography of a working man. Above all, it formed a substantial contribution to the debate about the slave trade. Pamphlets, books, sermons, lectures, pictures – all had been flying off abolitionist presses for the previous two years. Much of the evidence against slavery in that literature was also autobiographical – from sailors, surgeons and West Indian residents – but this time the argument was advanced by an African, who wrote with the unique authority of the former slave.

Equiano wrote that he was born an Igbo, had been captured in a slave raid along with his sister, and was transported on a slave ship first to Barbados, and then to Virginia.[10] His account of Africa was obviously influenced by what he had read and in the process Equiano shaped for himself an African identity. Recently, however, evidence has come to light that has raised doubts about the authenticity of a critical section of the book. In both baptism and naval registers, Equiano's birthplace is given as Carolina, which has led some scholars to denounce the book and its author.

Yet there is an abundance of evidence that seems to confirm his African origins. When he arrived in England as a boy his English was poor and his patrons had to teach him. He was often used to act as an interpreter for newly arrived Africans on slave ships, in Montserrat, Jamaica and on the Mosquito Coast. Large numbers of contemporaries and, above all, those who knew him best, called him 'an African'. Supporters who provided testimonials for him when he travelled the country, declared him to be 'an African'.[11]

In the late eighteenth century, however, the concept of being African was not as straightforward as it may seem. The adoption of the term by people of African descent had taken root by the early 1790s, although previously Africans themselves had had no concept of the continent as a whole, and had their identity shaped by much tighter, more particular characteristics – by language, religion, kinship, tribe. Europeans and Americans talked about Africans and Africa, but Africans did not. But from 1787 onwards leading black spokesmen, in London and Philadelphia, described themselves and the organisations they had created – political groupings, churches and schools – as African. It was a deliberate effort to identify themselves with their origins, even though they may have been born in the diaspora.

This may be the key to Equiano's story, and to the image he cultivated after 1787. His description of his African birthplace may have been literally true, although some details of his *Narrative* are demonstrably wrong, and some relied on literary, not personal, sources: as with other sections of the book – the voyage to the Arctic, for example – he cross-checked memory against published information. But there remains a likelihood that Equiano was, like millions of others, an African of the diaspora: born to African slave parents in the Americas. Even so, he would have been raised in an African environment, where language, customs, worship and kinship were African in all but location.

Despite these problems of authenticity, the importance of Equiano's *Narrative* transcends its details, arguments and flaws. It refuted the argument of the slave lobby that Africans were fated, by birth and colour, to occupy only the lowest rungs in any society, which denied black humanity the possibility of civilised or educated achievements. Anyone who read the book could not help but be impressed by a man of considerable talent, perseverance and strength. Who was to say that many others might not be able to thrive like him, if only they were freed from slavery? Equally, who was to say what the continent of Africa might be able to achieve if it could be cleared of the scourge of outside slave traders?

Over the next few years, Equiano continued to promote his book. Wherever he went – Birmingham, Manchester, Sheffield, Huddersfield – he was heeded by the local literati and reformers. Throughout this time, his home base was London, though he flitted restlessly between lodgings, sometimes living with his friend, the radical shoemaker

Thomas Hardy, a Scot who founded the London Corresponding Society. It was a taxing schedule, and the regular setbacks – personal insults on the road, the annual defeat of abolition in Parliament – must have depressed him. By 1792 Pitt's government had become hostile towards reformers and their sympathy for French ideas. After the outbreak of the terror in France, and the even greater bloodshed in Haiti, support for the 'Rights of Man' looked subversive. In this atmosphere, the prospects of abolition had faded. Nonetheless, Equiano pressed on undeterred.

In April 1792, Equiano married the thirty-one-year-old Susanna Cullen, who came from a family of modest means in Soham, Cambridgeshire. She had subscribed to Equiano's book and it is likely that the two met in 1789 on one of Equiano's tours. Their marriage caught the eye of the London press: the *General Evening Post* thought Equiano 'well known in England as the champion and advocate for procuring a suppression of the slave trade'.[12] Equiano had made no prior mention of Susanna, nor of any other women in his life; he referred to his marriage only in the fifth edition of his book, and even then allotted a mere two and a half lines to it. It is curious that a man who devoted so much attention in the early part of his autobiography to his African family background makes so little mention of his marriage to Susanna Cullen.

Susanna took the married name Vassa, not Equiano, and their two daughters, Ann Mary (Maria, born on 16 October 1793) and Joanna (born on 11 April 1795) were also named Vassa; this suggests that the name Olaudah Equiano was really a nom de plume. But it was a short-lived marriage: Susanna died in February 1796. She bequeathed Equiano some land in Cambridgeshire, but it was wrapped up in legal complexities and yielded him little. A year later, their firstborn died, aged almost four; their second child, Joanna, married an Independent minister and lived to the age of sixty-one.

Marriage did not deflect Equiano from the abolition cause. He attended the anti-slavery debates in Parliament before taking his bride on a book tour of Scotland. His life followed the same pattern of press publicity, speeches at gatherings, and reports back to his friends in London on the political climate north of the border. However, he continued to fall victim to tricksters and rogues: he failed to recover £232, which he has loaned to a 'Rascal'. It appears that Equiano was now handling substantial sums of money, most of it generated by his book.

In April and May 1792 his success was threatened by hostile press reports in London, which focused on the accusation that he was not African, but had been born in the Americas. It was, as Equiano admitted, an assertion that 'has hurted the sales of my Books'.[13] The allegation was designed to undermine his authority and diminish his power as the African voice of abolition. It is likely that these attacks were orchestrated by supporters of the slave trade. Equiano drafted a new preface for the fifth edition of his book, denying the accusations levelled against him. Most persuasive of all, he named people who 'knew me when I first arrived in England, and could speak no language but that of Africa'.[14] Equiano paid scrupulous attention to revising the text of his *Narrative* for each new edition, taking heed of what had been said about him and the book since its last edition. His autobiography had developed its own dynamic.

By 1793–4, however, abolition had begun to fade in the teeth of growing hostility to political change of any kind. The year 1792, which had seen 519 abolition petitions, and a narrow defeat in Parliament had proved the high-water mark of the movement in its initial phase. Pitt's government, once sympathetic, became ever more hostile, pursuing radicals and their organisations. Thomas Hardy, Equiano's old friend and landlord, found himself tried (unsuccessfully) for treason; even the God-fearing

Wilberforce was denounced as a Jacobin. The fact that France abolished the slave trade in 1794 merely confirmed the link, in the eyes of its British opponents, between subversion and abolition.

It speaks of Equiano's perseverance that he stuck to the abolitionist cause when others drew back. Yet he now tended not to recruit subscribers from among the ranks of the more prominent radicals: he had become conscious of his own political safety in a dangerous climate. The ninth and last edition of his book was published in 1794, the year of the famous 'Treason Trials' which, though largely unsuccessful, effectively halted the British reform movement.

From late 1794 Equiano fell silent, possibly distracted by the obligations of two small children, and, soon after, by his wife's declining health. His book had brought financial security, but happiness eluded him. After Susanna's death in February 1796 he left his baby daughters in Soham and moved back to London, keen to consolidate his estate and ensure that his children would be provided for. He drafted a will which bequeathed his money and property to his daughters, but if they should predecease him, he left money for a school in Sierra Leone and for training missionaries 'to preach the Gospel in Foreign parts'.

Equiano died on 31 March 1797. One of his last visitors was his old abolitionist friend Granville Sharp, who commented: 'He was a sober, honest man, and I went to see him when he lay upon his deathbed, and had lost his voice so that he could only whisper.'[15]

When his surviving daughter Joanna inherited Equiano's estate at the age of twenty-one in 1816, she received £950, most of which derived from her father's book. By then, the British slave trade had been abolished by an Act of Parliament in 1807. The changed political circumstances of the early century, the dogged persistence of abolitionists, and the growing public sense of outrage about the trade had finally won through, and Parliament, despite persistent opposition in the Lords, voted overwhelmingly to end the trade.

Equiano's had been a remarkable story. The most puzzling aspect of his life, however, was his rapid and almost total disappearance from public memory after his death: within a few years both he and his autobiography had been utterly forgotten. It seems that abolition had simply removed his importance and relevance. Equiano and his book would reappear briefly half a century later, in the arguments over slavery in the United States, but it was to be another 160 years before Equiano's memory was revived in Africa, Britain and America. In the 1960s and 70s, a small band of scholars, most notably Thomas Hodgkin, Paul Edwards and Philip Curtin, breathed new life into the man and his book.

Equiano is now an icon. As a man with a shrewd awareness of his own standing and achievement, he would surely have loved his current fame. He would also have relished the fact that a black man of such humble origins, a man who had tasted the unique bitterness of slavery, could become so famous, so long after his death. Today, Equiano is regarded as one of the greatest black voices before the twentieth century, a man who spoke for the millions of fellow Africans whose voices had been stilled by the brutality of Atlantic slavery.

Epilogue

These three very different men, emerging from diverse locations and cultural backgrounds, were all shaped by the world of African slavery. Though Africa was a distant continent which barely registered on the consciousness of most contemporary Britons, the lives of John Newton, Thomas Thistlewood and Olaudah Equiano reveal the centrality of Africa in Britain's Atlantic empire in the eighteenth century. Above all else, it was the gravitational pull of slavery which held their lives together. Equiano had been a slave, and spent his life struggling against slavery. Even so, slavery presented Equiano and others like him with confusing dilemmas. He hated it, fought against it, but at the same time he was able to emerge from it and make something of himself. John Newton came to share Equiano's view that African slavery was an abomination, though at first Newton's was a very different story. Newton's time as a slave trader had been his dark days, a period he looked back on with contrition and shame. Equiano, however, had no need to ponder the issue: he knew the horrors of slavery from excruciating personal experience. Yet both he and Newton converged, late in life, in denouncing the slave trade as a religious outrage. They were not alone, for by 1787 they were to be counted among large numbers of British people who viewed the slave trade as an affront to Christian values.

This shifting view presents us with a remarkable historical puzzle: if slavery was un-Christian in, say, 1787, why had it not been in 1687? Something had clearly changed: there had been a seismic shift in the way the British viewed the world. The nation that had throughout much of the eighteenth century perfected and profited from Atlantic slavery, now turned against it with a vengeance, deciding that it offended their religious sensibilities.

There were many, of course, who remained untouched by this sea change in attitudes; people who clung to the old ways and to the old values, and who remained immune to the suggestion that the whole slave system was morally rotten. Thomas Thistlewood remained an unrepentant slave owner to the end of his days. Like many around him – planters, slave shippers and merchants – Thistlewood viewed the benefits of slavery as obvious, and unchallenged by morality or religion. For such people slavery and the slave trade continued to provide well-tested material benefits. Whatever its flaws and difficulties, the slave trade continued to yield good profits and buoyant commerce to people on three continents. Those closest to the Atlantic slave system, whose livelihoods were entangled with slavery, tenaciously resisted the rising moral and religious sentiment against the slave trade. They soon discovered, however, that what had been their greatest strength – the rock of economic stability and prosperity – was being rapidly eroded by a rising tide of outraged abolition opinion. Thistlewood went to his grave unaware that his lifetime's work was being undermined by the strength of moral opposition 5,000 miles away.

All three men were creatures of the literate culture of the mid and late eighteenth century. Indeed, we know so much about them because of their addiction to writing.

Thistlewood recorded the data of his life in unusually fine detail. He also loved to read, and amassed a considerable library. Newton and Equiano were similarly bookish, and were both keen writers who became authors of considerable importance. Some of the words they crafted have embedded themselves in the collective memory. Newton's hymn 'Amazing Grace' is sung today by millions of people the world over, and Equiano's *Narrative* has become, by the early twenty-first century, one of the most quoted and remembered testimonies to African slavery. Much of what they wrote – the experiences they described, the changes they sought, the dreams they had – were defined by their personal familiarity with slavery. Though Newton (reluctantly) abandoned slave trading and turned to religion, his life nonetheless remained overshadowed by the slave trade. Much of his later life and work was a struggle to redeem himself from the sins of his slaving days.

But they were also men who transcended their own distinctive lives. When viewed together they form a biographical map that spans the world of eighteenth-century slavery. They covered all points of the enslaved Atlantic, and embraced all the key economic and social activities of contemporary slavery. Newton was one of thousands who shipped goods to Africa, Africans to the Americas and slave-grown produce back to Britain. Thomas Thistlewood, in common with other slave planters and managers, eagerly received the Africans disgorged by the slave ships. The labour of the Africans and their descendants made Thomas Thistlewood a prosperous man. The Africans on the other hand gained little or nothing from the system of Atlantic slavery, though some were able, through hard work and luck, to improve themselves. Few did so more dramatically than Equiano, who left a rich literary and political legacy. But how are we to set such meagre returns against the sufferings of enslavement for so many people?

Today, all three men are well-known, but a mere

generation ago only John Newton was known outside a tiny circle of specialists. Thistlewood's diaries remained hidden in an archive; Equiano had just begun to emerge from a century and a half of total obscurity. Today, each occupies an important position in the history of the eighteenth century. In part this is a reflection of the way slavery has shifted from the edges to the centre of historical attention. The lives of Newton, Thistlewood and Equiano speak both to the world of slavery at its mid-century peak and to the remarkable changes which threatened, by the end of the century, to destroy the entire slave system. Each was born into a world where slavery dominated the Atlantic economy; they died at the point where the slave trade was doomed. And it was doomed because the British Parliament turned against it. Exactly why and how this happened – why the British transformed themselves from the dominant Atlantic slave traders to the world's most aggressive abolitionists – is a curious and confusing story, but it can be teased out from the lives of these three men.

All the major ingredients in this profound political change were prefigured in their lives. Most obviously, Equiano and Newton both helped to give voice to the complaints against the slave trade. Though the two men could hardly have been more different, both had known the horrors of the Atlantic slave ships, and both paraded their experiences before the British public. They were, at once, carried along by the rising tide of abolition after 1787 and yet were also major contributors to the rise of abolition sentiment.

On the other side of the Atlantic, Thistlewood represented the face of the beleaguered planters, utterly reliant on their enslaved labour force, but always uncertain about how the slaves would behave. His violent dealings with his slaves, his descriptions of the Africans' sufferings at his hand, provide vivid illustrations of everything abolitionists railed against. Thomas Thistlewood saw – and was almost destroyed by – the violent upheaval of enslaved people in western Jamaica. Slave revolts, slave violence and slave resistance formed a defining experience for black and white in the colonies. And the more the British learned about these revolts – and especially about their brutal suppression and aftermath – the less they liked slavery itself. Thistlewood's diaries speak not only to the terror and uncertainty experienced by white people living through slave upheavals, but they provide detailed, repeated and, at times, scarcely believable evidence for why slaves periodically rose so violently against their masters. The bloodshed in the British slave colonies had its roots in the world of Thomas Thistlewood and his friends. It was the persistent, random violence doled out to his enslaved labour force, his sexual assaults and calculated sadism, which made slave reaction inevitable. Though the particularities of Thistlewood's brutality may have been unusual, the lives of enslaved people throughout the British colonies were defined by levels of viciousness which prompted angry slave reaction. And that, in its turn, caused further white reprisals. This apparently endless cycle of brutality and bloodshed, horribly outlined in Thomas Thistlewood's diary, formed the backcloth to the growing sense of British outrage about the true nature of slavery in the last decades of the eighteenth century.

For all the influences from the Caribbean, the British abolition movement had local, specific origins. The small band of pioneers who had set out to end the British slave trade and, eventually, slavery itself, came to the task outraged by what they learned about the slave trade and slavery. The long-term origins of this British revulsion had been the slave cases in English courts in the 1760s and 1770s, and a growing awareness about the plight of poor blacks in England itself. Here, Equiano was essential, for he formed a bridge between black people in Britain and their small band of British friends – led by Granville Sharp – who defended black interests, inside and outside the courtroom. Equiano told Sharp horrifying stories of kidnapping, brutality and enforced removal from Britain to the slave colonies; he repeated them in 1789 in his abolitionist *Narrative*. Here was an unbroken link between the first, ad-hoc efforts to defend individual black cases in the 1760s and the full-scale assault on the slave trade twenty years later. Of course, Equiano has a broader importance than simply linking these events, for his book spoke for Africans throughout the diaspora. He wrote not only about his personal experiences, but his book resonated with that elemental force – African agency – which opposed the slave trade from first to last.

At the height of the abolition campaign, the overwhelming bulk of the arguments against the slave trade were couched in moral and religious terms. This was hardly surprising because religious organisations – churches, chapels and clerics – dominated the campaign. The pioneering abolitionists in 1787 had been inspired largely by religious feelings, and they ensured that religious organisations rallied to the cause. However, abolition quickly spilled beyond the world of religious sentiment to become both secular and popular – though without ever losing its sense of religious outrage and inspiration. This was the world of John Newton.

By the time he agreed to add his voice to the abolitionist cause in 1787, Newton was a much-respected and celebrated cleric, famous alike for his sermons, his spiritual advice and for his hymns. Newton added a distinct resonance to the calls for abolition: he was, at once, a revered clerical figure and a man with a tainted past – a born-again abolitionist. No other prominent abolitionist could match Newton's unique personal blend of the grim, hands-on experience of a slave trader and the charismatic presence of an inspirational preacher. He raised his voice against the slave trade as a preacher, but he spoke with the calloused worldliness of a slave trader.

Since the end of the Second World War, the historical arguments about abolition have returned time and again to the confused issue of profit and loss – though it is no easy matter to draw up an accurate balance sheet of the British slave trade. Did the British end the slave trade on economic grounds? Had it ceased to be a profitable form of trade and investment? It is now clear that those most intimately involved in the slave trade – on and around the ships and their trading outlets in Africa and the Caribbean – were most fiercely opposed to ending the slave trade. The West India lobby, that powerful federation of planters and merchants, based in London and with many prominent friends in Parliament and government, fought a bitter rearguard action to defend the slave trade in the twenty years to 1807. There is little evidence in their arguments to suggest they felt they were defending a trading system which had lost its economic vitality, or its ability to yield good returns. Those with most to lose from abolition clung to the belief that slave trading remained profitable. Of course, once the slave trade had been abolished, major economic consequences quickly followed. Nonetheless it remains much less certain that the end of the British slave trade was inspired by arguments about profit and loss. The current evidence simply does not sustain an argument that the British ended the slave trade for economic reasons.

This is not to say, however, that there were no economic criticisms of the slave trade before 1807. Various critical voices were raised against the economic orthodoxy of slavery. Best remembered is of course Adam Smith's argument in *The Wealth of Nations* (1776), though it is unclear what influence he exercised on the course of abolition before 1807. Other less exalted opponents made similar critical points. Thomas Clarkson, the indefatigable and valiant foot-soldier for abolition, travelled thousands of miles in the company of his famous display chest, which contained a wide range of African produce. Such produce, he argued, could form the basis for a more legitimate trade to and from Africa. Equiano himself, in later editions of his *Narrative*, also argued that the slave trade on the African coast be replaced by other forms of commerce. Yet the overwhelming bulk of the debate about the slave trade between 1787 and 1807 was not about its economics; if abolitionists in the country at large and in Parliament felt that the slave trade had become unprofitable, they rarely said so. Indeed, if the debate had been solely, or even largely, about the profitability and potential of the trade, the argument would not have gone the way of abolition. All this was to change, in the next generation, when the abolitionist movement began to attack slavery itself. Especially from the 1820s onwards, the most persuasive and politically-influential attacks on Caribbean slavery were economic.

The ambition of the early abolitionists of 1787 had been fulfilled by 1807. In that year Parliament outlawed the British slave trade, though colonial slavery itself survived until 1833. (Moreover, an illicit Atlantic slave trade continued well into the 1860s, defying the best efforts of the American and the Royal Navies, and delivering one and a half million Africans, mainly to Brazil and Cuba.) It had taken twenty years to win Parliament over to abolition. It had been delayed by the impact of the French Revolution, by the slave revolt in Haiti in 1791, and by the comings and goings of political and governmental changes. The Lords remained doggedly resistant in support of the trade, and the progress of abolition in the Commons was uneven. But abolition was driven forward by popular pressure, especially through massively supported abolitionist petitions, and by the persistent lobbying of William Wilberforce and his friends.

Then, in 1807, Parliament decided not only to end the slave trade but also that henceforth the British should be an aggressively abolitionist power in the world. At a stroke, the slave trading poacher of the eighteenth century became the abolitionist game-keeper of the nineteenth century. It is hard to think of another example where Britain undertook so complete and fundamental a reversal of political and economic policy.

John Newton, Thomas Thistlewood and Olaudah Equiano lived out their lives under the shadow of this great transformation and, in their own ways, all three contributed to it. Their individual lives depict in miniature many of the factors that brought about the broader changes: the unwavering brutality of the slave system, the remarkable emergence of a new religious sensibility towards slavery, the role of Africa and Africans, the voice of humane learning, of widening popular literacy, even the early economic doubts about slavery itself – all could be seen in the lives of these three very different men. Moreover, their parallel lives underline the central role of Atlantic slavery in British history in the eighteenth century. But as their lives drew to a close the British experienced a fundamental change of heart and decided to turn their back on the nation's old addiction to buying and selling Africans.

Notes

Chapter 1: A Wayward Youth

1. Steve Turner, *Amazing Grace: John Newton, Slaver and the World's Most Enduring Song*, London, 2005 edn, p. 110.
2. Ibid. p. 114.
3. 11 December 1752, *The Journal of a Slave Trader*, Bernard Martin and Mark Spurrel, eds, London, 1962, p. 71 (afterwards, *Journal*).
4. Roy Porter, *London: A Social History*, London, 1994 edn, p. 144.
5. 13 January 1763, *Letter II*, in *An Authentic Narrative of Some remarkable Particulars in the Life of* ... [John Newton]. 1764, in *The Life and Spirituality of John Newton*, Bruce Hindmarsh, ed., Vancouver, 2003, p. 19.
6. Turner, pp. 42–3.
7. 13 January 1763, *Letter II*, p. 21.
8. 17 January 1763, *Letter IV*, p. 33.
9. Turner, p. 43.
10. 15 January 1763, *Letter III*, p. 28.
11. Ibid., p. 28.
12. Turner, p. 48.

The Trader, the Owner, the Slave

Chapter 2: In Africa

1. Quoted in Steve Turner, p. 54.
2. 17 January 1763, *Letter IV*, p. 35.
3. *The Works of John Newton*, 6 vols, Edinburgh, 1988 edn, I, p. 13 (afterwards, *Works*).
4. 19 January 1763, *Letter VII*, p. 50.
5. 17 January 1763, *Letter V*, p. 43.
6. *Works*, I, p. 14.
7. See Daniel Shafer, 'Family Ties that bind: Anglo-American Traders in Africa and Florida. John Fraser and His Descendants', in *The Slavery Reader*, Gad Heuman and James Walvin, eds, London, 2003, Ch. 37.
8. *Works*, I, p. 16
9. 17 January 1763, *Letter V*, p. 41.
10. Quoted in Turner, p. 66.
11. *Works*, I, p. 20.
12. Ibid., pp. 22–3
13. 19 January 1763, *Letter VII*, p. 50.
14. *Works*, I, p. 27.
15. Ibid., p. 31.
16. 20 January 1763, *Letter IX*, pp. 64–5.
17. Richard Cecil, *The Life of John Newton*, Marylynn Rouse, ed., 2000 edn, Fearn, Ross-shire, p. 58.
18. Turner, p. 78.

Chapter 3: Slave Trader

1. James A. Rawley, *London: Metropolis of the Slave Trade*, London, 2003, p. 39.
2. For details, see James Walvin, *Atlas of Slavery*, London, 2005, Chs 11–12.
3. Quoted in William E. Phibbs, *Amazing Grace in John Newton*, Macon, Georgia, 2001, p. 29.
4. Steve Turner, pp. 82–4.

Notes

5.   For details, see *The Atlantic Slave Trade*, CD-Rom, D. Eltis et al., eds, Cambridge, 1998.

6.   Emma Christopher, *Slave Ships, Sailors and Their Captive Cargoes, 1730–1807*, Cambridge, Ch. 6.

7.   22 January 1763, *Letter XI*, p. 74.

8.   *Works*, 5, pp. 317, 319.

9.   Rawley, p. 39.

10.   24, 27 October 1750, *Journal*, pp. 12–13.

11.   1 November 1759, ibid., p. 14.

12.   31 January, 1 February 1751, ibid., p. 33.

13.   26 April 1751, ibid., p. 48.

14.   Ibid.

15.   9 January, 13, 23 February, 6 April 1751, ibid., pp. 29, 35, 38, 44.

16.   28 November 1750, ibid., p. 20.

17.   *Works*, 5, p. 338.

18.   Ibid., p. 343.

19.   Ibid., p. 354.

20.   13, 20 June 1751, *Journal*, p. 56.

21.   *Works*, 5, p. 363.

22.   17 August 1751, *Journal*, p. 59.

Chapter 4: Finding Grace in Slavery

1.   *Works*, 5, pp. 331, 343, 345–6.

2.   Ibid., pp. 355, 360.

3.   Quoted in William E. Phibbs, p. 44.

4.   *Works*, 5, p. 377.

5.   Quoted in Steve Turner, p. 93.

6.   11 December 1752, *Journal*, p. 71.

7.   23 February 1753, ibid., p. 77.

8.   24 August – 24 December 1752, *Journal*. pp. 67–73.

9.   6 January 1753, ibid., p. 74.

10.   12 August, 11 December 1752, ibid., pp. 66–72.

11.   14 December 1752, ibid., p. 72.

12.   30 January 1753, ibid., p. 75.

13.   9 February 1753, ibid., p. 75.

14.   31 January 1753, ibid., p. 75.

15.   24 December 1752, ibid., p. 73: 15 December 1752, *Works*, 5, pp. 402–3.

16.   5 March 1753, *Works*, 5, pp. 408–10

17.   21 March 1753, *Journal*, p. 78.

18.   26 April 1753, ibid., p. 80.

19.   Ibid.

20.   3 June 1753, ibid., p. 81.

21.   6 June 1753, ibid.

22.   8, 12 June 1753, *Works*, 5, pp. 420–2.

23.   Quoted in *Journal*, p. 81.

24.   Ibid., p. 84.

25.   Letter to David Jennings, 7 June 1754, quoted in Richard Cecil, op. cit., p. 79.

26.   Cecil, pp. 78–80.

27.   Turner, pp. 96–7.

28.   Ibid., p. 97.

Chapter 5: From Slaving to Preaching

1.   23 November, 21 December 1754, *Journal*, pp. 87–8.

2.   4 January 1754, ibid., p. 89.

3.   25 January 1754, *Works*, 5, p. 450.

4.   25 January 1754, ibid., pp. 450–1.

5.   10 January 1754, *Journal*, p. 90.

6.   27 January 1754, ibid., p. 90.

7.   27 March 1754, ibid., p. 92.

8.   7 April 1754, ibid., p. 93.

9.   8 August 1754, *Works*, 5, p. 486.

10.   6 July 1754, ibid., p. 468.

11.   11 July 1754, ibid., p. 472.

12.   Eugene D. Genovese, *Roll Jordan Roll*, London, 1975, p. 252.

13.   Richard Cecil, *John Newton*, p. 71.

Notes

14.   Cecil, p. 71, William E. Phibbs; and p. 65 see also Steve Turner, p. 100.
15.   20 August 1754, *Works*, 5, p. 494.
16.   Phibbs, p. 67.
17.   Bruce Hindmarsh, *John Newton and the Evangelical Tradition*, Oxford, 1996, p. 15.
18.   Adam Hochschild, *Bury the Chains*, New York, 2005, p. 74.
19.   Quoted in Cecil, p. 80.

Chapter 6: The Slave Trader as Cleric

1.   William E. Phibbs, p. 88.
2.   Ibid., p. 89.
3.   Josiah Bull, p. 135.
4.   Bruce Hindmarsh, *John Newton and The Evangelical Tradition*, Oxford, pp. 1–12.
5.   Ibid., p. 31.
6.   Quoted in Steve Turner, p. 119.

Chapter 7: Reluctant Abolitionist

1.   David Richardson, 'The Atlantic Slave Trade,' in P.J. Marshall, ed., *The Oxford History of the British Empire: The Eighteenth Century*, Oxford, 1998.
2.   The most recent discussion of these issues can be found in Simon Schama, *Rough Crossings*, London, 2005. The best broader analysis of Sharp, English slavery and abolition is Christopher Leslie Brown, *Moral Capital: Foundations of British Abolitionism*, London, 2006.
3.   Quoted in Kevin Belmonte, *Hero for Humanity: A Biography of William Wilberforce*, Colorado Springs, 2002, p. 83.
4.   Quoted in Steve Turner, p. 124.
5.   Quoted in Adam Hochschild, *Bury the Chains*, p. 89.
6.   Brown, pp. 341–53.
7.   Ibid., pp. 342, 72, 243.

8. Judith Jennings, *The Business of Abolishing the British Slave Trade, 1783–1807*, London, 1997, p. 35.

9. Turner, pp. 135–6.

10. John Newton, 'Thoughts Upon the African Slave Trade', 1788, *Works*, 6, p. 523.

11. Ibid., pp. 1–2; my italics.

12. Ibid. p. 13.

13. *Hansard's Debates*, 1066–1918, vol. XXVII (1788–9) cols 495, 501.

14. Quoted in John Pollock, *Newton the Liberator*, Eastbourne, 2000 edn, p. 177.

15. 'Thoughts Upon the African Slave Trade', p. 7.

16. For the latest and most persuasive interpretation of abolition, see Brown.

17. Bull, p. 301.

18. *Works*, 5, pp. 304–644.

19. Turner, pp. 139–40.

Chapter 8: A Jamaican Apprenticeship

1. 26 April 1759, Monson 31/1 f.289. The Thistlewood Diaries form 37 volumes of the Monson papers (Monson, 31/1–37) in the Lincolnshire County Archives, Lincoln. I have used the microfilm version, kindly loaned to me by Trevor Burnard. All subsequent references are to *Diary*.

2. Trevor Burnard, *Mastery, Tyranny and Desire: Thomas Thistlewood and His Slaves in the Anglo-Jamaican World*, Chapel Hill, 2004, p. 22.

3. *Diary*, 15 July 1750.

4. Ibid., 14 April 1750.

5. David Watts, *The West Indies*, Cambridge, 1987, pp. 378–81.

6. *Diary*, 27–29 April 1750.

7. See essays by David Richardson and Philip Morgan, in P.J. Marshall, ed., *The Oxford History of the British Empire: The Eighteenth Century*, pp. 459, 468.

Notes

8. Watts, p. 311.
9. *Diary*, 16 July 1750.
10. Ibid., 2 October 1750.
11. V.A.C. Gatrell, *The Hanging Tree: Execution and the English People, 1770–1868*, Oxford, 1994, pp. 255–8; M. Dorothy George, *Hogarth to Cruikshank: Social Change in Graphic Satire*, London, 1967, pp. 92–7.
12. *Diary*, 1 August 1750.
13. Ibid., 8 June 1751.
14. Burnard, pp. 3–5.
15. *Diary*, 10 September, 3, 8, 9 October 1751.
16. Burnard, pp. 5, 156.
17. Ibid., p. 5.
18. *Diary*, 6 July 1751.
19. Watts, pp. 405–23.
20. *Diary*, 11–13 September 1751.
21. Ibid., 1 November 1751.
22. For naming process among slaves, see Cheryll Ann Cody, 'There is no "Absolom" on the Ball Plantatons...', in Gad Heuman and James Walvin, eds, *The Slavery Reader*, Ch. 15.

Chapter 9: Sugar and Slaves

1. Trevor Burnard, p. 183.
2. *Diary*, 25 November 1751.
3. Ibid., 22, 26 February 1752.
4. Ibid., 29 May 1753.
5. Douglas Hall, pp. 59–60, 61, 68.
6. *Diary*, 23 July 1756.
7. Ibid., 30 July 1756.
8. Ibid., 1 August 1756.
9. Ibid., 10 October 1766, 2 July 1768, 24 May 1768; Trevor Burnard, pp. 96–7.
10. *Diary*, 16 February 1757.
11. Ibid., 18 June 1757; 3 January 1756.

12.   Ibid., 19 June 1757.

13.   Ibid., 23 June 1757.

14.   Ibid., 4 July 1757.

15.   Hall, pp. 81–2.

16.   Burnard, pp. 103–15.

Chapter 10: Tacky's Revolt

1.   Edward Long, *History of Jamaica*, London 1774, 3 vols, II, pp. 447–8; Michael Craton, *Testing the Chains: Resistance to Slavery in the British West Indies*, Ithaca, 1982, p. 127.

2.   *Diary*, 14 March 1760.

3.   Craton, *Testing*, pp. 136–7.

4.   Hall, pp. 106–38.

5.   Craton, *Testing*, p. 138.

6.   Ibid., pp. 138–9.

7.   *Diary*, 30 December 1760.

Chapter 11: An Independent Man

1.   David Eltis, *The Rise of African Slavery in the Americas*, Cambridge, 2000, table 44, p. 105.

2.   *The Journal of a Slave Trader (John Newton), 1750–1754*, Bernard Martin and Mark Spurrell, eds, London, 1962, p. 80.

3.   Douglas Hall, p. 119.

4.   *Diary*, 5 April 1765.

5.   Trevor Burnard, p. 186.

6.   The details have been exhaustively analysed in Burnard's study of Thomas Thistlewood; see pp. 156–64.

7.   *Diary*, 21 January 1772.

8.   Hall, pp. 209–10.

9.   *Diary*, 1 April 1775; Hall, p. 213.

Notes

Chapter 12: A Refined and Prospering Man

1. I have been influenced by reading Christopher Browning's brilliant study, *Ordinary Men*, London, 2001. Browning's account of how a battalion of middle-aged reserve policemen were transformed into a group of savage killers in Poland in 1942 is a critical text for any student keen to understand how ordinary men can be persuaded to do terrible things.

2. See essays in John Brewer and Roy Porter, eds, *Consumption and the World of Goods*, London, 1993.

3. Trevor Burnard, p. 109.

4. Ibid., pp. 112–13.

5. David Watts, pp. 504–5, 433–4.

6. Ibid., p. 120.

7. *Diary*, 29 March 1772.

8. Ibid., pp. 125–6.

9. *Diary*, 7 September 1780.

10. See the meticulous calculations made by Trevor Burnard in *Mastery, Tyranny and Desire*, Table 2.2, p. 61.

11. For the finances of the slave trade, see Kenneth Morgan, 'Remittances in the Eighteenth Century British Slave Trade', *Business History Review*, 79, Winter 2005.

12. James Walvin, 'The Colonial Origins of English Wealth: The Harewoods of Yorkshire', *Journal of Caribbean History*, 2005, vol. 39:1, 2005.

13. Burnard, p. 64.

14. Douglas Hall, p. 242.

15. Andre Jackson O'Shaughnessy, *An Empire Divided: The American Revolution and the British Caribbean*, Philadelphia, 2000, p. 152.

16. Watts, p. 279; J.R. Ward, *British West Indian Slavery, 1750–1834*, Oxford, 1988, pp. 41–2.

17. *Diary*, 2 October 1780.

18. Hall, p. 278.

Chapter 13: The End to It All

1.   *Diary*, 4 January 1784.
2.   Ibid., 20 July 1786.
3.   Ibid., 22 August 1786.
4.   Ibid., 31 October 1786.
5.   Ibid., 14 November 1786.
6.   Trevor Burnard, pp. 194–207.
7.   Douglas Hall, p. 313.
8.   See Christopher Browning, *Ordinary Men*, Ch. 18

Chapter 14: An African in England

1.   Vincent Carretta, *Equiano the African: Biography of a Self-Made Man*, Athens, Georgia, 2005, p. 44.
2.   *The Interesting Narrative*, Penguin, p. 67.
3.   Ibid., p. 63.
4.   Ibid., p. 64.
5.   Christopher Bowes, *Medical Log of Slaver the 'Lord Stanley', 1792*, Library of the Royal College of Surgeons, Lincoln's Inn Field, London.
6.   The Opinion of Sir Philip York and Mr Talbot (Attorney and Solicitor General), 1729, in M. Craton, J. Walvin and D. Wright, eds, *Slavery, Abolition and Emancipation*, London, 1976, p. 165.
7.   Slave advertisements, in Peter Fryer, *Staying Power*, London, 1984, pp. 58–64; James Walvin, *The Black Presence*, London, 1971, pp. 70–80.
8.   *Narrative*, p. 65.
9.   Ibid., p. 68.
10. Ibid., p. 64.
11. Ibid., p. 65.
12. Ibid., pp. 77–8.
13. Ibid., p. 78.
14. Quoted in Carretta, *Equiano*, p. 81.
15. *Narrative*, pp. 84–5.

16.   Ibid.
17.   Ibid., pp. 91–2.
18.   Ibid., p. 94.

Chapter 15: Kidnapped

1.   'Shanley v. Harvey, 1762', in Craton, Walvin and Wright, p. 168.
2.   Details of this case in Vincent Carretta, *Equiano*, pp. 86–8.
3.   For one Quaker businessman's dealings with slavery, see the letters of Thomas Corbyn, in *Letterbook, Corbyn and Company Papers*, Western Manuscripts 5442, Wellcome Institute Library, London.
4.   *Narrative*, p. 99.
5.   Ibid., p. 100.
6.   James Walvin, *Atlas of Slavery*, London, 2006, p. 47.
7.   Equiano's birthplace is currently the subject of intense academic discussion; see www.brycchancarey.com.

Chapter 16: In Miserable Slavery

1.   See Marcus Wood, *Slavery, Empathy and Pornography*, Oxford, 2002.
2.   For a fuller discussion, see Marcus Wood's brilliant study, *Blind Memory: Visual Representations of Slavery in England and America, 1780–1865*, Manchester, 2000, Ch. 2.
3.   *Narrative*, p. 104.
4.   John Newton, 'Thoughts Upon the African Slave Trade', 1788, in Martin and Spurrell, *Journal*, pp. 101–5.
5.   *Narrative*, pp. 104–5.
6.   Ibid., p. 105.
7.   Ibid., p. 107.
8.   Simon Schama, *Rough Crossings: Britain, the Slaves and the American Revolution*, London, 2005, p. 25.

9.   *Narrative*, p. 107.

10.   *Abstract of the Evidence ... (1790–1791)*, reprinted, Cincinnati, 1855, pp. 44–5, 51.

11.   Trevor Burnard, pp. 263–4.

12.   *Narrative*, pp. 105–6.

13.   The story of VD among black and white in one corner of enslaved Jamaica is a refrain in the diaries of Thomas Thistlewood: Burnard, pp. 218–19.

Chapter 17: Prospering in Slavery

1.   For their story, see Gad Heuman, *Between Black and White*, Oxford, 1981.

2.   *Narrative*, p. 116.

3.   Ibid., p. 94.

4.   Ibid., pp. 116–17.

5.   Ibid., p. 118.

6.   Ibid., p. 119.

7.   Ibid., pp. 121–2.

8.   Ibid., p. 128.

9.   Ibid., p. 129.

10.   Ibid., p. 130. There may be some confusion about the precise date; see Carretta, p. 276, n. 359.

11.   *Narrative*, p. 131.

12.   Ibid., pp. 131–2.

13.   Ibid., pp. 135–6.

Chapter 18: A Free Man

1.   *Narrative*, pp. 136–7.

2.   Ibid., pp. 150–1.

3.   Ibid., p. 159.

4.   Ibid., p. 164.

5.   *Diary*, 29 July 1767.

6.   All details from my own database, 'Black people in Britain', available from the author on request.

Notes

7. *Narrative*, pp. 165–6.

8. *Felix Farley's Bristol Journal*, 12 March 1757; J.J. Hecht, *Continent and Colonial Servants in Eighteenth century England*, Northampton, MA, 1954, p. 48.

9. Quoted in Paul Edwards and James Walvin, *Black Personalities in the Era of the Slave Trade*, London, 1983, pp. 226–8.

10. *Narrative*, p. 166.

11. Ibid., pp. 167–9.

12. For details, see David Richardson, 'The British Empire and the Atlantic Slave Trade, 1660–1807', in P.J. Marshall, ed., *The Oxford History of the British Empire, The Eighteenth Century*, Oxford, 1998.

13. Quoted in F.O. Shyllon, *Black Slaves in Britain*, Oxford, 1974, p. 110; see also James Oldham, *The Mansfield Manuscripts and the Growth of English Law in the Eighteenth Century*, University of North Carolina Press, Chapel Hill, 2 vols, 1992, II, Ch. 21.

14. *Narrative*, p. 172.

15. N.A.M. Rodger, *The Command of the Sea: A Naval History of Britain, 1649–1815*, London, 2005 edn, pp. 327–8.

16. Carretta, *Equiano*, pp. 147–8.

17. *Narrative*, pp. 176–7.

Chapter 19: Religion, Redemption and America

1. *Narrative*, pp. 178–9.

2. Ibid., p. 190; the use of the word 'Ethiopian' was common usage to describe Africans.

3. Ibid., pp. 192–3.

4. Ibid., p. 202.

5. Ibid., pp. 203–4.

6. Ibid., p. 205.

7. Ibid., p. 206.

8. Ibid., p. 211.

9. Ibid., pp. 217–18.

10. Ibid., p. 220.

11. Ibid., pp. 221–3.

12. William St Clair, *The Grand Slave Emporium: Cape Coast Castle and the British Slave Trade*, London, 2006, pp. 117–20.

13. Andrew Porter, 'Religion, Missionary Enthusiasm, and Empire', in Andrew Porter, ed., *The Oxford History of the British Empire, The Nineteenth Century*, Oxford, 1999.

14. James W. St G. Walker, *The Black Loyalists*, London, 1976, Ch. 1.

15. Simon Schama, *Rough Crossings*, London, 2005.

16. N.A.M. Rodger, *Command of the Sea*, pp. 335–8.

17. *Narrative*, p. 223.

18. Ibid., p. 224.

19. Letter in *Commonplace book*, MS Box X3/2, Library of the Society of Friends, Meeting House, Euston Road, London.

20. Letter also reproduced in *Narrative*, p. 225.

21. *Narrative*, p. 226.

Chapter 20: Africa, Abolition and the Book

1. Stephen J. Braidwood, *Black Poor and White Philanthropists*, Liverpool, 1994, pp. 28–9; Cassandra Pybus, *Epic Journeys of Freedom: Runaway Slaves of the American Revolution and Their Global Quest for Liberty*, Boston, 2006, pp. 208–9.

2. Peter Fryer, *Staying Power*, pp. 193–4.

3. Braidwood, *Black Poor*, pp. 22–4.

4. Fryer, *Staying Power*, p. 195.

5. Ottobah Cugoano, *Thoughts and Sentiments*, p. 106.

6. James Walvin, *An African's Life*, p. 148.

7. *Narrative*, pp. 229–31.

8. Ibid., pp. 231–2.

9. Vincent Carretta, *Equiano*, Ch. 12.

10. Alexander X. Byrd, 'Eboe, Country, Nation and

Notes

Gustavus Vassa's *Interesting Narrative'*, *William and Mary Quarterly*, vol. 63, no. 1, 2006.

11.   Carretta, *Equiano*, Ch. 14.
12.   Ibid., p. 347.
13.   Ibid., p. 350.
14.   Ibid., p. 353.
15.   Ibid., p. 365.

Bibliography

Readers who wish to follow up the rich literature on slavery and abolition could begin by consulting the annual bibliography compiled by Joseph C. Miller and colleagues, 'Slavery: Annual Bibliographical Supplement', in the journal *Slavery and Abolition*, edited by Gad Heuman. The books I used in the text can be traced through my notes.

The materials for John Newton's life can be found in *The Works of John Newton* (6 vols, Edinburgh, 1988 edition). His slave-trading journals are available in Bernard Martin and Mark Spurrell (eds), *The Journal of a Slave Trader (John Newton) 1750–54* (London, 1962). The manuscript journal is kept in the National Maritime Museum, Greenwich.

A good introduction to Thomas Thistlewood's life and diaries is Douglas Hall, *In Miserable Slavery: Thomas Thistlewood in Jamaica, 1750–86* (Kingston, Jamaica, 2000). Trevor Burnard's *Mastery, Tyranny and Desire: Thomas Thistlewood and His Slaves in the Anglo-Jamaican World* (Chapel Hill, North Carolina, 2004) is the standard study of Thistlewood. The thirty-seven volumes of Thistlewood's manuscript diary are located in the Lincolnshire County Record Archives, Lincoln, Monson 31/1-37. I have used the microfilm version kindly loaned to me by Trevor Burnard.

Olaudah Equiano's writings have been reproduced and

The Trader, the Owner, the Slave

anthologised many times, but by far the best edition is Olaudah Equiano, *The Interesting Narrative and Other Writings*, edited by Vincent Carretta (London, 2003). The major biography is Vincent Carretta's important book, *Equiano the African: Biography of a Self Made Man* (Athens, Georgia, 2005), but see also my study, *An African's Life: The Life and Times of Olaudah Equiano, 1745-97* (London, 1998). The debate about Equiano's birthplace can be studied on various websites, beginning with www.brycchancarey.com/equiano.

Index

Index

Index

Index

291

Index

Index